Death in the Midst of Life

Christian Explorations in Psychology
Edited by David G. Benner and Hendrika Vande Kemp

*Wisdom and Humanness in Psychology: Prospects for a
Christian Approach*   C. Stephen Evans

Family Therapy: Christian Perspectives
Hendrika Vande Kemp, editor

*Death in the Midst of Life: Perspectives on Death from
Christianity and Depth Psychology* Lucy Bregman

Death in the Midst of Life

Perspectives on Death
from Christianity and Depth Psychology

Lucy Bregman

BAKER BOOK HOUSE
Grand Rapids, Michigan 49516

128789

Copyright 1992 by
Baker Book House Company

Printed in the United States of America

Library of Congress Cataloging-in-Publication Data

Bregman, Lucy.
    Death in the midst of life : perspectives on death from Christianity and
depth psychology / Lucy Bregman.
        p. cm. — (Christian explorations in psychology)
    Includes bibliographical references and index.
    ISBN 0-8010-1017-9
        1. Death—Religious aspects—Christianity. 2. Death—Psychological
aspects. 3. Psychoanalysis and religion. 4. Death—Biblical teaching. 5.
Bible. N.T.—Criticism, interpretation, etc. I. Title. II. Series.
BT825.B73 1992
236'.1'019—dc20   91-39617
                                                                                          CIP

Contents

Acknowledgments

The material in Chapters 2, 7, and 10 was presented as lectures for the 18th Annual John G. Finch Symposium at Fuller Theological Seminary, January 18–20, 1989. I wish to thank the respondents to these lectures—Eddie Elliston, Hendrika Vande Kemp, and the late Paul Jewett—as well as all the other participants in the symposium, for their helpful comments and criticisms. I am indebted to Arlene Miller and Sara Thiermann for their help with the material in Chapter 1.

Introduction to the Series

Christian Explorations in Psychology is a series of books designed to explore the interface of contemporary psychology and Christianity. All the volumes in the series are intended for those in the field of psychology (either the upper-level undergraduate, graduate student, or professional) as well as those thoughtful Christians who have interest in issues in psychology and a desire to examine those from a Christian perspective. Each volume presents a scholarly treatment of the issues in one field of psychology; future volumes in the series will address such matters as epistemological and methodological aspects of psychological research and practice, cognitive psychology, family therapy, psychotherapy and culture, and personality theory. It is hoped that these volumes may make a significant contribution to the ongoing dialogue between psychology and Christian theology, a dialogue which has often been better developed at the level of popular and journal article-length works and is somewhat deficient in book-length treatments of a more scholarly sort.

David G. Benner
Hendrika Vande Kemp
Series Editors

Introduction

When Jesus died on the cross, he cried out, "My God, my God, why hast thou forsaken me?" (Mark 15:34).

"For he who has died is freed from sin" (Rom. 6:7).

"The last enemy . . . is death" (1 Cor. 15:26).

"For you have died, and your life is hid with Christ in God" (Col. 3:3).

At the death of Jesus, the dead came out of their tombs and appeared to many in Jerusalem (Matt. 27:52–53).

"The wages of sin is death" (Rom. 6:23).

"To live is Christ, and to die is gain" (Phil. 1:21).

These statements from the New Testament can be augmented by the following anecdotes and images.

A student who spent his summer in a monastery helped to bury a dead monk in the cemetery where, in unmarked graves, all of the brothers lie buried.

A northern Renaissance painting depicts in exquisite detail two rotting corpses, who stand as lovers with arms intertwined.

In an intentional religious community, a woman's lingering death becomes a sign of blessing for the group, for to be near death is to draw near to heaven and God.

All of the above, whether familiar or strange, share two features. First, they insist upon a closeness between life and death, the living and the dead, that defies our common-sense

11

boundaries. Second, they are all "strange" in the sense of distant from the categories our middle-class North American culture uses to grapple with death and dying. There is something foreign and incomprehensible about them. Even the statements that have served to validate our fears and agendas are probably more experience-distant than we recognize.

This is a work that takes "perspectives" on death, those generated by contemporary psychology and those arising from Christian sources and tradition. We will present, examine, and interrogate this rich variety of materials in hope of making the strange at least halfway comprehensible. In the process, we will also look at theories and images and claims that appear much more obvious and closer to our ways of thinking, and try to gain some distance from these. The most popular and plausible psychologies of dying may not be the most adequate. The most popular and oft-repeated theological renditions of Christian faith may not be the most authentic, nor the most truly guided by revelation.

The plural "perspectives" is important in several senses. Psychology is not Christian thought, and vice-versa. Psychology has its own *logos,* its own rules for generating and supporting meaningful statements. In our view, it is a misguided hope to squeeze psychology so completely into Christian theology that a "Christian psychology" can emerge. Most often, this hope has been expressed as that of a "Christ-centered psychology" or a "biblical psychology." But indeed the Bible itself is not a psychology text, and what "psychology" can be drawn from it almost always involves a theological reading of Pauline categories such as "body," "spirit," and "flesh," which are then treated doctrinally. Although it is true that Paul, like all ancient authors, holds some views about persons and their motives and "nature," we cannot say that he or any of the other New Testament authors was "really" a psychologist. Even writings of a much later period that do seem to be more explicitly "psychological," a work such as Teresa of Avila's *Interior Castle*, for instance, are not best grasped as direct and clearcut alternatives to Freud, Jung, and other practitioners of "psychology" as we can come to know it.

Instead, our view will be one that lets psychology be psychology, and that regards the key texts of the Christian faith as remaining somehow outside the restrictions of modern thought-forms. We may legitimately ask that psychologies leave room for the human possibilities that such texts hold out for us; indeed this theme of "leaving room" and "providing space" will be one of the major motifs of this book. But we can hope for an integration that is not the assimilation of one perspective wholesale into the other.

Indeed, within "psychology" pluralism of perspectives exists as well. As the title of this work indicates, we have selected depth psychology from among these as the option within contemporary psychological theorizing that best conveys this capacity to "leave room" for death. Depth psychology is that tradition within personality theory that depends fundamentally upon the imagery of multiple levels, hidden meanings that lie "underneath" the words and acts of human beings. Although as we shall see, the original form of this commitment was a fervent belief in "the unconscious" as a reified entity, understood mechanistically, the contemporary representatives of this tradition prefer other formulations. Due to the focus of the central metaphor on multiple and hidden meanings, depth psychology considers itself a psychological hermeneutics, a discipline of interpretation. We will note the qualifications and ambiguities of this self-location during our discussion of the Freudian and Jungian traditions. The plurality of psychological voices, within as well as outside the boundaries of depth psychology, must simply be acknowledged as a fact of the current situation of this discipline.

A third sense of "perspectives" in the plural is that death is precisely one of the topics about which Christians have never been forced to say one and only one word. The various words of Paul, some of which are cited at the opening of this chapter, suggest a large tract of territory with many different trails leading through it. In a remarkable little book entitled *The Shape of Death* (1961), Jaroslav Pelikan documents how five different early Christian intellectuals expanded and elaborated upon the core of their faith, by developing particular "theologies" of death. Some relied upon the most prestigious and plausible philosophy of the day, Neo-Platonism, to restate the underlying truth of the gospel as they grasped it. Others rejected this, and went in an entirely different direction. As this work reveals, death is indeed a central theme of Christian reflection, but it is not one that requires unanimity.

Moreover, if ancient Christians borrowed from what made sense of their intellectual milieu, then it seems that they were able to set a precedent for a centuries-long engagement with whatever thought-forms each culture produced. In our century, these have included existentialism, a movement that greatly influenced both theology and some of the "death and dying" literature. Today, psychological theories can also be included as potential partners in such ongoing religious reflection. To suggest this is not to destroy the integrity of Christian faith or the theological tradition that emerged from it. It is to acknowledge that the biblical images give rise to thought, and that to make this thought accessible and intelligible is an ongoing task of Christians. As with the ancient thinkers about whom Pelikan wrote, the occasion for this may be sudden awareness of how heavily and unwittingly Christians are being influenced by available thought-forms. If this already happens, then it behooves the Christian to inspect the degree of influence, and the ultimate compatibility or adequacy of whatever these thought-forms have to offer, against a norm drawn from Scripture as interpreted through Christian tradition.

Examples of this process are plentiful in regard to our topic. The remarkable success of Elisabeth Kübler-Ross and the death-awareness movement—about which we will have a good deal to say—led to immediate enthusiasm on the part of many Christian clergy and others. A spate of pastoral care writers produced works that might uncharitably be described as "Kübler-Ross for chaplains." Another reaction was to attack head-on some of Kübler-Ross' particular claims, by contrasting these with what the critic held to be the central teaching of the gospel. But a more thorough critique looked at the underlying assumptions behind the popular psychologized accounts of dying as a process, and saw that perhaps neither the embrace nor the repudiation was a sufficient response.

Because in the last two decades or so, a gigantic quantity of literature has been produced on the subject of death and dying, it will be impossible to pretend that this book will be comprehensive in scope. I will not attempt a total literature review, although massive bibliographies do exist and more are on the way (Southard 1991). There are already many works that try to include *all* possible approaches, with a chapter on psychology, a chapter on sociology, a chapter on medical ethics. Although one of the strengths of thanatology as an area of knowledge is its willingness to be interdisciplinary, intensity rather than breadth will be my goal, although as in any work of "integration" there will be at least two primary bodies of material to handle.

Given the fact of sheer quantity, a word should be said in advance about my principle of selection. One of the dominant arguments in this book will be that death requires "myth" as the proper framework within which to develop any kind of response at the level of thought or life. Death requires "myth" not in the sense of "untruth" or "prescientific worldview," but myth as scholars of religion have used this term. "Myth" means a comprehensive world-vision, a "landscape" of reality that serves as a model of how things are, and a model for acting within such a "how." Myth in this sense places the human drama upon the widest possible stage, expands our everydayness so that the boundaries we ordinarily accept are transcended or shattered. Christian faith, I believe, is irrevocably "mythic" in this sense. So—and this is where a more surprising and controversial claim can be made—are any of the depth psychologies that truly try to apprehend death as a human reality. It is not necessary to claim with William Law (the eighteenth-century religious writer) that "The greatness of those things which follow death makes all that goes before it sink into nothing" (Law 1978 [1728]:71) to stress death's awe and ultimacy. Death is a link with what lies beyond, and its power to reveal the triviality and falseness of the everyday receives new testimony in our midst. But how adequate are the available and popular "myths" of psychology, even a form of psychology committed to uncovering "hidden meanings"? Can these newer "myths" convey death's awe and ultimacy? This is one of the major debated issues that this work will address.

"Myth," landscape, world-vision, and worldview: these are some of the categories I will rely upon throughout this presentation. Christian faith is not to be equated with holding an intellectual position about God, Christ, and humanity. It is at its core dependent upon an encounter with God through Jesus Christ his Son. Yet this encounter requires—at least so I believe—a landscape of faith within which the believer dwells. When Karl Barth wrote of "the strange new world within the Bible" (Barth 1957 [1928]:34) he wished to express just this

sense of alternative vision, of reality reseen and remolded
through revelation as conveyed in Scripture. Living God, central narratives, key images, and then a tradition of intellectual
formulations: these follow from each other. Their relation to
each other is not arbitrary, but it is also not so water-tight logical as much theological tradition has insisted. There really are
some points where images could have given rise to alternative
patterns of thought, or where alternative features of the narratives can be developed as clues to the character of God the
redeemer. As we shall see, which details of the Passion narratives are selected for theological development is a choice upon
which some thinkers rest their vision of the role of death in
Christian faith.

As a Christian, I am committed to a landscape whose contours are at least hinted at by the Bible. As a contemporary
person steeped in psychological categories, I am aware of how
these form my "first language"—a fact of life for many persons
today. As a scholar of religion, I dimly sense that death is a
subject that potentially challenges the very pervasive assumption that we today know more than peoples of the past. North
Americans of the middle class seem to be more ignorant and
inarticulate in the face of death than any other culture or
group known in history. Perhaps it is not true that the authors
of the New Testament and their original readers knew "more"
about death than we do. But they knew differently, more truly.
In that, they have the edge on us. To learn from their writings
is not to revert back to "premodern" and "prescientific"
thought-forms ourselves, but to gain an entrance into the landscape of faith, and to gain in perspective on the roles of death
in that landscape.

1

Testimonies

In order to give the reader an idea of the "database" for this chapter, the following "testimonies" are listed here:

Author	Title	Relation of Writer to Deceased	Cause of Death
Albertson, S.	*Endings and Beginnings*	wife	cancer
Cousins, N.	*Anatomy of an Illness*	self (recovery)	rare muscle disorder
Gould, J.	*Spirals*	wife, daughter	cancer
Gunther, J.	*Death Be Not Proud*	father	cancer
Hostetler, H.	*A Time for Love*	mother	AIDS
Lear, M.	*Heartsounds*	wife	heart disease
L'Engle, M.	*Two-Part Invention*	wife	cancer
Lewis, C. S.	*A Grief Observed*	husband	cancer
Monette, P.	*Borrowed Time*	friend	AIDS
Perry, S.	*In Sickness and in Health*	wife	AIDS
Rollin, B.	*Last Wish*	daughter	cancer (suicide)

Author	Title	Relation of Writer to Deceased	Cause of Death
Schreiber, L.	*Midstream*	daughter	cancer
Stringfellow, W.	*A Second Birthday*	self (recovery)	cancer
Truman, J.	*Letter to My Husband*	wife	unknown
Watson, D.	*Fear No Evil*	self	cancer
West, J.	*The Woman Said Yes*	sister	cancer (suicide)
Whitmore, G.	*Someone Was Here*	journalist	AIDS

merican society represses death." How often this claim has been made! It is one of the major themes of both technical literature in the field of thanatology and popular writings. "Ours is a death-denying culture," or "In America, death is taboo" are alternative wordings. That, by now, a vast quantity of literature exists on the subjects of dying and death does not seem to affect the plausibility of this statement. For indeed, most of the literature exists for the purpose of breaking the silence and going beyond the ignorance that pervades this culture. Contributors have their own pictures of what the culture permits us to think about, and what it forbids. Each has a possible cause for the repression that all, in one fashion or another, perceive. This is the language that most authors use when they wish to justify their own focus on dying or death. The general verdict on our culture's inability to encounter death is shared by religious and secular thinkers.

Narratives of Grief

To explore this paradox of repression amidst widespread talkativeness, the most compelling evidence lies in the "testimonies" of various individuals who have written from firsthand experience. They tell of how difficult it is to die in contemporary North America. These tales of grief, courage, and denial are autobiographical narratives of survivors, mourners, and, occasionally, those who did not survive. Such narratives are numerous. They together constitute evidence for the phenomenon of massive denial of death in our world. Yet that they are written at all shows that the denial is imperfect. That some of them are read shows how much concern there is to hear what others who have "been there" have to say. For that is the most basic function of such stories. One collection's title says this: *Someone Was Here* (Whitmore 1988). "How I lived through the death of the one I loved most dearly" is the theme of all of them. "I have been there, I have endured the grief, I can bear witness to it." This, more than any particular plea, is the message behind such works. Some are authored by professional writers, some by journalists, and some by "amateurs," yet all can have power as testimonies to the role or nonrole of death in America today.

Why would anyone—professional writer or not—share with the public the very intimate tale of how a relative or beloved one died? Or a record of personal mourning? The answer most often given is: to help others who are in the same boat, who must struggle through what the author has already endured. In short, such narratives can serve as inspirational "how to do it" books, filled with advice. The autobiographical genre simply adds authenticity and readability. But although this is a worthy goal, the authors' underlying intentions appear to be more complex.

There is something about the first-person singular that fits the stories these persons have to tell. Each author is also a mourner, who in writing memorializes the dead other. A unique life, a special relationship, is now gone, lost forever. Yet it can live again in the prose of a narrative. To tell the story is part of the work of grief, and perhaps a step toward recovery. Partial evidence for this view of these narratives is that some of the relationships "memorialized" were very ambivalent, or ended in a manner that left the author with guilty awareness of unfinished business. To write the story is to untangle the skein, and to reweave it for oneself and posterity. Where the relationship itself was not deeply troubled, the author urgently wants to communicate how unique, how irreplaceable, this particular individual now dead really was. Because our culture has no publicly recognized period of mourning, and rituals such as funerals are soon over, the need for structure in "grief work" and memorialization is unmet except on such an individual, private basis. Even in those narratives that tell a tale of "recovery," where the author celebrates *A Second Birthday* (Stringfellow 1970), there is still a strong recognition of something past and gone, and a need to memorialize an experience of overwhelming personal significance.

The extreme privacy of the situations described for readers gives the lie, on one level, to all statements about Americans' repression of death. The details of a last illness, medical treatments, and final emotions are laid out again and again in these testimonies. They are our culture's attempted equivalent to Renaissance death-bed scenes, where not just the family but the general public was invited into the death-chamber to witness a "good dying." And this may be the third function of such narratives: to reveal by example how a good dying is indeed possible, in spite of everything society can do to hinder it. Scenes of heroism—or at any rate, what the narrator presents as heroism—are contrasted with the false, destructive expectations set for the dying. Few or no "role models" exist for us, the authors say; nevertheless, some individuals do manage to make it through the dying process as the kind of people we would want to be under similar circumstances. Anne H. Hawkins finds these narratives of "regeneration" parallel to accounts of religious conversions (Hawkins 1990:553). Yet these persons died not as "converts" to something new, but as themselves—a central goal that is more suited to our culture's individualism than any generic ideal. It is certainly a goal for which the autobiographical genre is fully appropriate.

When we try to make generalizations about the views of dying and persons and illness found here, we should not forget the limits of such testimonial evidence. The nature of the genre itself means that it is unrepresentative as sociological "evidence" for how we die in America, or even how everyone thinks about death. The authors are all, basically, white middle-class persons whose writing skills may vary but who have access to educational and cultural resources denied to others. The narratives that we are considering as "testimonies" therefore miss the experience of homicide, infant mortality, and death from drug overdose among the inner city underclass. We cannot read them to grasp how America's many ethnic subcultures cope with dying. Perhaps groups that value family over individual, or who have retained traditional patterns of mourning, may not need the intense private retelling of a particular person's dying. Or perhaps publishers simply will not believe that a book reflecting distinctive ethnic or cultural patterns will sell to a general audience (i.e., white middle class) in search of guidance and inspiration.

Medicalized Dying

Although it is true that autobiographies of dying and mourning are not sociologically inclusive, they do reveal both the sameness and the variety of North Americans' perceptions of themselves and death. The sameness comes when we recognize a standard pattern or plot to these narratives. The storyteller's "other" becomes sick, receives medications, has surgery, and finally dies. The encounter with death occurs within a medical context, where news about life and death is conveyed via words about chemotherapy, radiation, and new procedures. It is conveyed by doctors, and actions are implemented by a health-care team. The decisions to be made are at one level decisions about medical treatments for which the one most affected is usually unprepared both emotionally and cognitively.

Simultaneously, as the medical tale of pain, anxiety, and defeat unfolds, there is another story: how to respond to what is happening in one's life, with one's own existence and relationships. Very often, these two tales are thoroughly intertwined. A decision not to continue "aggressive" treatments is a decision to remain a certain type of person, holding fast to a firm vision of what counts in life (L'Engle 1988:220). Information about an illness also has this double meaning. It is needed to help make a choice about medical strategies, but it is also a tool to regain some power or control over one's destiny (Monette 1988:92). Because for so many persons in America "control" is a paramount virtue, the helplessness brought on by illness is thoroughly demoralizing. Hence, the underlying approach of death is transformed into a battle to wrest control from doctors and others, and so restore some sense of self-worth (Schreiber 1990:196–97). When this happens, an element of reductionism creeps into the narrative. To assert that the problem resides only in the health-care system is to distort something about the limits of control and individual freedom, and reduce mortality to politics. Not that politics are irrelevant to health and illness, but they are only part of the human drama of human dying.

Medicalized dying is also long-term dying. Overwhelmingly, the disease that is involved in these narratives is cancer, and to die from cancer takes time. The narratives of AIDS also cover a time-frame of a year or more, and the uneven and mysterious progress of this disease makes it parallel (for narrative purposes) to the strange sequence of remissions and returns of cancer. The stories abound with these unpredictable ups and downs. After a horrendous description of chemotherapy treatments, the narrator can tell of six happy months of recuperation, travel, optimism, only to be followed by the return of the symptoms, and—this time—no reprieve (Rollin 1985:89). This sequence, or some variation of it, creates human turmoil for the sufferer, the storyteller, and all those around them. "Preparatory grief" is premature, as remission is at least a possibility. Everyone in these situations lives on "borrowed time" (Monette 1988:285), although each responds to this fact differently. Moreover, if the sequence of illness-treatment-remission has been completed once, it becomes fixed as a pattern of expectation, so that a second round that ends differently is even more devastating than it would have been at the start.

Amid this confusing and demoralizing up-and-down of the disease and its treatment, narrators and those who are dying must rearrange their lives. The world contracts into visits to the hospital, time spent on basic routines, a near-incarceration of caretakers to the sick. Since the majority of the authors were active persons with jobs and responsibilities that took them well beyond the confines of home and family, this change of world-space is especially harsh. Travel plans must be cancelled, and instead of a vacation in Egypt, a quiet weekend with friends must substitute. For the caretaker, a free afternoon in the park becomes a treasured event, to one whose usual routine had included frequent traipsings across the continent (Schreiber 1990:218). Remember that these narratives are not inclusive sociologically. For many persons, the sense of "curtailment" would not be so great, since vacations in Egypt were never part of their plans at any stage.

Another rearrangement is financial. Few of the accounts dwell on this, and it may be that a narrative that stressed this would not find a publisher. Nevertheless, it is obvious that illness is expensive. Even for those with complete hospital and health insurance, the expenses begin to mount. Home nursing care, visits from specialty therapists, and nonorthodox treatments may not be covered by insurance or by agencies established to meet the special needs of the sick. It takes time, effort, and imagination to learn about such resources. Moreover, expenses for air travel between New York and Minneapolis (Schreiber 1990) or Kansas and San Francisco (Hostetler 1989) mount up after a while. It is a staple of these narratives—no doubt accurately reflecting middle-class residential patterns— that close family members rarely live together or even in the same part of the country. Brother and sister take turns flying in to be with mother, but brother has a medical practice that he can't leave and sister has a job that requires her presence. Presumably, there may be other families where everyone is geographically available, but rarely does this seem to be the case in the narratives. Each person had led a separate life, away from the others, until illness struck.

The negative correlate of such individualism is the risk of isolation. At times of illness and dying, each of the narrators was closely involved with the sufferer. Often the text is rich with supportive friends, helpers, an entire network of persons who shared the experience of caretaking, and even considered it a privilege. Yet for certain persons, it seems, to be very sick was a source of intense shame and embarrassment. To appear before others—even relatives—looking bad, was too threatening to one's identity. The solution was to break off all contacts except those needed for caretaking, severing relationships before one was rejected (Rollin 1985:125–26). This strategy, which appears in several narratives, leads naturally to increased pressure on the immediate caretakers to "be there" continuously.

However one wishes to interpret it, women provide the clearest instances of this pattern. For them "to appear without my makeup" is tantamount to being dead already, and so is unthinkable (Rollin 1985:35). Sense of self dependent upon physical appearance is precarious, obviously, and reveals the fragility of both identity and the relationships supposedly so dear to the sufferers. Men, at least in these stories, are never so concerned with appearance, and are willing to maintain relationships even when grotesquely swollen or emaciated. For men, what seems to matter most is the capacity to work; so long as a man can function on the job he is, in his own eyes, "the same person" as before (Gould 1988:124; Whitmore 1988:65–67). When this is no longer possible, then the illusion of being "the same person" is shattered, and new forms of identity must be found. Among the many devastations of AIDS is the fact that its victims are often at the stage in their careers where "work" matters most in establishing a stable identity (Monette 1988:28). In the end, neither appearance nor work preserves the self from its own impending end.

In these narratives, religion sometimes functions as a "support community" or extended family. The "support" includes visits from beloved pastors (L'Engle 1988:160), or money for airplane tickets (Hostetler 1989:166). Some autobiographies could be "testimonies" in the sense of advertisements for religious membership. Churches can indeed provide help for the ill and their caretakers. But not inevitably. Where participation in religious services had been a family habit, or a sign that "everything is right with us," the shallowness of such a role will be revealed quickly.

Moreover, the social support function of religion depends in part upon the nature of American religion as "voluntary association," and on the "like attracts like" quality of religious participation. Scholars such as Catherine Albanese see in such "voluntarism" the role of religion in creating and maintaining social boundaries (Albanese 1979:93, 253). In times of crisis, these boundaries can become barriers to intergenerational support. For example, a Mennonite community of small-town Kansas may do its absolute best to support the parents of a gay AIDS victim, but for the young man himself the friends and services of San Francisco proved necessary (Hostetler 1989:133–41). This was in part because of the patient's specialized medical needs, but also because the nature of group "support" requires a shared sense of values, or at least the absence of direct value conflict, for it to be genuinely supportive. In another example of religious "voluntarism" a young dying husband's experimental Quaker service and spirituality meet his need for fellowship, but depends upon a degree of emotional expressivity that appears strange to an older generation (Albertson 1980:82–83). Because voluntarism and "like attracts like" transcend the lim-

its of formal religious organizations, *lack* of such religion does
not necessarily mean lack of a support community, as some of
the AIDS narratives testify (Whitmore 1988:20).

The Quest for Meaning: Three Frameworks

Beneath the surface of the plot, there is an urgent, sometimes frantic quest for meaning, for a framework within which
to place one's sufferings. Not just "Why me?" but "What have I
learned about myself? Who am I in the light of these new experiences?" are questions that arise again and again. The narrators ask these questions, as do those they tend, who die sometimes with answers and sometimes without answers. But, to
borrow from William James' famous insight, one real bite of
food is more nutritious than all the words on a menu. One real
piece of meaning, wrested from personal suffering, is more solid
than an elaborate blueprint or ideal that no one can follow. No
matter if the meanings are precarious, idiosyncratic, or dubious.
An intrinsic part of the case built by these autobiographies is
that in our world, even a tiny bite of real meaning, of any kind,
will be a major feast. To die in America today is to struggle
within a medicalized milieu to discover such a treasure.

Given this precarious and highly privatized sense of meaning, it is far from surprising that not all autobiographical narratives succeed in communicating it. Some sound "inauthentic"
or idealized, just plain phony. Those that succeed, do so not by
hitting readers over the head with inspirational messages, but
by connecting whatever "meaning" occurs with the actual lives
and characters of the people in the story. Religion, at this level,
can appear as one framework for meaning, but it is no more
"objective" or immune to inauthenticity than are other frameworks. Because of this, a question such as "Does Christianity
help persons face death?" receives an equivocal answer from
these narratives. Does ethical naturalism or existentialist focus
on inner freedom help persons face death? These appear to be
the three available "frameworks" for meanings, but in all three
cases there is no guarantee that any particular individual will
be able to live and die truthfully within such a framework. Or
rather, there is no guarantee that an autobiography reliant
upon a framework will necessarily be "truthful," as the reader
receives and responds to its message.

There are narratives where the author has a clear self-designated "religious" worldview and the story fits within it. The protagonists have relied over their lives upon forms of faith that are both identifiably religious and intrinsic to their own identities. They did not start "being religious" when illness struck, and their faith provides categories through which the particular realities of dying can be grasped. For Madeleine L'Engle, Christian faith left plenty of space for suffering and pain, yet within a wider field of hope (L'Engle 1988:195–97). Her husband's dying drew upon a relationship with Christ formed over many years. Moreover, that relationship had already guided her and Hugh to leave behind the glamorous world of theater, and live a quiet and restricted life in a small New England village for a decade. They knew that who they were as a couple did not depend on work or money. By the time Hugh was sick and near death, they had learned all this and more. The illness did not threaten faith, and their decision not to request "heroic" life-prolonging methods of treatment became a spontaneous outgrowth of their relationship to God and to each other. Another example of such long-term faith that succeeds as a framework for meaning is the devout, conservative Hostetler family, whose son's death from AIDS called them to *A Time for Love* in the midst of grief (Hostetler 1989:215–19). In such cases, the religion fits the people and their actions; it helps them grapple with reality and yet be themselves.

The "ethical naturalist" framework is one that finds in "nature" a global perspective to comprehend and accept the reality of death. We will examine this more deeply when we turn to the work of thanatologists in the next chapter. As an autobiographer's framework of personal meaning, it may succeed even if it fails as a general philosophy. Joan Gould's *Spirals: A Woman's Journey Through Family Life* relies upon it to recount two very different deaths (Gould 1988:125–26). The first, that of her husband, is told with straightforward affection and admiration. Her husband was not the extraordinary idealistic (and idealized?) person that other widows write of, but he maintained courage and humor and concern for his family through a long illness. Her mother's death, on the other hand, was far more problematic, as the relationship had been fraught with conflict and bitterness. This leads Gould to consider the "spirals" of generations. Her mother dies physically, but will remain alive in memory until Joan's own grown daughter perishes, for one generation of women interlocks with several others (Gould 1988:245ff.). The narrator is grand-daughter, daughter, mother, and grandmother simultaneously, and receives her sense of identity from acknowledging each of these relationships. "Nature" is the web within which these are formed. Nature lies behind the mysteries of human embodi-ment, provides these continuities, noticed and appreciated pre-cisely because persons are so often failures at continuity and presence (Gould 1988:212–15). Gould's mother fails at this level of "persons" but a more universal, fundamental bond endures, like it or not, to be "memorialized." A more upbeat instance of "ethical naturalism" is Sandra Albertson's *Endings and Beginnings* (1980), which tells of the death of her young husband. Nature includes both endings and beginnings, both death and renewal. There is no need for any life beyond death in the sense of immortality, and in fact such a hope would be "unnatural," a denial of the terms upon which the gift of life rests (Albertson 1980:87). To accept death and to hope for per-sonal continuity beyond death appear incompatible within this vision. Albertson's naturalism is optimistic and idealized, Gould's is somber and compassionate. Yet can "nature" alone tell us how to die? Or only *that* we die?

How to die? And how to live while facing death? These ques-tions must be answered by narrators who recognize that humans alone can prepare for death rather than just let it hap-pen to them. Humans alone seem to have a choice: to struggle against impending death with all one's might, or to "accept" and give in to it. To seek it on one's own terms, or to let it come on a time-table not set by the self. Here we have the central themes of the existentialist ethos, and there are autobiogra-phies dominated by such choices. What counts in them is that someone consciously says "Yes," or "No," and death becomes a free act and not a fate that just "happens."

Jessamyn West's *The Woman Said Yes* (West 1976) is a pow-erful and persuasive example of this existentialist framework. "The woman" of West's title is her mother, Grace, and the entire text is a tribute to her. In part 1, Jessamyn the daughter lies dying of TB in her twenties. Miraculously, the mother nurtures, bullies, and lures her into recovery, faithful to a vision of life as worth preserving and death as a foe (West 1976:102–3). Part 2 tells how Jessamyn assisted Carmen, her sister, in committing suicide. Carmen, dying of cancer, did not want to face ugliness, pain, and humiliation. The mother who had said "Yes," to life, would—so Jessamyn believes—now say "Yes" to death under such circumstances. And so Jessamyn continues the task bequeathed her by Grace, and helps to end Carmen's life (West 1976:220–21). What counts is not whether we—the readers—find this right or wrong, or like Carmen as a person. What matters, in the author's eyes, is that knowledge of how to live and when to die are part of the same picture, the wisdom of a Grace who faced both life and death as a human being who loved.

Grace's rural Quaker background could not be in greater contrast with the affluent, flamboyant world of gay Los Angeles, but Paul Monette's *Borrowed Time* (1988) contains a message curiously similar to that of West. As Monette unfolds the story of how his best friend/lover Roger dies of AIDS, he tells how they moved from that world they had known and enjoyed, to "the moon" of AIDS (Monette 1988:83). Bitter anger and medical uncertainty are part of this "moon" existence, a vivid image of exile and lifelessness. But as Paul and Roger move closer to Roger's death, they discover a way to say "Yes," while at the same time to say "No" to whatever was superficial and destructive in their lives. They begin to read Plato, not to become Platonists, but because "Whoever Socrates was, we read the blue book to see how a man of honor faces death without any lies" (Monette 1988:303). In this work of preparation for death, they find a liberation from the materialism, concern with appearances, and fragmentation that had marked their milieu.

What all of the above works share—and there are others, of course, in this category—is a sense of compelling authenticity. These persons have truly *been there*, and the stories they tell are worth hearing, even when the reader deeply disapproves of some of the actions and attitudes of the narrators. In fact, the genre of autobiography may work as a relativizing force, since one is able to recognize oneself in the lives of such a diversity of persons, and empathize if not sympathize with their acts. The small and particular bite of meaning wins out over every general but unnutritious ideal.

Autobiographies that "fail" and that appear as "inauthentic" are almost as useful to reveal the obstacles to an encounter with dying and death. If genuine personal meaning is hard to discover and appears at a level so private and personal that it is precarious to communicate, no wonder authors do not always succeed in doing so. Some of the sources of "untruth" in auto-biography are the lack of fit between the expressed framework of meaning and the characters and motives of the protagonists. For instance, Shireen Perry's *In Sickness and in Health: Love in the Shadow of AIDS* (1989) purports to retell the author's courtship, marriage, and early widowhood. The author and her husband were both Christians, and one hopes for the inner story of their relation to God, of guilt and hope, of repentance and renewal. Yet this remains hidden. We do not learn how a Christian man faces death without lies; we do not learn how a Christian woman says "Yes" to death and loss. It is as if their religion does not touch upon such realities, or it does so at a level that fails to convince.

"Nature" too can "fail" in an autobiography, especially when the human dilemmas remain only partly understood. LeAnne Schreiber's *Midstream* (1990) is another narrative of a mother's death, alternating with the mid-life transition of the daughter. LeAnne quits her career and embarks on a life of solitude in the country. Simultaneously, her mother falls sick with cancer. The periodic returns to "nature" do not provide insight into the reality of the illness or of the family dynamics. The world of nature is there, yes; but it is no substitute for a level of connectedness unachieved in this narrative. Because of the high level of isolation and denial, the mother's death is in some way more tragic than any of those where someone discovered how to face death without lies (Schreiber 1990:249).

Finally "failure" can occur when the level of meaning desired and found seems blatantly inadequate to the power of the situations described in the story. Life and death are reduced to something much less, and the most basic and ultimate human situations are treated in a manner that degrades both protagonists and narrator. For North Americans, this path seems to lead directly into diatribes filled with slogans ("the right to die") against the medical establishment, in the name either of individual rights or some other seemingly unquestionable value. What makes such narratives impoverished is not the particular courses of action taken, such as active euthanasia (Rollin 1985), but that the human realities have been blurred or denied so that what might have been the inner story of one person's dying is never told. And so, it is lost to us forever.

Privatized Struggles

As testimonies to American society's repression of death, all of these narratives have some value, even some that are false and fail as autobiographies. Religion competes with other meaning systems, none of which can be guaranteed to provide a pattern for "good dying" that will convince protagonists, narrators, or readers. Persons both die as they live, and discover themselves in new ways when near to death. They respond with fight, flight, and acceptance, in ways that clearly replicate their general personal patterns of behavior. Many of the relationships described are ambivalent at best, and the task of "memorializing" that the narrator intends does not always produce the desired result.

To find a way to think or write about the self that does not make death a meaningless accident, or an entirely externalized catastrophe, or a punishment meted out by villainous doctors is not easy. The world of the dying contracts, but is this a merciful simplification, a paring down to essentials? Or is it an imprisonment, a humiliation too bitter to be borne? Is it possible to live and face others without makeup? Without one's job? How can we admit that relationships that were filled with anger during life, will never in this world be healed? That there are limits to our rights, our will-power, our ability to control—and if so, is denial or defiance of these heroic or pathetic?

Within such a landscape, contemporary Americans struggle to learn the wisdom of Grace, of Socrates. Theological questions rarely appear as such, or in familiar, traditional forms. But neither do ethical naturalism or other secular ideologies—at least, not in their traditional forms. The privatized world of bewildered individuals struggling toward meanings, which are themselves private and precarious, is the space set aside for these discoveries. That such a space now exists at all shows how silence and repression are not the only realities at work today in regard to death. But as the plethora of testimonies reveal, no firm, publicly shared, objective framework now exists within which all can find a role for death in their lives.

2

Elisabeth Kübler-Ross: An Ethical Naturalist's Approach to Death and Dying

In the previous chapter, the term "ethical naturalism" was used to identify a perspective in which human fulfillment is tied to harmony with "nature" and meaning is discerned in the rhythms of the organic world. This chapter examines the psychological perspective that depends upon such a view, one most often associated with "death and dying" as a field of research. The view, as we have seen, lies very close to the experience of many North Americans. An elderly widow confided: "When my husband died, nothing anyone at church said made any sense to me until a therapist told me, 'It's a natural part of life.'" A seminary student summed up his own practice by saying, "You listen, you offer emotional support, you let people go through the process. . . . I mean, what more is there really to say?" These two persons reflect exactly the perspectives of ethical naturalism. And also its limits, its "repression," if you will, of certain other agendas or perspectives, such as the theological.

It is convenient to focus on the work of Elisabeth Kübler-Ross, by far the best known figure in the field, and especially representative of this perspective. Her assumptions and vocabulary have been repeated and borrowed by many others without revision. Not a few of the autobiographies rely upon them. It may be fair to say that in Kübler-Ross, American society got the view of dying and death it could accommodate, congruent with its worldview. Even those thinkers who have criticized Kübler-Ross' particular ideas have most frequently shared her basic assumptions. True to our approach, we will examine her central images. These include dying as natural process, as individual "growth," and her goal of "acceptance." Then we will contrast Kübler-Ross' work with that of an alternative "ethical naturalism," which, although closely related, expresses a different moral and spiritual ethos. The work of Erich Lindemann, John Bowlby, and Colin Parkes on mourning provides an interesting and instructive contrast.

The most distinctive feature of Kübler-Ross' thinking on dying is to imagine it as "process" rather than as a "state." Her work, like that of many other researchers, was done in hospitals with the terminally ill. Her patients had plenty of time to reflect on their situations, for as we have noted, dying in America can take a long time. Kübler-Ross speaks of the "stages" of dying as distinctively psychological happenings, and organizes her data into a schema of progression. That most empirical studies have not entirely validated this idea, or have revealed only unsurprising conditions such as denial and depression, does not make the idea of stages less attractive. A process heads somewhere, and this fact in itself implicitly promises an order and a goal. Is this what made Kübler-Ross' work so uniquely popular? Perhaps. An equally readable, sensitive, and inspirational book on *Counseling the Dying* by Margaretta Bowers and others (1981 [1964]) remains in relative obscurity perhaps because it lacks this promise of progress toward a goal. Even if every patient's "progression" is unique (as some want to argue) the motif still appeals. Is such a phenomenon actually a function of the hospital setting within which Kübler-Ross and others worked? Some think so (Kamerman 1988:42–43). But this seems unlikely, given the wide applicability of such a model.

The "Stages" of Dying

If dying is a progression, and this is a psychological process and not just a way to describe the course of the fatal disease, then the process has a start and a goal. "The five stages" of dying are Kübler-Ross' major contribution to the American culture's perspective on death. The stages begin with "denial," when the person first hears the diagnosis, generally, and proceed through anger, bargaining, depression, and acceptance (Kübler-Ross 1969:264). Overall, what this process accomplishes is to acknowledge the reality of impending loss, conclude one's "unfinished business," and finally let go of life. This schema requires an attitude of renunciation, expressed perhaps in the ancient near-death posture of turning one's face toward the wall and away from the living. But the term "renunciation" forms no part of Kübler-Ross' vocabulary. Instead, she transforms this into the very positive-sounding goal of "acceptance."

On Death and Dying begins with such American-Freudian generalizations as "In our unconscious, death is never possible in regard to ourselves . . . in our unconscious mind we can only be killed" (Kübler-Ross 1969:2). "Fear of death is a universal fear" (Kübler-Ross 1969:5). Denial and projection are seen as universal responses to the frightening power of death. Children are not aware of death's irreversibility; like the unconscious, they simply do not believe in it (Kübler-Ross 1969:3). From this, one would hardly imagine that the goal of "acceptance" could possibly be its conclusion, nor even what such a goal could mean. Most often, such generalizations have served to legitimate American society's own repression of death.

Kübler-Ross then shifts to factors within contemporary culture that exacerbate the denial of death. Among these are the elaborate medical technology and the impersonal bureaucracy of hospitals, the setting that turns human mortality into "management of the terminally ill patient." She then relates a story that plays a key role not only in her book, but for the ethos of the movement that embraced her work. When she was a child in rural Switzerland, she remembers, a farmer had an accident and died a few days later in his bed at home. His family was with him; even she, the neighbor's child, was present. He had time to say good-bye amid familiar surroundings. This is the way most people once died, and this—she claims—is the way people ought to die, even today (Kübler-Ross 1969:5–6). Such a death is "natural"; it forms the peaceful and unterrifying end to life. In such a setting, death can be "accépted," not just by others but even by the dying person. This kind of death thus functions as an ideal, an ideal that fuels the hospice movement and many other efforts to detechnologize the dying process. Curiously, according to historian Philippe Ariès, ever since the era of the high Middle Ages Westerners have had a more complex and disrupted relation to death than such a picture promotes. This "tame death" (Ariès' term) cannot encompass the Western need for individuality, subjectivity, and self-awareness (Ariès 1981 [1977]:28).

The task for the rest of *On Death and Dying* is set: to see that patients in a high-technology research hospital, in the midst of an urban, death-denying society, achieve that same degree of harmony with nature and interpersonal, intrapersonal peace this nostalgic ideal promises. Is this a possibility? As Kübler-Ross' discussion of the stages unfolds, the reader senses this moral vision undergirding the case presentations. Each patient is to be taken as an individual; no one is to be pushed through denial or anger just to reach the goal more quickly. That is one side of Kübler-Ross' argument. The other side is that, given a supportive environment and relieved of the fear of emotional abandonment, dying persons move away from denial and through other emotional states until they spontaneously reach acceptance. Even the quasi-psychotic patient who is the case history for the "denial" chapter eventually in symbolic fashion recognized her oncoming death (Kübler-Ross 1969:45). Far from being a universal, static response to death, denial is only a step along the way.

Kübler-Ross' five stages are defined as emotional states. Denial, anger, bargaining, depression, and acceptance can have any variety of cognitive contents, she insists. What is constant is the need of the dying patient to express the emotions appropriate to each stage. Unlike a denying patient, an angry patient disrupts hospital civility and routine, and will often be deliberately avoided and isolated by the staff. Kübler-Ross' strategy for dealing with anger is to stress to its human targets that it is not meant personally, and to encourage its expression for emotional catharsis. Screaming, hitting a pillow, raging at God are all okay; they express, but in such a way that no one will be hurt. (God is big enough to take our anger, she assures readers.) But at all stages, emotional expression is healthy; suppression and a "stiff upper lip" are not.

In addition, some of the responses most widely accepted as proper—such as fighting one's illness to the end—are by Kübler-Ross' criteria unhealthy and unnatural. If dying is a process that unfolds spontaneously, then "the will to live" can impede the process. To cheer up patients, to encourage them to fight, is counter-productive (Kübler-Ross 1969:86–87). So is pressing them to continue treatments when they are "ready" to die. Kübler-Ross deliberately challenges the language of heroism, of military resistance to death. After all, the entire medical profession relies on a military model of conquest, of "unlimited unconditional war," in the words of ethicist William F. May (May 1983:66); medicine sees in any patient's death its own defeat. Although May, deploring this "warfare" imagery, suggests "covenantal" alternatives, today there is a resurgence of support for "fighting" illness, for resistance in the face of AIDS or cancer. At the time Kübler-Ross wrote *On Death and Dying*, the Vietnam War raged and many Americans shared her revulsion against military heroism as a human ideal.

Even in the midst of her treatment of "depression," Kübler-Ross omits certain topics that—on the basis of the autobiographies—one would expect to find. The problem of physical pain, or contemplation of suicide, plays no role in *On Death and Dying*. The pain of depression is psychological, "reactive," and "preparatory" (Kübler-Ross 1969:86). The former deals with specific emotional sources of pain, usually unfinished emotional business from the past. Preparatory depression is focused on the future impending loss of everything and everyone the patient has loved. Here there is little the therapist can do except be present in silence.

For now Kübler-Ross sees the patient's task as decathexis, loosening the ties to the living. The dying person loses interest in more peripheral relationships, and will receive visits only from close family members. Kübler-Ross does not use the term "renunciation," which implies an act of will; decathexis proceeds as a letting go, a relaxing, and not (at least according to Kübler-Ross) a deliberate decision. It leads spontaneously into the last stage of "acceptance."

Kübler-Ross claims that almost all of her patients reach this state, that it does not require any kind of joyous enthusiasm for death, and that it is not the same as bitterly giving up (this would be "resignation"). "Acceptance is not a happy stage; it is

almost void of feelings" (Kübler-Ross 1969:113). The patient
has decathected, is ready to die, and has returned to a prere-
lational condition. In one of her most striking images, Kübler-
Ross cites Bettelheim on infantile narcissism—a time when
nothing was asked of us, "when we experience the self as being
all." She concludes: "And so, maybe at the end of our days,
when we have worked and given, enjoyed ourselves and suffered, we are going back to the stage that we started out with
and the circle of life is closed" (Kübler-Ross 1969:120).

"Acceptance" in this sense has become an ideal, a goal, a
moral achievement, a hope. It appears that in acceptance the
unconscious at last makes room for death. The death that is
accepted is not one of "being killed"; it is nonviolent, nonintru-
sive, the final ripening of the fruit. It may correlate with the
body's own exhaustion, but as a psychological reality it has its
own integrity. Acceptance as a goal, defined in this context,
supposedly has absolutely nothing to do with beliefs. The pious
patient and his wife who are the examples of "acceptance" hold
beliefs entirely different from Kübler-Ross' about what to
expect after death. The man himself sees ahead two good
options. "I do look forward to meeting the Lord, but at the
same time I would like to stay around on earth as long as possible" (Kübler-Ross 1969:122–23). Even the dramatic and well-
publicized shift in Kübler-Ross' own beliefs, after *On Death
and Dying*, does not seem to have altered her definition of what
"acceptance" as psychological condition means. In *On Children
and Death* she repeatedly invokes the image of the caterpillar
becoming a butterfly to describe death as a transition (Kübler-
Ross 1983:141, 220).[1] It is no longer a loss, it is no longer an
ending, it is no longer even a reality. Yet the five stages still
stand, acceptance among them—although the "what" of acceptance has dramatically changed. But this is precisely the point
of Kübler-Ross' formulations; not only "acceptance" but all of
the stages are construed so as to minimize attention to the
ideational "what." They are emotional states, feelings, seemingly detached from any specific cognitive content, and so capable of universal application (Bregman 1989:66–68).

1. In a public lecture attended by the author, Kübler-Ross displayed an
ingenious toy that she used to teach this to her patients: a fuzzy stuffed caterpillar that, once turned inside out, becomes a butterfly!

Readers of *On Children and Death* do not need to be philosophers to recognize the discrepancy between the five original stages and the view of death its author proclaims. One does not ever normally speak of "accepting" a pleasant and nonthreatening event. The original scheme of five stages assumes that death is loss, and that in spite of this humans have the resiliency and the psychological capacities to come to terms with it. If death is no loss at all, but gain (and who would not rather be a butterfly than a caterpillar?), then should not the original framework be adapted to account for this? For no emotion, not even a supposedly "primitive" one such as anger, is really a matter of content-less feeling. The same is true, and has been more frequently noticed, of "acceptance." Kübler-Ross tries to define it strictly as emotional state, but it is impossible to avoid its object, death.

Death and Nature

Kübler-Ross' theory of dying is simultaneously an image of death. Is death as an ending, the view of her original work, truly "acceptable"? Is the letting go and the "closing of life's circle" a stance dependent on a particular view of death that finds it "natural"? When Kübler-Ross was directly asked, "What does death mean to you?" she replied, "Peace" (quoted by Branson 1975:464). Such a view is grounded on the belief that human life is fulfilled only when one lives and dies in harmony with what is biologically natural. But then, what image of "nature" is expressed here?

For Kübler-Ross, and for most psychological ethical naturalists today, "nature" is envisioned as a self-balancing ecosystem. All individuals exist within a prevailing harmony and order. Thus to live and to die in accordance with nature is peaceful, yet includes acceptance of change, of rhythms that are stronger and older than humankind's. Ethical naturalism has taken other forms in the past. For "social Darwinism," nature was "red in tooth and claw." Predation was the lesson to be learned, and conflict in nature validated competition in society. In Freud's view of nature, as we will see, repetition and the principle of homeostasis dominate. But in Kübler-Ross' more optimistic vision of ethical naturalism, the "closing of the circle" is gentle and fulfilling. It does not matter that no "beyond death" exists for us as individuals. Nature itself continues. To wish for continuation when none is given would be to imitate the doctors who insist that patients "keep fighting" even when such a goal defies the body's natural ending.

Perceptive critics have seen in this view of death and nature the seeds for Kübler-Ross' own later views. From this benevolent vision of nature and life's closing circle, she moved to adopt what appears to many to be blatant denial of death. If death for the ethical naturalist is never truly, necessarily a threat, then we can "accept" it without fooling ourselves about the nature of reality. Still, it is the ecosystem and *not* the individual that continues. This system, "nature," is filled with conflict, corpses, and premature death. From any one individual organism's point of view, if predators don't get it, the winter weather will. The ecosystem itself is harmonious and endures, yet for the individual death remains the end of everything. Hence the shift to a view where it is not "the end" at either level does represent a significant change. Kübler-Ross now opts for "natural immortality"—as the caterpillar-to-butterfly image reveals. This is disturbing, but perhaps not so entirely unanticipated.

For all along Kübler-Ross' theory presupposes a fulfillment and self-actualization model of human existence, which combines with ethical naturalism in the metaphor of "growth." This model organizes the clinical data into *stages* and not merely a typology of responses, thus revealing strong value judgments and her own underlying view of "maturity." The fulfillment paradigm makes Kübler-Ross akin to Rogers and Maslow as a personality theorist, and distant from the psychoanalytic tradition. It is the fulfillment model that has dominated popular psychology, the human potential movement, and the self-help genre; Kübler-Ross may find her place here, as the title of an edited book, *Death: The Final Stage of Growth* (Kübler-Ross 1975), reveals. At the level of imagery, this use of "growth" is congruent with naturalism. Objectively, of course, the natural cycle of living organisms includes both growth and decay, birth and death. It is simply misleading to assume that "nature" can be reread as perpetual "growth."

In a very incisive discussion of this dimension of Kübler-Ross, Bonnie Miller-McLemore notes how the assumption of preexisting natural harmony can serve to legitimate individualism. Even the popular image of an ecosystem works in this direction at the level of ethical outlook. If indeed all individuals fit within such an "ecosystem," then true conflict among their needs or desires appears ultimately impossible. All will harmonize "naturally" (Miller-McLemore 1988:86). This pervasive, hidden assumption gives not only Kübler-Ross but many contemporary psychologists a degree of ethical blindness. For then one's own needs and wants are guaranteed a "rightness" that can never be challenged. In fact, Miller-McLemore states, in all the popular "death-awareness" literature, one's appropriate death, needs, experiences, and timing are treated as moral absolutes, and the prospect of conflict with any other commitments or requirements dismissed as negligible (Miller-McLemore 1988:94). Even those who argue against Kübler-Ross' stages as imposing a time-table upon patients hold to this restricted ethical vision of an individual whose own subjectively determined needs are paramount. The hopeless inadequacy of such a viewpoint for serious medical ethics is forcefully argued by Miller-McLemore.

Mourning and Grief-Work

Our concern, however, is to recognize and examine the major images for death and dying used by ethical naturalist theories. Ever since Kübler-Ross' initial work, the study and treatment of mourning—as distinct from dying—have been closely related by all, including Kübler-Ross. Long before her work, in 1944, Erich Lindemann had described grief as a process. In an article on symptomatology and management of acute grief, he suggested that grief was not only a syndrome with a distinct cluster of symptoms, but that as a response to death it formed a process of "grief-work." Grief-work included coping with anger, guilt, and isolation. Since many of Lindemann's subjects were survivors of the infamous Cocoanut Grove fire, a tragedy of mass death at a night club that received much publicity at the time, guilt over having lived while loved ones perished, and sudden shock, were prominent reactions.

The grief-work Lindemann describes requires coping with loss. The bereaved is preoccupied with the image of the deceased, is subjectively certain of that person's continuing presence, and performs actions that presuppose that individual. Established patterns of action, communication, and meaning are all disrupted. Sometimes, behaviors of the deceased are adopted, inappropriately. Actions are initiated and never completed. The bereaved's world is incomplete, and must be reconstructed minus the presence of the deceased. Eventually, however, this is accomplished. The loss may never be forgotten, but the person (it is hoped) develops new patterns of behavior, and begins to live anew.

Lindemann's research establishes certain themes continued in the perspective of Bowlby and Parkes. It is also possible that Kübler-Ross borrowed and adapted it for *On Death and Dying*. But the "process" view of mourning (grief-work) has one firm fixture to it. Its goal is to return the bereaved to connection with life, to let the past go (Lindemann 1944:147). The person who cannot accomplish this appears crippled and disabled, in need of help. We assume that grief is a terminable state, a stage to move through on the way back to full living. At this point, the parallel with one's own dying fails; "acceptance" will have different meanings and implications for the two situations.

The most thoroughgoing "ethical naturalist" of mourning is Colin Parkes, whose work derives from that of John Bowlby, the developer of "attachment theory." Bowlby begins from an ethological, evolutionary stance. Attachment to others is part of human survival. All infants have an inborn capacity to attach themselves to a protective other—not necessarily the biological mother—and we have most often taken this for granted. In the dim prehistory of humanity, individuals who lacked this would have been more vulnerable to accidents, predators, and other dangers (Bowlby 1969:58–64). Only when attachment is secure can the young child venture forth to explore; "independence" is not the enemy of attachment, but its correlate.

When separation and loss occur, both children and adults mourn. The process—the same as that described by Lindemann—is a form of search to restore the lost other (Parkes 1972:39–56), followed by a gradual recognition that this is impossible. Eventually, the attachment fades. Young children restored to their parents after lengthy separations often require time to reattach themselves, much to the parents' dismay. In studies of widows, Parkes showed how mourning was indeed one phase in the overall history of the attachment itself. Insecure or conflictual attachments could generate especially distressing responses to their loss. It is worth mentioning that these studies began in England, where an earlier war had left widespread widowhood and separation (Newcombe and Lerner 1982). The initial research was done on children displaced by the blitz of London. Bowlby raised a strong moral protest against the institutionalization of small children, which had been justified on the grounds that "they're too young to miss their parents," too young to mourn (Bowlby 1969:xii–xiv). In fact the devastation of such separations, and the harm done by threats of separation (especially when made by parents to children), are well documented in the case histories of his books.

Thus the Bowlby–Parkes studies have an entirely different picture of selfhood, reality, and even of nature, from that made familiar by Kübler-Ross. The world—whether of wartime London or the primordial "environment of evolutionary adaptedness" (Bowlby 1969:59)—is a place of dangers and losses, from which persons can protect themselves in part by bonding together. There is no individualism of the sort noted and criticized by Miller-McLemore. Instead, persons depend upon each other; but attachment is risky. To become attached is to become vulnerable to separation and loss. And death is loss from all sides. It is never "the final stage of growth," and there never was a time when "the self was all." Read in contrast to Kübler-Ross the somber picture of life's vulnerabilities—particularly the vulnerabilities of children—is striking.

This approach, significantly, has never enjoyed the popularity of Kübler-Ross or the other "fulfillment" theories. Although it does not claim that grief is inconsolable, it holds out no promise of "peace" in the form of Kübler-Rossian "acceptance." Yet it fits the overall testimony of the autobiographies far better than hers does, since these tales, after all, are stories of attachments and losses. Even if "to die as oneself" is a major theme and goal, this self is supported by the presence of others. The dark picture of nature as filled with losses and unexpected blows also fits the atmosphere of the narratives, where illness strikes and disrupts plans, identities, and lives. "The moon" of AIDS (Monette's image) is in fact Bowlby and Parkes' "nature." It is the ordinary world of health that is illusory. No wonder Parkes' studies never could be used to present death as "acceptable," nor dying as growth.

Both theories rely upon the image of death as loss. Yet neither confines itself to physical death. Bowlby includes all separations in his analysis. And the success of Kübler-Ross' model
of dying has probably been due to its flexibility. It can cover a
wide range of other situations, interpreted as losses. Although
the dynamics are different, separation and loss also occur in
cases of divorce, for example. If one uses Kübler-Ross' "five
stages" as the process whereby persons come to accept any
form of deprivation, then a very wide variety of experiences can
be encompassed. Factory closings (Raines and Day-Lower
1986:43), the responses of the city of San Francisco to the AIDS
epidemic (Shilts 1987:569), amputation of a limb (Parkes
1972:182–89), one's status as an adopted child: all these can be
viewed through the lens of the five stages.

Yet there is something misleading in this wide applicability,
going back once again to the ethical naturalist premises of the
theory. The deaths and losses charted by Kübler-Ross and
Bowlby are unwanted, and certainly unchosen by those who
suffer them. Yet other losses are in part the consequences of
our own decisions, or the result of others' decisions. A factory
closing is as unchosen as an earthquake for most of the work-
ers, an external calamity over which they have no control. But
it is also very different, since someone intended and planned
for it, and probably benefits from it. To treat as similar a loss
that falls upon us as part of "nature's" rhythms, and an outcome caused by human actions and their consequences, represents a serious interpretive decision. Significantly, Kübler-Ross
is astonishingly weak in discussing death due to suicide, or the
suicidal impulses of terminally ill patients. As for death due to
murder or warfare, in these cases the "loss" theme seems most
inadequate, and the human causality most apparent.

Death and Justice

Because of the benign naturalistic framework of "loss,"
death cannot be called an "injustice," let alone a "punishment."
Such terms not only do not appear in Kübler-Ross' work, but
would be vigorously rejected by her. Her ethical naturalism
eliminates the use of "political" or "legal" categories right from
the start, for such ideas as "punishment" do not arise within
"nature" as a biological system. Even if Kübler-Ross' vision of

nature included predation, which it does not, such a phenomenon could not be described as "just" or "unjust." Here,
Bowlby's form of "naturalism" is curiously more capable of
including "justice" as a category; it is "natural" for the young
to expect and receive protection, and "unjust" if they are unnec-
essarily left isolated and defenseless, stripped of their support
and attachments. Still, nature itself is "unjust" in that much
separation and loss are built into reality.

Traditionally, the deaths of human beings can and have
been described as just or unjust. The deaths of soldiers and
civilians in warfare, death by capital punishment, and deaths
through genocide all directly raise this question of justice.
Justice here is not an extraneous imposition of an artificial concept onto a natural event, but a human concern relevant to
understanding and dealing with a human event. The language
of "loss" to some extent avoids this, and, as we have seen, to
assume an ultimate "ecological harmony" of individual aims
deepens this avoidance.

But the language of "justice" is extraordinarily unsettling
and controversial. "Nature" just exists—at least according to
ethical naturalism—whereas "justice" must be established and
argued. Even a small foray into the ways that "justice" might
relate to dying demonstrates this. Although 100 percent of us
will die, the life-expectancies and causes of death will vary
depending upon our race, income level, and place of residence.
Even more unsettling are questions over "personal accountability" in regard to one's health, illness, and death. We
increasingly recognize that some of our fatal diseases are fur-
thered if not actually caused by factors such as environmental
pollution, diet, and lifestyle. Are cigarette smokers to blame
when they sicken with lung cancer? Are cigarette companies
and the media to blame for advertising smoking and trying to
make it glamorous? Are smokers to blame when nonsmokers
in their homes become sick? All of these deaths can be
described as "losses." But "loss" and "nature" will never help us
sort through these other real and important questions con-
cerning them.

A grim if curious testimony to this inadequacy of the "death-
awareness" movement's model of loss, and its ethical naturalism, is that it flourished simultaneously with the rise of medical malpractice suits by patients and their families. Perhaps

Kübler-Ross presented doctors and their technology as villains and so abetted an atmosphere of mistrust. Yet the foundation of "malpractice" is the claim that some hospital deaths are not just sad, but "unjust." They should not have happened, and are someone's fault. Negligence and malpractice are legal categories, and in this model for handling death and suffering almost any outcome less than full recovery can potentially be seen as someone's fault. It is ironic that this perspective seems to be the most prevalent way our society has found to include "justice" categories in its approach to death, to fill the gaps left by a psychological image of "death as loss" to which it seems so radically opposed.

If one doubts this opposition, recall Kübler-Ross' discussion of the dying patient's preoccupation with guilt. Traditionally, dying might have been a time to assess the moral quality of one's own life, one's own accountabilities and failures of response. The autobiographies bear witness to this, although without reports of dramatic reversals and conversions. But recall as well that the categories that define the "stages" of dying are emotional states. Like "anger," "depression" evokes only the amorphous, noncognitive emotion of sadness, and so withdraws attention from the cognitive and moral categories required to make sense of "guilt" as a human experience. Moreover, as Miller-McLemore and many other critics of psychotherapeutic ethics have noted, "guilt" is itself treated as "an inappropriate emotion" (Miller-McLemore 1988:108) and rarely if ever connected to what one can label "objective" circumstances and actions on the part of the self. It is the task of psychotherapy to be "nonjudgmental" rather than accusatory, yet in this case reliance upon an emotional category, "depression," obscures the moral categories that seem appropriate to the situation of the dying.

What would happen if one were to say that death itself is an injustice? Or a punishment? No ethical naturalist would accept such statements. Death is "a natural event." It is, in fact, childish and petulant to protest against it. To use a word loaded with connotations for the movement advanced by Kübler-Ross, it is "undignified" to do so (Morison 1975:99). To die with dignity is to accept that death comes as natural event. The autobiographies, discussed in the previous chapter, reveal how utterly certain traditional Christian theological statements have vanished from the landscape of American thought and imagery regarding death. Ethical naturalism, in contrast, permeates our lives and patterns of thought, as the two persons whose words began this chapter illustrate. Although almost all Christian therapists and chaplains would clearly reject the spiritualism of the later Kübler-Ross, the overwhelming response to her original work has been favorable, and often an unqualified endorsement of her basic theory. As a result, much of the literature produced by this group duplicates secular psychological writings, and makes no attempt to discover underlying incompatibilities between historical Christian theological assertions and Kübler-Ross' ethical naturalism. Although a reaction has now set in against uncritical use of secular psychotherapies among Christian counselors, in this area there are not the kind of clear alternatives to Kübler-Ross that one might imagine. Moreover, until certain fundamental theological and ethical issues are addressed, nature, growth, and acceptance will probably be our vocabulary for dying, our imagery, and our myth of death.

Depth Psychologies of Death: Three Legacies

$\mathbb{A}$lthough it has been through the ethical naturalist myth of harmony with a natural ecosystem that many Americans have been able to "accept" dying as an intrinsic part of life, if not "a final stage of growth," there are alternative mythic frameworks for visioning death within psychological theory. In fact, as we move away from the popular "healthy-minded" form of naturalism with which Kübler-Ross is associated, we find ourselves confronted more clearly with the "mythic" dimensions of psychology. When it takes the form of grandiose speculations on "the death instinct," such thought can become "mythic" indeed. In this chapter, we will examine three "legacies," all of which can be grouped as "depth psychologies of death." For us, they provide alternative perspectives to the dominant form of ethical naturalism, the seemingly easy accommodation to death that Kübler-Ross' goal of "acceptance" promises.

The Freudian Legacy

Depth psychology may not have historically begun with Freud, but in the twentieth century's intellectual landscape, he is surely its founder. True, Freud's infamous, overt, and untempered hostility to all religious formulations makes him an unpromising candidate for a work that attempts to integrate psychological perspectives with Christian faith. Additionally, on the topic of death, some of Freud's ideas are not only bizarre, but were never accepted even by those who followed his other theories "religiously." Americanized Freudianism managed to exclude "the death instinct" entirely.

But such considerations ought not to deter us from taking Freud's legacy seriously, whether or not we wish to claim it for our own. Freud's own hostility to religion has not prevented several generations of theorists and counselors from attempting to sift out from his theories that which is in essential contradiction to religious commitment, and that which is only accidentally so. There is a long tradition already established of trying to "integrate" what is valid within psychoanalysis with what is central within religion, Christianity in particular. Obviously there is the potential of a dialogue between Freud and religious faith, if not a full conceptual integration. If there remains a basic disjunction between the work of Freud and virtually all forms of religiousness, disjunctions are what good religious reflection is used to encountering.

The roots for that disjunction illuminate much about religious faith that might have lain hidden had it not been for Freud's work. There are forms of faith that duplicate the conflicts of childhood, and others that manage to move the individual beyond childhood dynamics in some significant, positive way. Freud's perspective on interpretation and symbolism helps us discern the dynamics and ambivalence of all religious symbols. The "gender asymmetry" of Freud's thought on masculine/feminine development subtly correlates with his evaluations of cultural endeavors, including religion. And the many strands of Freud's thought include several relevant to a religious perspective on death.

It is true that psychoanalysis, in spite of Freud's claims about it, cannot be considered a "science," nor do its statements correspond to the criteria for scientific claims. It is certainly not "value-free" as a form of therapy. At least since 1964, when Perry London showed in *The Modes and Morals of Psychotherapy* that no therapy really could be considered so, the issue of psychoanalysis' status as theory and clinical practice has been viewed in other terms. Since all therapies presuppose some ideal toward which the patient/client must move, some desired goal, it is impossible to uphold an ideal of "scientific" value-neutrality. Hence, if psychoanalysis and other therapies are based upon values and visions of the human, then they are not really different than other, more traditional systems of insight, including those of religion.

The Death Instinct

In this light, we should reconsider the meaning of Americanized Freudianism's refusal to accept the founder's later speculations about death. Freud wrote, after 1920, of the "death instinct." It is fair to say that this idea has played virtually no positive role in the American appropriation of Freud. Is this because such an idea is genuinely "unscientific" in contrast to the earlier theories, such as the Oedipus complex? No, that answer is insufficient and misleading. What was adapted from psychoanalysis in America was exactly the theme of "denial" with which Kübler-Ross began. "In the unconscious, death is never possible in regard to ourselves." For the deepest level of the self, death simply does not exist. Perhaps that is why, in Philip Rieff's excellent *Freud: The Mind of the Moralist* (1961), there is no chapter or even systematic discussion of Freud on death. It may well be that this particular rendition of Freud legitimates at the level of theory American society's overall denial of death. If death does not exist in the unconscious, that somehow makes its invisibility in our culture seem more normal, less deviant from its presence in other societies and historical eras. Ironically, Freud's own work claimed just the opposite: how pervasive, if elusive, "death" as human possibility is within the deepest level of the psyche. However improbable Freud's ideas, their unpopularity on this issue says more about our society and its prejudices than about the intrinsic worth of Freud's concept.

Having allowed for this sociological bias, however, it remains true that Freud's account of the "death instinct" is as speculative and distant from clinical material as can be. The "death instinct" is never linked directly to death as human event, to the kinds of phenomena captured in the autobiographies or in Kübler-Ross. *Beyond the Pleasure Principle* is

Freud's exposition of this idea. It begins with a focus upon the compulsion to repeat, as in the horrible dreams of those who survive a traumatic experience and repeat it at night. Freud then moves to the role of repetition in psychoanalysis, particularly the manner in which "transference neurosis" is a forced repetition of the original relationships of the patient's childhood. Almost immediately, from these starting points, Freud postulates a force that strives toward return, toward a primordial stasis. Like other Freudian "forces," it is entirely "internal," however alien to consciousness its aims may be. Such a force encompasses all of "natural" reality, however, not just human psychic reality. The final goal of all organic striving is a return to an inorganic state. This is the equivalent of death—not decayed yet once-living organic matter, but "inorganic" primordial inert stuff. "If we are to take it as a truth that knows no exception that everything living dies for *internal* reasons—becomes inorganic once again—then we shall be compelled to say that '*the aim of all life is death*' and, looking backwards, that '*inanimate things existed before living ones*'" (Freud 1955 [1920]:38). Freud then discusses various theories about the origin of death in multicelled beings, and whether indeed it is true that "everything living dies for internal reasons." He reviews work on one-celled animals, and concludes that although individual death may not have been the primordial situation for such creatures, the thrust toward a return to the inorganic could have been active even before the origin of "death" as the means to achieve such a goal. "Aim," "destiny," and "goal" are all equated with "final end," so that the theme of a force at work striving toward death turns the fact of death into an "instinct." Death is not "the final stage of growth," but the triumph of this instinct for return to primordial unliving stasis.

The "death instinct" meets its match in its opposite, the sexual instinct. Freud traces the origin of sexual reproduction in lower organisms and links sexuality to the "life instincts," which strive toward union. Previously, Freud had associated sexuality with tension reduction, but the latter now appears as the "goal" of the death instinct. He comments: "Our views have from the very first been *dualistic*, and today they are even more definitely dualistic than before—now that we describe the opposition as being, not between ego instincts and sexual instincts but between life instincts and death instincts" (Freud 1955 [1920]:53).

Freud, working to construct a mythology of instincts (a term he himself was willing to use in this context!), considers and rejects an alternative formulation. Suppose one were to postulate a "regressive" instinct and a "progressive" one, the first reaching back to the inorganic, the second questing forward to some "higher" or more spiritual goal for organic life. One thinks of all the "progressivist" or "evolutionary" theories that have flourished during the past 150 years, which depend upon such an idea and hope for a "New Age" when the progressive instinct will triumph over the regressive. Freud's words on this possibility bear quoting:

> It may be difficult . . . to abandon the belief that there is an instinct toward perfection at work in human beings, which has brought them to their present high level of intellectual achievement and ethical sublimation and which may be expected to watch over their development into supermen. I have no faith, however, in the existence of any such internal instinct and I cannot see how this benevolent illusion is to be preserved. The present development of human beings requires . . . no different explanation from that of animals. (Freud 1955 [1920]:42)

Even at his most "mythic" Freud could not tolerate this version of Enlightenment eschatology, rejecting it as a "benevolent illusion." It would make cultural achievement and ethical sublimation real and direct expressions of "instinctual" forces rather than secondary phenomena derived from instinctual repression. Nowhere can we see Freud's "hermeneutic of suspicion" in regard to culture, ideals, and moral achievement more clearly displayed. The only "progress" permitted is the "aim" of all organic matter to return to its original inorganic, dead state. The future is never other than a return to the beginning, in disguised form. Moreover, no separation of the "human" from "animals" is to be introduced in order to serve the benevolent illusions of humankind—although Freud is elsewhere anything but a simplistic biological reductionist.

Here at Freud's most mythic, "the death instinct" makes death a pervasive, enormously powerful force, an active agent that kills "internally" rather than from outside. As "return" it is the remote past, reappearing as *telos*, as aim. Freud must then explain why we strive to resist and postpone this goal with all our might. To see death as a return is part of the pervasive Freudian sense that everything we do is in some sense a return. The unconscious is "timeless"; we never grow beyond it, our childhood never vanishes from our adulthood, and the past is a perpetual burden that we are doomed to carry around throughout our lives. If so, then death is the final triumph of the past over the organism's futile attempt to stake out a present for itself. We may recall a vestige of this idea from the Bettelheim quote of Kübler-Ross. Dying is like a return to infancy, a return to one's individual beginning. Yet the difference in the tone of the two observations is absolute. Freud speaks of the futility of consolation in this ending, while Kübler-Ross tries to bring exactly that. Infancy may be romantically glorified, whereas no one can do much with "the inorganic state" as a source of hope.

The "biological" nature of these speculations is abundantly obvious. Freud leaves psychological levels of discourse completely behind. Defenders of Freud, or even cautious critics, allow that Freud's use of "instinct" is intentionally ambiguous. It is a biological concept, yet the representatives and representations of instincts are psychological. Once Freud abandoned the hope to found psychological functioning on neurology—which he did very early—the terminology he develops proceeds as if he were dealing with a level of autonomous psychic events not reducible to physiology. But this does not appear to hold true for the death instinct. Freud's plunge into biology makes it seem as if he at last has found a direct mooring between human instincts and organic processes. Nor does *Beyond the Pleasure Principle* ever link clinical data directly to death.

Nevertheless, "the death instinct" does, somehow, suggest that death remains an invisible yet ever-present *psychological* as well as biological fact. That organisms always die because of "internal causes" is certainly false, but that something internal ties us to death seems an important insight. Moreover, although death may not be literally a return to an inorganic state, to so envision it is to reveal death as a potential psychological force operating "behind the scenes" of psyche and culture. For Freud, in contrast to Kübler-Ross, death is *not* the final stage of growth; it is a consummation of that which tends toward *un*-growth, and which will therefore never be compatible with cultural progress or achievements. Even the biological tie-in may have another meaning. As David Bakan points out (Bakan 1966:160), Freud created his idea of the death instinct when he developed cancer. Is his acknowledgment of a drive toward death the psychological correlate of his cancer? Perhaps Freud himself was experiencing in his own body, in a new manner, that "the goal of life is death." This link may be the missing "clinical data" for *Beyond the Pleasure Principle.*

Castration and Death

Were "the death instinct" the sole constituent of the Freudian legacy in regard to the psychology of death, the legacy itself would be far less valuable. Two other principal themes must be mentioned alongside it. One we may label the "castration connection" and the second is *Ananke* (necessity). Both of these have actually been more directly significant to American psychoanalysis than the death instinct.

As is well known, Freud believed that the central conflict concerned the male child's desire for his mother, and jealousy toward the father. The little boy's murderous rage against the father is balanced by his love and admiration; Freud stresses the ambivalence inherent in all such family bonds. The child is therefore able to internalize his father's condemnation of incestuous desire, resulting in guilt, an intrapsychic condition. The father does not actually have to threaten the son with punishment; the child will fantasize such a threat if one is not actually made. The "punishment" involved here is inevitably castration, violence against the organ associated with the boy's desire, and so with his fantasized "offense" against the father. In the paradigm case of Oedipus, his self-blinding (a symbolic substitute for castration) is an act of expiation inflicted not by external authority but by the guilt-ridden self. Freud's use of this story is so pervasive, so "mythic," that no account of his ideas would be complete without it. There are also certain peculiarities in his version of the Oedipus story. Foremost is that in Sophocles' original drama the seeds for tragedy are sown through the father's murderous hostility against his baby son. Whereas Oedipus' crime of patricide is unwitting, his father's

infanticidal attempt is all too deliberate and conscious.[1] Another
peculiarity is the loss of any role for "Jocasta," the mother,
except that of desired object. A baby's first tie is to its mother,
and this relation must condition all its later experiences; Freud
never denied this. But again and again, he found this "pre-
Oedipal" bond impenetrable, or else believed it to be of little
interest compared to the conflict generated by the Oedipal crisis. Although post-Freudian psychoanalysis has rectified this
gap, Freud's own view of murder, guilt, and punishment is thoroughly tied to the Oedipal conflict and the motif of castration.

It is taken for granted by Freud and his followers that
Oedipus' self-blinding is a symbolic castration. Here we see
Freud's theory of symbolism as well as his preoccupation with
the penis as organ of male identity and power. Castration itself
could never be a substitute for blinding. Symbolism requires
that the less acceptable, sexual, meaning is the one repressed.
Such a bias virtually identifies all punishment with castration
and the latter's symbolic equivalents. It introduces gender
directly into the psychology of death, as no other psychological
theory dares to do so starkly.

When Freud came to adapt this myth to the situation of
women, the Oedipus tale eventually proved faulty as a guide.
The drama for girls was how to transfer their first love, for
their mother, to the "appropriate" object, their father. Women
do not grow beyond the father-qua-love-object, as men grow
beyond the Oedipus complex. For a female, there is no "dissolution" of the complex through identification with the father.
Instead, she simply substitutes husband and eventually son for
the father, thus remaining bound to paternal authority
throughout her life. The real crisis for her is the early move
from mother to father, in conjunction with the discovery of her

1. It is David Bakan who noticed how Freud's filiocentrism ignores and
represses the theme of the paternal "infanticidal impulse" in myth (Bakan
1966:205ff.). Bakan, however, turns to the biblical story of Abraham and Isaac
as exemplary of this motif, leaving Oedipus be. A defender of Freud might
point out that Sophocles as well focused on the psyche and tragedy of Oedipus
the son, not his father. Perhaps internally experienced guilt holds more fascination than actual offense for the Western psyche, even before Paul and
Augustine. Nevertheless, this issue continues to haunt all those who confront
family violence, where Freud's filiocentrism and intrapsychic emphasis seem
to distort the actualities of child abuse through denial and projection.

own inferiority, namely, her lack of a penis. Castration, for the girl, has already happened; it is not a threat or a punishment, but a fate to which she must become resigned. Recognizing her mother as castrated makes it possible for the little girl to scorn her, and transfer her own affections to her intact and potent father (Van Herik 1982:131).[2]

If the Oedipus complex is simultaneously a psychological theory of death, with its mix of castration, guilt, and punishment, then what of death-fears and guilt in women? Freudian thought sees death directly as murderous wish on the part of the son, answered by the half-death of castration. The latter is punishment for the male but fate for the female. Does this mean that women will somehow be more "resigned" to death? Less driven by unconscious guilt, since they have not internalized the father's prohibition? Perhaps, more plausibly, death as bodily mutilation will mean something different for men and women, although not even this would be directly supported by the autobiographies. What seems the least productive route to take is to assume that all references to death are "really" disguised references to castration. Such wooden use of Freud's ideas clings to the postulate that sexual meanings must be the most basic. They cannot be "symbolic" of something else. As a claim about the anxieties of Kübler-Ross' dying patients, this seems absurd.

The "castration" theme plays a major role in Freud's understanding of religion. *Totem and Taboo* (1957 [1913]) is his attempt to trace back the "origin" of religion through the myth of a primal humanity dominated by a tyrannical father. The band of sons who overthrow, kill, and eat the father are then themselves consumed by guilt. Although their revolt had as its goal to obtain the women of the group for themselves, their guilt leads to renunciation of this good (and the start of exogamy). Out of guilt, they reinstate the murdered father at the level of group fantasy, and create a ritual whereby they

2. Judith Van Herik, together with Juliet Mitchell, is a feminist interpreter of Freud. They believe that a full portrait of "femininity" as it has been defined in Western culture is needed before alternative psychologies can be developed. Freud, they find, provides such a portrait, and for this reason his writings are worth close study. This stance is in contrast to the majority of American feminist thinkers, although French feminism is much more closely associated with psychoanalysis.

both reenact the crime against him (the totem meal) and seek to appease his wrath. For Freud, the very stuff of religion is guilt and attempted atonement, and all forms of religion do little more than reenact this primordial drama of crime and retribution. Freud repeats this message in *Moses and Monotheism* (1964 [1939]). Thus death as murder, rather than as "internally caused," dominates Freud's portrait of religion. Religion, far from being easily outgrown, is a primordial destructive legacy, "internal" to humanity rather than imposed.

These ideas may be as far-fetched at their literal level as is the death instinct. But the "castration connection" provides an experiential matrix for a link between death and punishment that Kübler-Ross' brand of ethical naturalism entirely ignores. "Punishment" here links the family to the legal order, for father as internalized by the son is not acting as arbitrary vindictive tyrant, but as the representative of law. It is in this symbolic capacity that the son seeks identification with him, to become his imitator and cultural heir. The Oedipus and castration themes provide exactly that bridge between body and society, nature and culture, growth and guilt, which strict ethical naturalism negates or ignores. At this level, Freud's death-imagery transcends the biology of "the death instinct," without leaving "nature" behind entirely.

In formulating such thoughts, we already may be anticipating the theological section ahead. Although Christians have had many things to say on death in addition to the thought that it is a punishment for primordial transgression, this idea has been at least one ingredient in traditional theology. To exclude all reference to guilt in a theological discussion of death may abandon the field of discourse to ethical naturalism, as Miller-McLemore claims. Curiously, Freud's "castration connection" becomes a strong twentieth-century reemergence of this classical theological motif, albeit in altered guise.

Ananke

The third element in the Freudian legacy may actually be a function of Freud's personal *Weltanschauung* as much as of his theories. A strong sense of the need for reconciliation to the harshness of fate and reality runs through his writings and his life. We have seen this already in his refusal to grant a "progressive instinct" any status as an ultimate principle, and instead to label it "benevolent illusion" (Freud 1955 [1920]:42). In *The Future of an Illusion* (1961 [1927]) Freud makes this stance toward death, disappointment, and suffering even more clear by contrasting it with religion's reliance on illusory consolation. This is Freud's most simplistic book on religion. Published in 1927, it relies exclusively on Freud's earlier pleasure/reality dualism. In the debate Freud admits that an illusion may not be false, but it is held because it is what one desires, and is therefore suspect. In contrast, "education to reality" (Freud 1961 [1927]:49) holds out the promise of exchanging illusion for actual practical gains, however limited. The latter are to be achieved through science, the human cultural endeavor that corresponds to reliance on the reality principle. Nowhere else does Freud's simplistic positivism, his use of the Enlightenment cliché of the war between science and religion, play such a large role.

But amid the hope of progress through science, another theme is part of "education to reality." It is the honest encounter with suffering that life without illusions demands. "The gods retain their threefold task: they must exorcize the terrors of nature, they must reconcile men to the cruelty of Fate, particularly as it is shown in death, and they must compensate them for the sufferings and privations which a civilized life in common has imposed on them" (Freud 1961 [1927]:18). Without gods, these features of human existence do not vanish, but remain starkly in place. *Ananke*, necessity, is Freud's term for them (Freud 1961 [1927]:53). The triumph of *Logos* (reason) never exceeds what *Ananke* sets as its limits. Once again, for Freud, death could never be "the final stage of growth." It will remind us how all growth is limited in duration and in scope. Just as Freud's hopes for what psychoanalysis could accomplish grew more and more restricted, so his view of *Ananke's* power seems to have grown.

This attitude toward death and life's limits is often labeled "stoicism," and it appears to have dominated Freud's own experience in facing his long, very painful illness and dying. Stoicism is, of course, assimilable into ethical naturalism. To die with dignity is to face one's biological ending knowingly, dispassionately, and with a certain reconciliation to nature's (*Ananke's*) relentlessness. As indicated, this is apparently how

Freud faced his own death: not as a substitute for castration, or as the triumph of the death instinct, but as the irrevocable and invincible working of Fate. Is this "acceptance"? Whatever his actual words, the psychic meaning of this attitude clearly differs from that of Kübler-Ross, even in her earlier work. The difference lies not only in Freud's reliance upon the pleasure/reality dichotomy, but in the entire view of "nature" the two hold. Kübler-Ross' "nature" consoles, for as life's circle closes the "self" becomes "all" as it was in the beginning. Freud's "nature" disappoints, disillusions, and finally kills.

We can see this Freudian motif functioning as legacy in the work of thanatologists other than Kübler-Ross. For Avery Weisman the contrast between death and illusion retains its Freudian meaning. "If ultimate dissolution is absolute, then it is the *Future*, any future, which is the true illusion. . . . What death means, however, is that the future does not exist" (Weisman 1972:213). Weisman like Freud holds that "It is completely within human potentiality to greet death ruefully, but without regret" (Weisman 1972:226). This form of dignified death mixes a stark sense of renunciation of the illusory future with a significance found in the very act of refusing the denials offered by religion and other illusions. "Denial at too great a price is an encumbrance" (Weisman 1972:224) and paradoxically in the spurning of traditional consolations one achieves the only real consolation: the dignity of one who submits to reality. It is not surprising that Weisman's very Freudian vision of a "good death" could not be translated into an inspirational best-seller, nor serve as the grounding for a popular movement of "death awareness."

Freud advocates the renunciation of illusions, of narcissistic satisfactions, of wish-fulfillments. An instrinsic part of this is the lesson of *Ananke* that death is universal, inevitable, painful. Yet there are certain satisfactions that are never renounced; the pride of whoever manages to live without the illusions of religious consolation is one of these. Perhaps smug superiority of masculinity is another, given the tone of Freud's writings on gender. If there is a Freudian ideal of the good person and the good death, it combines these two themes. The one who can renounce illusions is clearly a psychically masculine figure whose reliance on *Logos* is the correlate of freedom from the Oedipal conflict through identification with the father (Van Herik 1982:103).

This "stoic" ideal is genuinely "heroic," as have been its precursors down through the centuries. It is also just as clearly an ideal distinct from what Christianity has cherished, however much that has varied. Nor does it truly seem to animate the autobiographers, perhaps because so many of them are women (who, given the "gender bias" of the theory behind the ideal, might not be capable of sufficient "renunciation" of their illusions). The "heroism" of a Grace West was of a warmer, far more enthusiastic sort. She who said "Yes" to life, might even have found a way to befriend and so transform *Ananke*. The Freudian perspective would consider such a hope another instance of "benevolent illusion," along with the religious beliefs of many of the other writers. Still, the Freudian hope for triumph over the need for such illusion represents an idealized self, mythic in the ability to acknowledge fate truthfully and to face death without lies.

The Jungian Legacy

Freud and Jung stand together as co-giants of depth psychology. Although Freud has been immeasurably more influential in American culture at large, Jung is equally important for anyone interested in religious issues. His works all touch on religious motifs, symbolism, and ideas. It is through such topics that the Jungian legacy in regard to death emerges. The primary aspect of this legacy is his reliance on "death" coupled with "rebirth" as a symbol for a universal pattern of psychic transformation. This idea plays a core role within his psychological theory. A second and far more peripheral aspect of the legacy concerns Jung's own peculiar beliefs about the dead and life after death. As in the case of Freud, the theorist as individual experiencer and sufferer plays a role here.

Unlike Freud, Jung was never preoccupied with finding biological correlates to psychological processes identified in his theory. Although he made occasional references to analogies from biology or chemistry, no equivalent to Freud's focus on death in amoebas clutters Jung's writings. If anything, analytic psychology, the system he developed after his break with Freud, pushes the "symbolic" dimension of life, death, growth, and sexuality so heavily that one easily loses sight of how these as *symbols* connect to the embodied person. Another aspect of this shift toward the "symbolic" is Jung's replacement of Freud's focus on the individual's early childhood, by references to "primordial" archetypal consciousness, or to archaic humanity. Similarly, instead of references to men and women with differing genitals and gender identity, one finds "feminine" and "masculine" frequently used as principles, or as psychic orientations without regard to physiology. One may appreciate Jung for his emphasis on symbolism, and his move away from biological reductionism and pan-sexuality. Nevertheless, the results can occasionally be muddled.

Jung's understanding of symbolism is itself an important aspect of his legacy. Whereas for Freud symbols occur as part of defense and disguise, Jung insists that dream images and figures in myths *reveal* (Jung 1953 [1943]:#162[3]). There are kinds of meanings that can be conveyed only via pictorial, nondiscursive vehicles. Jung's theory of symbols puts him squarely within the early twentieth-century approach of Ernst Cassirer, Rudolph Otto, and G. Van Der Leeuw, all of whom sought to recover a sense of the nonrational, mysterious, and sacred as a distinctive "way" to know reality (Jung 1958 [1938]:#6). In this sense, Jung is a practitioner of what Paul Ricoeur calls "hermeneutics as the restoration of meaning" (Ricoeur 1970:28–32). Although Jung denies that symbols function purely as "defenses" against repressed unacceptable meanings, however, his own "psychologizing" of mythic and religious imagery is in its own way as "reductionist" as Freud's. Jung was often thoroughly aware that he had "seen through" traditional understandings of religion, and freely translated claims about God and Christ into statements about psyche and the Self-archetype. This simultaneous sense of "restoration" and "reduction" marks much of what he says about "death" and "the dead."

Death Symbolism and Transformation

Death enters Jung's thought through the gateway of psychological transformation. According to Jung, the major psy-

---

3. All references to Jung's *Collected Works* cite the numbered paragraphs.

chological process accomplished in therapy is that of "individuation." This goal is actually a spontaneous development of "the
second half of life" (Jung 1933:106) for which the therapist can
serve as midwife. Therapy is more than freedom from the past;
it is progressive or purposive. The person had hitherto lived as
if ego or consciousness were all there is, a naiveté in regard to
psychological matters that Jung saw pervading Western rational culture. The typical Jungian patient had been a rational-
ist, until things started to go wrong. Neurotic suffering in the
form of irrational urges, embarrassing symptoms, and other
inroads against the hegemony of the ego, brought the person
into therapy. The therapeutic process takes the form of the
ego's conscious separation from parts of the psyche now
revealed as "not-ego." The easiest to recognize is the persona,
or "mask"—what we would ordinarily call the "social self." This
is the first to go; with the collapse of the persona comes that
distinctive Jungian moment when the true, deeper powers
within the psyche begin to make themselves known (Jung 1953
[1943]:#243–53; Homans 1979:96). In a sense, then, the separation of ego from persona, the recognition that I am not my
social role, is the first of many "deaths" within Jungian analysis. The persona for Jung, however, is never particularly valuable. It is simply, as the term itself implies, a mask that, once
shed, frees the person for deeper access to unconscious contents, and to more interior "deaths."

The next aspect of the person to be identified as clearly distinct from the ego is "the shadow," the feared negative qualities previously denied or projected onto others. This shadow
corresponds most closely to "the repressed" in Freud's theory,
although Jung personifies it into a secret, dark "other."
According to Jung, the shadow is not "really" evil, just unde-
veloped, socially awkward, and different from the rational ego's
aspirations (Jung 1958 [1938]:#134). In a sense, although once
again "humiliation" might be a better term, an encounter with
the shadow is a "death" to the individual's pretensions to perfection.

It is only when one moves beyond the "personal" unconscious
of the shadow, and into what Jung refers to as the collective,
objective, or archetypal unconscious, that the true power of
"death" as symbol emerges. When patients have dealt with the
shadow—I am schematizing here more than Jung himself ever

did—they then encounter a mysterious contrasexual figure, in
dreams and waking fantasies, who represents the powers and
presence of the deeper unconscious realm. This figure is "the
anima" or "the animus" and through her/him (always personified) the ego meets the primordial collective energies of the
objective psyche (Jung 1953 [1943]:#296–340). Most of Jung's
examples deal with men—rational egos—confronting their ani-
mas; the confrontation with the animus for women is less
clearly specified (Jung 1953 [1943]:#328–33). Other unconscious powers deep within the objective psyche emerge as a
series of "archetypal" figures: Wise Old Man, Great Mother,
Divine Child, and finally the Self, symbolized by a mandala or
quaternity figure of some kind.[4] The goal of therapy as "individuation" is to recenter the psyche away from the ego, and
within the Self-archetype, which can then serve as a "mid-
point" between conscious and unconscious (Jung 1953
[1943]:#365).

Jung relies heavily upon a balance model, between conscious
and unconscious "halves" of the psyche. The goal may be
described as the union of opposites, the meeting of ego and
anima, to produce the Self (Jung 1953 [1943]:#274). In fact,
that is Jung's most frequent metaphor. All sorts of symbols
appear as paired sets of opposites within the framework of this
balance model. The preference for geometrical shapes dia-
gramming this process, in books by Jung's followers, adds to
this fascination with balance and the union between opposites.
Individuation as a process is goal-oriented, however, and the
end result will be a "new being," the Self. The S should be capi-
talized, because Jung made it clear that this is a numinous,
symbolic reality rather than what we ordinarily think of as a
psychological concept (Jung 1953 [1943]:#399).

At this point, Jung's theory is closer to a "fulfillment" model
than one of "balance." Instead of a union of opposites, the
emphasis shifts to the "new being" of the Self, and so, by this

4. Jung neither offers a systematic inventory of these figures, nor gives any
absolute numerical limit to them. For example, is "the maiden" an archetype
separate from "the anima," or an expression of the latter? Is "the trickster" an
archetype on his own? Do some archetypes reflect directly the dimension of
"soul" about which Hillman (see Chapter 4) speaks, while others fall more into
the domain of "spirit"? My own view is that had Jung wished to provide
unequivocal answers to such questions, he would have done so.

path, to death and rebirth as the symbolism of its appearance. The ego must "die" so that the Self may be born. Here is where Jung's mechanical balance imagery proves too static and depersonalized, inappropriate for what he wants to convey. He turns to religious symbolism because that alone fits the processes he describes. But he never frees himself entirely from geometry: the Self as "mid-point" is best symbolized by the mandala, a geometrical quaternity figure with a clearly marked center (Jung 1968 [1952]:Part 2, Chapter 3, #122ff.).

When Jung seeks for suitable religious symbols of the ego's death, he relies on those of Christianity. Christ as a symbol of the Self replaces the "I" of the individual ego, as in Paul's famous declaration of Galatians 2:20: "It is no longer I who live, but Christ who lives in me" (Jung 1953 [1943]:#365). But although at least one entire book has been written by a Jungian on this theme (Cox 1959), Jung never found the Christian context for it comfortable. Orthodox Christianity, however powerfully it provides us with a paradigm of ego-death and a hope for a new center of personal existence, seemed flawed to him on other grounds (Jung 1958 [1938]:#103).

Jung sought alternatives in the symbolism of alchemy. Why? In the alchemists, Jung believed he had found his true precursors. The alchemists projected their own psychic transformations onto the metals and other substances with which they worked. In alchemy, substances were "reduced" or "killed," mixed with other substances, or "married" and distilled, so that their spiritual essence was released from its material bondage. In other words, alchemists freely mixed language of death-rebirth, and mystical union, with chemical operations conducted on inorganic substances. They hoped for the redemption of matter, and not merely of the spirit. This was a goal whose inclusiveness appealed to Jung (Jung 1968 [1952]:#40). Their language fascinated Jung, perhaps because it seems to have lacked the "moral" overtones of the Christian usage.

Alchemical "death" relied upon two themes: dismemberment and self-immolation on the one hand, and dissolution through sexual union on the other (Jung 1968 [1952]:#333–34). This most esoteric pattern of death and rebirth imagery focuses upon death as the painful, violent destruction of the old self, and upon the power gained through this experience. Although the alchemists projected this death upon the metals of their experiments, they identified with the "torments" of these substances, and sought in such symbolic self-immolation a new and eternal identity. This was also symbolized by a stone or jewel, the *lapis* or "philosopher's stone" they sought through their work. These are Jung's interpretations, at least; whether or not he was correct about alchemy's symbolism is another issue.

The second alchemical death-image comes from the use of "sacred marriage" to express union with the numinous. Sol and Luna, king and queen, join together naked in a bed-cum-bath, within which they dissolve together. They give birth to a child, a stone, a new and spiritual entity of some kind—a symbol for the Self of the alchemist. This image of marital union fits with Jung's balance model and his preoccupation with the symbolism of contrasexual opposites. Whether alchemy was really less misogynist in its view of sexuality than other systems of thought contemporary to it is debatable, but Jung seems to have appreciated its "feminine" symbolic dimension.

Alchemical "death" is initiatory death; this is the chief religious parallel to individuation as a therapeutic process. If the union of matter and spirit forms the major quest of alchemy, Jung believed this to be parallel to the patient's quest for a union between conscious and unconscious. Symbolic, initiatory death, then, is the way in which "death" becomes an interior psychic reality. Death is simply not linked to embodiment. Nor is it ever connected with castration, by the way, so that alchemical dismemberment symbolism appears to be "gender-neutral" in contrast to Freud's fascination with bodily mutilation. Nor is death as psychic state tied to negative experiences such as physical illness. Indeed, death and sex become "spiritualized" to such an extent that they seem to refer exclusively to intrapsychic transformations (Wehr 1987:70).

The advantage of this approach, advocates of Jung's legacy will insist, is that it counters our culture's materialistic tendency to reduce everything to its physical, biological meaning. Freud wished to speak of giant cosmic forces of Love and Death mythically, but his materialist prejudices forced him to do so by way of examining the evidence for death among amoebas! For Jung, all symbols are viewed primarily as revelatory of truths that escape the rational intellect, and only secondarily and occasionally as disguises and distortions. For the sake of the numinous, Jung claims the primacy of the psychic over biological-literal meanings, when he deals with both sex and death as imageries.

This argument, which we will take up in more detail in later chapters, does help account for the very real variety of "death-language" used in Christian writings and spirituality. If there is *The Death in Every Now*, to cite the title of one theological work (Ochs 1969), it can only be because "death" has been loosened from its link to terminal illness, the dying of the body, and the entire ethos of ethical naturalism inhabited by Kübler-Ross and her patients. On the other hand, the same criticisms made about Jung's theory of sexuality and gender could be offered about this side of his legacy on death. Demaris Wehr, a feminist critic of Jung, finds that he confusingly jumps back and forth between describing "the anima" and making statements about women. The reader is kept guessing whether and how "real women" or "the feminine" or the man's anima is the topic (Wehr 1987:104). If we refuse to equate biological death with "real death" we still have a right to hope that death symbolism ought to be connectible with physical death, somehow or other. Jung does not do this at the level of his theory.

The Dead

The same may also be true of the other side of Jung's legacy, where not physical death but "the dead" become the focus. There is a definite presence for "the dead" in *Memories, Dreams, Reflections*, Jung's posthumously published autobiography. The dead appear in dreams, in night visions that Jung treats as psychic experiences, and as the congregation in "Seven Sermons to the Dead," reprinted as an appendix at the end of the book (Jung 1963:229–31, 305–10, 378–90). Jung's personal world is filled with paranormal and uncanny events, and shared by the living and the dead. The dead do not appear principally as corpses, but as visitors, spirits in search of something. In one dream of his dead father, the father asks his psychiatrist-son to recommend a book on marital therapy because soon Jung's mother will die, and rejoin her dead husband (Jung 1963:315). The dead are not all-wise; they are restive with the unfinished business of their earthly lives. More remote dead are ancestral spirits, either of Jung personally, or of all humans now alive. Jung accepts some form of postdeath existence, but it is not of a

conventional Christian blissful or punitive kind (Jung
1963:Chapter 11). Nor does his belief take the doctrinaire form
of the later Kübler-Ross' caterpillar-into-butterfly ideology. It
really is not clear how literally he takes these dreams and
visions of the dead, although he deals with them as serious psychic happenings. In *Memories, Dreams, Reflections* "the dead"
are never reduced to projections of the living. But whether they
are truly regarded as the literal spirits of individuals from the
past is not so clear. They hover around the edges of Jung's own
story, especially in his awareness of his ancestry and his experiences in the depths of the unconscious.

Americanized popular expositions of Jung focus upon individuation as the quest for "wholeness" and on the balance
theme of his psychological model. There is little room for any
concern with ancestors in this culture, and we lack almost
entirely Jung's pervasive sense of the present as an overlay
upon a past not our own. In this respect, the Freudian past of
personal childhood is much more real to us. Americans' dreams
of the dead most often take the form of injunctions to cease
mourning for them. Ours is a culture where the dead quickly
drop out of the picture. Perhaps this is why this entire theme of
the dead in Jung's autobiography appears so weird to many
American readers. It promises neither the hopeful tranformation of caterpillar into butterfly, nor release or consolation or
fulfillment. The dead return to raise unanswered and perhaps
unanswerable questions for us, their legacy of unfinished business. They remind the living that all, living and dead, exist in a
world bounded everywhere by mystery. At points such as this,
Jung's ideas expand the universe beyond the bounds of the ethical naturalist vision, or the view Freud took of religion as a
system of illusory consolation.

The Existentialist Legacy

Unlike Freudian psychoanalysis and Jung's analytic psychology, existentialism is not basically a school within depth
psychology. Its relation to psychology, and its legacy for
thought on death, is quite complex. There are indeed existential psychoanalysts, and in the work of figures such as Medard
Boss and Ludwig Binswanger, we can find examples of careful,
direct appropriation of existential philosophical frameworks

and vocabulary to clinical cases and psychoanalytic theory. But the real impact of existentialism as a movement is much more pervasive and harder to document.

Existentialism as a philosophical, literary, and theological movement arose in the early twentieth century as a response to the perceived devastating collapse of European Enlightenment hopes for peace and progress through science. It was prefigured in the thought of Søren Kierkegaard and a few other precursors. As a "movement" it offered an alternative to scientific positivism's and religion's hope, as well as to contemporary collectivist ideologies such as fascism. It sought truth through an intense awareness of individual freedom, alienation from nature and society, and authenticity in the face of death. In its literary exponents, particularly Jean-Paul Sartre, Albert Camus, and André Malraux, one finds these themes again and again in powerful form. Gaining strength from the horrors of Europe under nazism, this movement rediscovered "the individual" as unique and free, at a time when mass death and political ideology seemed to deny both qualities. The heroes of existentialist fiction and drama know that to be "a man" is to face the absurdity of existence without given meanings, yet to affirm one's freedom and selfhood in spite of this absurdity. To face one's own death, and so transform it from fate into self-chosen achievement, is the highest human possibility. In contrast, the "inauthentic" existence is one that lives only at the level of the mass, the generalized, the impersonal and anonymous.

Death is ever-present, as a threat to all that is false and inauthentic, and a threat to the ever-precarious freedom of the authentic individual. Anxiety in the face of human freedom is tied to fundamental anxiety in the face of certain death. If we recall the circumstances within which existentialism arose, it is not surprising that "death" is rarely linked to disease, and never to old age. Death in warfare or heroic, deliberate death is the most dramatic form, the most exemplary (Malraux 1934). Then there is death from torture or starvation, as in Part 1 of Victor Frankl's *Man's Search for Meaning*, originally published as *From Death Camp to Existentialism* (Frankl 1959). Death by suicide becomes an ever-present option in a world where one's fate is death sooner or later (Camus 1955 [1942]). Even the plague of Camus' novel of that name (Camus 1977 [1946]) is less a disease than a malignant symbol for the universality of death and evil. The human task is to achieve some form of meaning in the face of these kinds of death.

In addition, there is no guarantee that meanings staked out in one situation, for one person, will become permanent or universally binding upon others. There is no universal "human nature" that, if followed as a blueprint, will guarantee security and happiness in life (Sartre 1956 [1948]:289). "Nature" in fact has nothing to tell us as *human* beings, for as free, indeterminate beings we are in nature but never truly part of it. A self is not a natural entity, nor is it the product of history and culture. It is an individual, unique achievement (Sartre 1956 [1948]:300). Physical death brings it to an end—and can always do so at any minute—but awareness of physical death is a mark of the self's alienation from "nature." We are all beings-toward-death, but as free beings we can consciously exist within this knowledge and relationship to mortality. Other natural organisms just die. Human beings face death.

Awareness of our fragility, mortality, and freedom should draw us together in relations of compassion and solidarity. Although the basic language of existentialism is utterly individualistic, its exponents hold out the hope that an ethic of care, and of struggle against suffering and evil, may emerge from the vision of human existence facing death without lies. In Camus' novel *The Plague* (1977 [1946]), one finds these themes laid out in the allegory of a city's struggle against an epidemic. Evil and death destroy human meanings, and so must be fought, yet there is no hope of a permanent victory over them. Camus rejects vehemently all attempts to validate or legitimate suffering in the name of any higher good. Neither God nor nature can be invoked for such aim. Instead, the truly human response is courageous, sustained opposition to suffering and death, to the extent to which this is possible.

Nevertheless, the extreme individualism of this movement's vision of human beings can become severed from the ethic of solidarity in the face of death. Relationships, such as those of marriage or family, receive very minimal or negative treatment; they are perceived as traps for inauthentic self-definitions, or as obstacles to the self's freedom. Put most vividly, in the words of Sartre's *No Exit*, "Hell is other people" (Sartre 1949 [1944]:47). At its best, this movement represents the culmination of what Edith Wyschogrod calls "the authenticity paradigm" of individual death (Wyschogrod 1985:2–6). But it is an authenticity frequently bought at the cost of community and connection.

What is the relation of this movement to depth psychology? Clearly, its explicit preoccupations differ from those of Freud or Jung, and its vocabulary is distinct from theirs. Nevertheless, very early in the history of psychoanalysis, in the late 1920s, Ludwig Binswanger became convinced that existentialist conceptualization was actually more suited for psychoanalysis than Freud's own mechanistic vocabulary. Binswanger borrowed from Heidegger's philosophical system of *Being and Time* (published in 1927) in order to revise and dereify many of Freud's ideas (Binswanger 1968 [1955]:149–79). Instead of forces and agencies and analogies to an "apparatus" favored by Freud, one could take the same clinical data and restate them in terms of the free self as being-in-the-world. Binswanger's attempts to do so, as in "The Case of Ellen West," show how Freud's own concepts are indeed often counter-productive to his deepest intentions (Binswanger 1967 [1944]:226–28). Later, Medard Boss attempted the same project, in *Psychoanalysis and Daseinanalysis.* Freud's "scientific" outlook and vocabulary obscured his insight into the free acts and responses of the self (Boss 1963:75–129).

Thus, existentialism provides a means to reread Freud. It could be used to translate depth psychology into terms more congruent with the classical Western humanist tradition (Fromm 1950) or to make it more directly appropriable by average individuals (Frankl 1959; May 1967). The quest for authentic selfhood, and not freedom from mechanistically defined symptoms, becomes the context within which therapy is conducted. Existentialism's emphases demedicalized depth psychology, freed it from the determinism inherent in its model of scientific causation, and reaffirmed the freedom of persons to struggle toward meaning and selfhood. At its most popular level, it joined forces with humanistic psychology to emerge as a "third force" in clinical psychological theory (an alternative to both Freud and behaviorism). The themes of freedom, individuality, and the task of the self to create itself are integrated into this popular synthesis.

Yet the existentialist legacy itself remains distinct from such an upbeat synthesis. Especially in its focus upon the encounter with death and fascination with suicide as a human possibility

(Camus 1955 [1942]:3–8), classical existentialism is very far
from the inspirational "self-help" mood of popular humanistic
psychology. Anxiety or "dread" (Kierkegaard 1957 [1844]) is not
a condition one can overcome therapeutically, but a fundamental dimension of one's freedom. The flight from this freedom
into illusory certainties, or the quest for static happiness, are
ever-tempting forms of inauthenticity. Even the mythic-sym-
bolic link between death and positive personal transformation
found in Jungian thought would be, by Camus' standard,
merely a new version of a flight away from existence's inherent absurdity. Only in the face of death will all such strategies
be unmasked, and the self be left to face its potential nothing-
ness naked and without support. It is not death that is
"accepted," but the task of becoming a self under the threat of
death. Curiously the "stoicism" of Freud is closer to this mood
than are any of his specific theoretical formulations such as the
"death instinct." Freud's own demeanor in the midst of death
and suffering qualifies him for the heroism of the "authenticity" paradigm, even if his rejection of religion's consolation is
based on scientistic rather than existentialist grounds.

Existentialism functions as a movement, a mood, an ethos,
and a way to see the "human" and "meaning-making" concerns
embedded in the specialized vocabulary of depth psychology. We
will see it as a component of Ernest Becker's work in the next
chapter, and in theological writers such as Emil Brunner. Just
as it influenced the way many of us read Freud, so it influenced
the way religious insights were interpreted or the contribution
of religion was assessed. Its role in the "death-awareness" movement is far more difficult to assess, since implacable hostility to
ethical naturalism is one of its original hallmarks. Yet at the
level of concern for individual freedom, selfhood, and dignity, it
has merged with other psychological themes of naturalism.
Still, it retains a distinctive power, and offers a radically different image of how death figures in the total context of human
personal existence. It is best to consider it an independent element in the legacy of depth psychological perspectives, to whose
contemporary heirs we will now turn our attention.

4

Contemporary
Depth Psychologies
of Death

We now examine three recent thinkers whose works constitute genuine psychologies of death within the legacies of depth psychology discussed in the last chapter. Ernest Becker, James Hillman, and Robert J. Lifton all distance themselves from Kübler-Ross, thanatology, and the popular "death-awareness" movement. Two are implacable foes of ethical naturalism, and the third is a serious critic of its simpler formulation. All three rely explicitly on the Freudian, Jungian, and existentialist legacies, seeking in these sources an alternative to both American denial of death and the naturalist attempt to overcome this. And all three find themselves entering into an explicit use of "mythic" language in order to express adequately their perspectives on death and its relation to the entire sphere of human life. This "mythic" dimension is intrinsic, not accidental, to their work. It suggests how death as a topic may lead spontaneously and inescapably to such language, and how the quest for an adequate mythology of death is part of the depth psychological heritage itself. These authors present the most challenging options both for psychologists—as a springboard for rethinking their presuppositions about death—and for Christians who wish to integrate psychology and their own faith.

But the very direct use of religious and mythic language by these three depth psychologists raises questions for the entire issue of "integration." For psychology as represented by these three is already so deeply and intrinsically in the myth-making business that the metaphor of "integration" with Christianity is partly misleading. Instead, one might follow Paul Ricoeur, and speak of a conflict of interpretations (Ricoeur 1970:20ff.), or even a conflict of myths, in order to underscore this point. Insofar as Christian faith too makes use of "myth" as a special form of thought, and cannot be consistently "demythologized" without losing its central imagery and meaning, the hope for any integration with theories of depth psychology requires that we admit to the mythic character of both partners in the endeavor.

Ernest Becker

Ernest Becker wrote *The Denial of Death* shortly before his own death from cancer in 1974. The sense of existential crisis and urgency throughout the book makes this autobiographical tie-in seem more than poignant coincidence, although it remains unclear how much actual knowledge of his illness the author had when he began the project. *The Denial of Death* is a reinterpretation of Freudian depth psychology and existentialist perspectives, by way of Otto Rank, Kierkegaard, and Norman O. Brown's *Life Against Death*. All of these sources, however, are subordinated to Becker's own polemical, passionate vision. It is impossible, he proclaims, to write an "objective" and disinterested study of death.

Becker's book appeared during the height of the human potential movement, with its rhetoric of health, happiness, and wholeness, of fully actualized potentials and self-enhancement through perpetual growth. For many readers, *Denial of Death* was a sharp reminder of how far away popular psychology had moved from its links with existentialism's more somber view of the human condition. Insofar as Kübler-Ross' popularity was intrinsically tied to the same rhetoric of wholeness and fulfillment—with death as "the final stage of growth"—Becker's vision is also a bitter critique of that "healthy-minded" approach.

Becker gives readers a choice from the start: either hear what is real, however terrifying, or flee into healthy-mindedness, into all comforting illusions about oneself and the human condition. The first path is heroic and authentic, and allows for the unmasking of all those pseudo-solutions that disguise our horror of death. The reader is incessantly aware of the author himself struggling with this choice (or at least the author's "persona" within the text). Egocentric, outraged, grandly masculine, but in some ways pathetic: this may not be the "real Ernest Becker," but it is a self-presentation that emerges as a model for those who choose the "morbidly minded" and courageous path. It is not Becker's empirical arguments that convince the reader, but the degree to which the latter can identify with the author's style of being human.

Death and Denial

The central thesis of *The Denial of Death* is deceptively simple: "The idea of death, the fear of it, haunts the human animal like nothing else: it is a mainspring of human activity— activity designed largely to avoid the fatality of death, to overcome it by denying in some way that it is the final destiny of man" (Becker 1974:ix). All of childhood, all of culture with its "hero-systems," and all of everything that humans do are fundamentally expressive of this denial. Every nook and cranny of human existence is contaminated by death's terror. Death is not "acceptable," and words such as "terror" and "horror" and "fear" are repeated again and again. It is as if we the readers were always on the verge of slipping back into denial by mitigating the stark reality of death, and only such vivid verbal reminders could halt this process. Death is the constant dread presence discovered by Becker in every situation of vulnerability, humiliation, and violence. The task of author and reader alike is to strip away the levels upon levels of desperate lies, which attempt to deny this reality.

Becker claims to work from Freud's vision of the human condition, rereading Freud in the light of existentialism. For Freud, as we saw, every situation is construed as a conflict between two psychic forces; Freud was happy to admit that he was forever a dualist. Becker is also very definitely a dualist.

Yet unlike Freud, for whom (as we saw) "instinct" is both biological and psychic, Becker is a much more traditional
Cartesian dualist. He splits persons into mind and body far
more neatly and artificially than Freud. "Nature's values are
bodily values, human values are mental values" (Becker
1974:31), he asserts, claiming for his own one of the chief
themes of the existentialist legacy. Thus, Freud's duality of
mythic instincts is transformed into a mind/body relation of
continuous warfare, which ends only at death when both mind
and body lose, in simultaneous destruction. In contrast, Freud's
death instinct is actually a way to say that mind-cum-body
seeks its own ending, an idea Becker entirely rejects. Death
remains an external "horror" unbearable to the mind that
turns the body into threat.

Yet to speak this way is also to envision the two "halves" as
just that, easily separable in principle if not in actuality. Each
side in the civil warfare is relatively straightforward in what
it represents. The person is "Out of nature and hopelessly in it.
. . . His body is the material casing that is alien to him in many
ways—the strangest and most repugnant way being that it
aches and bleeds and will decay and die" (Becker 1974:26). The
spirit, on the other hand, is infinite in aspiration, eager to pursue its own "freedom-project" and imagine itself as "self-
caused" and self-created. This particular vision owes far more
to Sartre than to Freud.

Freud's view of the Oedipus complex is revised by Becker to
fit this yearning for self-causation. Following the earlier work
of Norman O. Brown, in *Life Against Death* (Brown 1959:118),
the real problem of the Oedipus situation is not erotic desire
versus punitive authority, but anxiety over one's own dependency and ontological grounding. The threat is no longer castration but nonbeing. The child wishes to be *causa sui*; his powerful parents reveal to him the impossibility of this project, so
he must protest and deny his metaphysical dependency all the
more. "The child wants to conquer death by becoming the
father of himself, the creator and sustainer of his own life"
(Becker 1974:36). Becker's reinterpretation, unlike Brown's,
turns sexuality into a torment rather than a pleasure; as an
activity where recognition of the self as embodied cannot be
escaped, it reveals the vulnerability of the inner self, the latter's dependence on the alien, material "casing" of the body.

This is particularly evident in what Becker writes about the role of the mother in Oedipal and castration fantasies. Although she remains an idealized love object, Becker finds her even more powerful as a source of horror, blood, and smells, who by her closeness to "nature" inspires disgust and loathing (Becker 1974:38). Since lack of a penis is no longer a differentiating factor, such attitudes are said to propel both girls and boys away from her for the same reason. Out of revulsion, children of both sexes flee from her into the world of the father. "He seems more neutral physically, more cleanly powerful, less immersed in body determinisms" (Becker 1974:40). Also, he presents the social world of cultural hero-systems, of organized defiance of nature. Freud's original "gender asymmetry," however difficult to accept literally, has been replaced with a view that on the surface denies gender differences. Yet, ironically, even more than Freud did, it seems that Becker has accepted male fantasy and gender stereotyping as a human norm.

The hero-systems of culture function defensively. They repeat the childhood denial of finitude, nature, and death, and at a level that society accepts and normalizes. Unlike the child's *causa sui* project, which will obviously fail, the systems of adult-level denial remain deceptively successful in masking the reality of death. Yet Becker's point is that ultimately nothing can reconcile the individual with the body and the death it bears within it. We may imagine that we might relinquish the heroic, and slip into a more "natural" outlook, but this is an impossible dream. Human nature can never be "natural" and it is not possible to live contentedly within our psychic means. At this point, the existentialist triumphs over the Freudian in Becker, for as we remember, Freud defended his "conflict of instincts" model by an appeal to solely "natural" evidence such as death in amoebas. When Becker derides "nature" in this way, we can hear him sneering at those same hopes cherished by Kübler-Ross and others, that because death is "natural" it couldn't be so bad after all.

Becker's Religion

Becker claims that the only sphere in which the human dilemma can even begin to find adequate expression, if not true resolution, is that of religion. Here is Becker's next surprising departure from the Freudian legacy—a much more explicit and acknowledged departure. Surely, of all cultural systems, religion is the least likely to appeal to Becker, who champions a hermeneutic of suspicion toward culture and symbols. Not only has religion generally advocated a life after death, the most transparent form of denial, but also it has been the implacable enemy of the individual's *causa sui* aspirations, the wish to be the ground of one's own existence. But Becker surprises us here. Since in his eyes *all* of culture rests on denial of death, religion is not qualitatively different from the rest of it—something Freud would have denied, since for him science could offer sublimation and resignation to reality, unlike religion's illusions. But for Becker, religion sets the human drama on the widest possible stage, the cosmos itself. It provides suitable grandeur for our basic situation. The traditional antithesis between religion and absolute human freedom is also reinterpreted.

> The personality can truly begin to emerge in religion because God as an abstraction does not oppose the individual as others do, but instead provides the individual with all the powers necessary for independent self-justification. What greater security than to lean confidently on God, on the Fount of creation, the most terrifying power of all? If God is hidden and intangible, all the better: that allows man to expand and develop by himself. (Becker 1974:202)

In other words, a transcendent God will permit, by his very transcendence, what the physical and immanent father and his equally immanent cultural stand-ins will not: the person can achieve "independent self-justification," the adult version of the child's *causa sui* project, after all.

And so the person expands, filling the space vacated by an otiose deity. Religion lifts the individual into alternative spheres of existence, "of heavens and possible embodiments that make a mockery of earthly logic. . . . In religious terms, to 'see God' is to die, because the creature is too small and finite to be able to bear the higher meanings of creation" (Becker 1974:204). Does the self, can the self, really "die" in this moment of cosmic awe? If so, it would indeed be a way beyond the denial of death. But is annihilation or self-deification the result? One thing is clear: Becker never connects such moments of "heavenly" apprehension back with the ordinary earthly, and earthly experiences of being an embodied spirit, so as to make embodiment itself more bearable.

Note Becker's resort to the explicit language of myth at this point. He wishes to provide a religious vision unabashedly rather than merely covertly. He realizes that a psychology adequate in its apprehension of death's power over human life requires a larger theater than this life, than "normal" psychologies focused upon interpersonal relations and emotional adjustment. Freud's legacy of demystification continues to operate, but no longer in the name of *Logos*, the rational voice of science, or *Ananke*, the spirit of resignation. Demystification is a step toward proper awe for the real mysteries of existence. Becker is therefore no "reductionist," however strongly his view of symbolism as defensive suggests this. On the other hand, once he has resolved to rely on myth at this point and for this reason, he becomes vulnerable to a very different critique. For not just the presence of myth, but the content of any particular myth, may be scrutinized. To what extent does Becker's own myth truly open up for us "the higher meanings of creation"?

Becker claims for himself the "Augustinian-Lutheran" tradition of Western thought (Becker 1974:88), clearly read through an existentialist lens. This tradition calls for the death of the self before it can become related to transcendence (Becker 1974:89), and is focused on the problem of identity, will, and anxiety. In this, perhaps, Becker is correct. Insofar as Becker's self in *The Denial of Death* is the grandchild of Augustine's in *Confessions*, he is certainly entitled to claim this theological legacy for himself.

On the other hand, the theologically trained reader will have noticed that Becker's body/spirit dualism is anything but "Lutheran" in its emphasis. "Mental values" and not the physical body were Luther's downfall, and justification by faith puts no faith in "higher human nature" or defleshed souls. A closer parallel would seem to be found in the outlook of the ancient gnostics. An intensified and anguished opposition between nonmaterial self and material, disgusting body-qua-casing characterized the gnostic outlook. These were the persons who took as their slogan "the body a tomb"—*sōma sēma,* a play on the two Greek words. Their solution, like Becker's, was a flight into a transcendent realm for the self, which claimed direct identity with the highest and most abstract "alien God," a divinity too remote and pure to have been responsible for the creation of matter. Like this alien God of the gnostic theologians, Becker's God confirms rather than thwarts the individual's aspirations for an entirely nonmaterial, nondependent identity.

Becker and "Naturalism"

Since Becker is not writing as a second-century near-Christian but a twentieth-century depth psychologist, such parallels should not be stretched too far. It still seems valid to ask: why has Becker reevoked a style of religiousness that few of his sources would support? What is Becker trying to say about the self and death? Why are nature, matter, mother, and the body so horrible, so bound up with the imagery of violence, death, and decay? Why does he find in religion not the reconciliation to those realities, but the triumph of a disembodied, self-justifying spirit?

Becker has found in humanistic psychology, including the healthy-minded ethical naturalism represented by Kübler-Ross, a superb target, against which his myth of disjunctive, tragic estrangement between self and "nature" cries out. Moreover, recall the date of *The Denial of Death*'s publication: 1974 was the aftermath of the Vietnam War, and the height of revulsion against traditional military models of heroism, or political categories altogether. It was easy to idealize and extol the "natural," the holistic, the ecologically harmonious, and the organic as alternative visions to a discredited heroic ethic of failed transcendence. Certainly, the language of popular psychology embraced such ideals, in the mode of an ethical naturalism relying on language of growth and health. As we saw in Chapter 2, Kübler-Ross' own vision of "nature," unlike Bowlby's, let alone Becker's, dismisses predation and violence as intrinsic elements within "nature."

Becker, in protest, writes a sustained attack on "nature" as an adequate human ideal, and an endorsement of heroism as the valid human mode. He does so by first removing the "heroic" entirely from the military and political sphere to which it had been reduced. The myth of the hero is not to be shunned, although in Becker's retelling it is indeed a tragic myth without happy resolution. As a result, however, the self of that myth is detached cleanly from all that "earth" represents; it is a self grandiose, but profoundly depleted. It is an entirely lonely, isolated self, for whom all encounters with others are fraught with potential threats to its freedom. Another mark of this depletion is Becker's complete neglect of cultural and contextual factors in favor of explanations at the level of universal human nature. His self lives ahistorically, everywhere and nowhere in particular.

But at a deeper level, the myth of the gnostic God and the heavenly self may be a profound and perennial response to certain agonizing failures in present cultural possibilities for meaning, heroism, and trust. Hence it is part of that myth, which Becker adopts, to demote most of culture to the realm of the hopelessly inauthentic, the earthly and the bodily. The very one-sided quality of Becker's vision makes it all the more powerful and provocative.

Yet the full degree of Becker's one-sidedness should not be underestimated. If Freud's view of Oedipus and castration seemed to introduce gender into the way death is imagined, Becker's theory nevertheless seems far more "gender asymmetrical." Although Becker claims that the views of mother as "nature" and father as "spirit" are shared by both boys and girls, it seems that throughout the book the vision of what is distinctively most *human* is identical to that which is masculine. Distant from nature and repulsed by it, intent on becoming self-caused ("the father of himself"), the Beckerian self builds identity by repudiating dependencies and relational ties. Although Becker could not deny that women can be "heroic," their doing so depends upon a thoroughgoing repudiation of the "feminine" or "maternal." Nor is it just an accident of Western culture that femininity is closely linked to despised "nature," because Becker treats this symbolic equation as a universal of human self-awareness. Since his persuasive power depends upon the reader's identification with this model of selfhood, it is not surprising that I have met virtually no women readers of *The Denial of Death* who really accept the book's arguments. Becker may have portrayed what death and its denial have sometimes meant for Western "man," but this tells us much less about "human nature"—and specifically about Western woman—than he ever realized.

And yet, the temptation to claim that men alone fear and deny death, and women do not, should be firmly resisted. Not just because there is no warrant for this leap into "healthy-mindedness" in any of Becker's sources. But the testimony of the autobiographies can be invoked to quash any such simplistic claim. According to the autobiographies, the death of the mother can be the most psychologically complex, forcing the narrator to confront not just her own mortality but the ambivalence inherent in the relationship. Moreover, it was for some women indeed a traumatic blow to the self when they experienced their bodies as "alien casings" that could no longer serve as the transmitters of selfhood. And, in at least a few cases, terminally ill women found the prospect of physical humiliation so unbearable that to reassert control over their own life and death became an obsession. Women's relationship to death, its imagery and symbolic substitutes, may not be identical to that of men, and neither one may correspond exactly to Becker's tormented split self. But for both sexes encounter with death lays bare the underpinnings of the self; for both sexes the issue of control and its loss appears repeatedly. Gender plays a role, but there are responses to the situation of impending death that transcend it.

Becker's self is one for whom his own death is indeed nothing less than the end of everything. Thus death is not just one problem out of many, but *the* problem for humankind. Becker claims that the problem of human nature is insoluble; there can be no resolution to the dilemma of a being out of nature but hopelessly of it. Becker so defines the problem, then, as to make any claimed "solution" a counterfeit. Even when the self "sees God," it is not reconciled to death at the level of ongoing existence. Yet Becker's analysis seems to rest on setting up one specific, culturally endorsed type of human identity into a universal norm, which in turn exacerbates the basic problem of death. His work ironically endorses a style of human being that contributes to the very outlook of frantic denial Becker himself claims to oppose. In contrast, the other two thinkers we will discuss in this chapter view the contemporary terror of death as a tragic anomaly, and by no means a revelation of an eternal "human nature."

James Hillman

James Hillman's "archetypal psychology" is a highly imaginative re-visioning of the insights of the Jungian legacy. Hillman's work expands on and considerably elaborates a distinctively "Jungian" approach to death as psychic reality. Like Becker but far more forcefully, he is explicit in his use of mythic and religious themes. In fact he occasionally reassures the reader that these are meant *psychologically*, and not as a call for new forms of worship. His writing is even more distant from conventional depth psychological discourse than Becker's. It is intrinsic to Hillman's re-visioning of psychology to break the illusory bond that has been forged between depth psychology and natural science, and reestablish the former's truer tie with myth. Here is a sample Hillman passage, demonstrating how (as with Becker) style is not separable from subject matter: "We ask: what is the purpose of this event for my soul, for my death? Such questions extend the dimension of depth without limit, and again psychology is pushed by Hades into an imperialism of soul, reflecting the imperialism of his Kingdom and the radical dominion of death" (Hillman 1979:31–32). This reference to Hades and the echo of the New Testament are central to Hillman's purposes.

The Jungian legacy gives Hillman several advantages. First and most important, he is not burdened with a defensive view of symbolism, one that assumes (as was the case with Becker) that all symbols are fundamentally mystifications to screen or shield the symbolizer from naked reality. Hillman insists that images, symbols, and myths are the true stuff of psyche, and should not be denigrated as poor substitutes for a "reality" stripped of imagery. Second, the Jungian perspective is not compelled to find in individual childhood the prototypes for all adult struggles. It is a relief when Hillman relinquishes the Freudian literalism of childhood origins along with so many other literalisms.

Hillman, however, rejects two central themes of the Jungian legacy: the balance model of "conscious" and "unconscious"; and the progressive individuation process, culminating in the archetype of the Self. "The unconscious," as reified entity, Hillman believes, rests on a false hope that depth psychology can duplicate the structure of scientific theory, and on a falsely mechanical style of explanation. "Balance" as psychological motif was always ill-served by such associations. Thus, gone are all those geometrical diagrams that fill the pages of Jungian expositions. But the disappearance of the individuation process and the Self-archetype is even more central. Jung's own religious hopes were pinned upon this symbol, and the Self with a capital S dominates his equation of mandala, Christ, the alchemists' *lapis,* and other images of "the God within" toward which psychic tranformation aims. The disappearance of the Self-archetype brings us into the heart of Hillman's own psycho-mythology.

Soul and Death

Hillman holds that the proper starting point for a psychology is soul, "a perspective rather than a substance, a viewpoint toward things rather than a thing itself" (Hillman 1975:x). Psychology, he believes, has been everything but soulish, taking its norms and methods from biology, sociology, and even theology rather than from psyche. Within soul, there are depths, death, dreams, and the whole "night side" of life, waiting to be discovered. And there are beneath all, Gods. These Gods are the personifications and powers who have always haunted inner life; Jung simply rediscovered and renamed them, as "archetypes of the collective unconscious." To capitalize the G permits Hillman to treat them seriously, giving them their proper due. Soul evokes inwardness, and a lovingly attentive approach to these powers within, emphasizing plurality and indeed fragmentation, as well as nonpossessiveness. These are not "my" archetypes; they are the true possessors and guardians of the soul and its depths. I should note here that soul, as Hillman uses this term, carries with it a feminine undertone, diametrically opposite from that of Becker's heroic inner self. Anima is the personification of the realm of soul, and "she" is present within both males and females. No longer is the mechanical balance idea linked to gender so as to make "anima" and "animus" parallels of each other.

The equivalent in Hillman's psychology to Becker's freedom-loving self is the "heroic ego," who plays the role of a villain in Jungian thought, and especially in Hillman. Ego psychology is the dominant form of contemporary clinical psychology, Hillman

says, because ego mirrors the literalism and materialism of contemporary culture, its fear and misunderstanding of the entire
realm of soul. The ego desires strength, light, height, one-ness,
and heroic conquest over all the other interior powers. Hillman
finds that Western monotheism has confirmed these aspirations, as has Western philosophy. Psychology simply perpetuates them. This is why, even when "self" or "spirit" is substituted for ego, Hillman suspects all systems based on "one-ness."
Unification, the sublime integration of all opposites—this basically Jungian theme is discarded by Hillman, by his equation of
all such hopes with the triumph of the heroic ego. The ego represents an alien intruder into the realm of soul, a Hercules in
the house of Hades, wielding a material sword against shades
(Hillman 1979:110).

For the realm of soul is spontaneously polytheistic; there are
many persons and powers acting within it. To emphasize this,
Hillman makes a return to "imaginal Greece" to describe the
powers of the soul, bringing to psychic life the myths and Gods
of classical culture. In contrast, the ego is consistently associated with the dominant Judeo-Christian strand of Western
faith, particularly in its Protestant manifestations. How literally Hillman takes his "imaginal Greece" and whether the
Greek pantheon functions as a true ontology for him, may per-
plex readers. He assures us that "We are not reviving a dead
faith. . . . Psychologically the Gods are never dead; and archetypal psychology's concern is not with the revival of religion but
with the survival of soul" (Hillman 1975:170). Still, one won-
ders, why Greece? Why not other polytheistic cultures?
Perhaps ancient Greece required a wide range of vivid female
as well as male figures in order to express its inclusive and plu-
ralistic vision of soul and world.

How does death come into this view of psyche as God-laden?
The link between soul and death is firm, not because of any
alleged immortality, but because through the soulish perspective death too is re-visioned. "Our emphasis upon physical
death corresponds to our emphasis upon the physical body, not
the subtle one; on physical life, not psychic life; on the literal
and not the metaphorical" (Hillman 1979:64). We find this distinction suggested in an early Hillman work, *Suicide and the
Soul*. There, Hillman examines all of the current approaches to
suicide—medical, legal, religious—and rejects them as insuffi-

ciently centered upon psyche. Death as symbolic transition is
the central focus for psychotherapy; in one way or another "the
death-experience" is necessary for therapy to be transforma-
tive. Death and rebirth are initiatory symbols, not to be by-
passed. In fact, "the more immanent the death experience, the
more possibility for transformation" (Hillman 1964:70).
Although suicide itself may involve the literalization of this
experience, and so a confusion between inner and outer, "The
mode to psychological experience seems not to matter to the
soul providing it has the experience. For some, organic death
through actual suicide may be the only mode through which
the death experience is possible" (Hillman 1964:83). Therefore,
far from being the automatic preventer of suicide and the
guardian of life, the therapist may on rare occasions assent to
suicide, or at least recognize it as a valid mode for psychic
transformation. For "We do not know if the soul dies. We do
not know if case history and soul history begin and end at the
same moment" (Hillman 1964:84). This is as close as Hillman
comes to equating what we normally call "death"—that is,
physical death—with what he means by psychic death.

For Hillman, it is abundantly clear that our culture's ignorance and silence in regard to death are not norms, attributable
to a universal human nature. They are abnormalities of the
ego's dominion, and the soul-loss this entails. His position on
this question is elaborated in *The Dream and the Underworld*, a
work based on an extended analogy: Hades is to earth's surface
as dream is to waking, as soul is to ego. Hades, the under-
ground home of dead shades, is the missing element beneath
every experience.

> All soul processes, everything in the psyche, move toward
> Hades. As the finis is Hades, so the telos is Hades. Everything
> would become deeper, moving from the visible connections to the
> invisible ones, dying out of life. When we search for the most
> revelatory meaning of an experience, we get it most starkly by
> letting it go to Hades, asking what this has to do with "my"
> death. (Hillman 1979:30)

Dying out of life, the realm of the external, literal, material,
and into soul: there is no less metaphorical way to state
Hillman's *telos*. Ironically, Hillman has rediscovered the most

controversial aspect of the Freudian legacy, the theme of internally sought death, now stripped of its biological reductionism and set forth as a perspective of psyche itself. If we hope for a nonmythic alternative, we are still caught in the realm of the ego, like Freud with his speculations on death among amoebas. Instead, Hillman uses phrases such as "the radical dominion of death," "the Resurrection of Death itself": these are the terms that suggest this sinking down to underworld, the realm of shadow, sleep, decay, and disintegration. This is a truly soulish version of the Freudian instinct of organic life to return to an inorganic state.

Hillman's shades, the traditional inhabitants of Hades, are also very real relatives to "the dead" of Jung's autobiography. Shades are not persons, literally; they are the remnants or dream-images of persons. They linger perpetually in the psychic landscape, lesser than the Gods but equally not to be confused with their flesh-and-blood, earth's-surface counterparts. Whereas Jung tended to literalize "the dead" into ancestors, Hillman keeps them strictly mythological. They tell us nothing empirical about "life after death"—only about death and soul as hidden dimensions that we commonly neglect in favor of life and ego. Hillman rediscovers the ancient category of "shade" from both Homeric and ancient Hebrew mythology, and relies on this in the same anti-ontological fashion that he refers to Gods.

Soul's Opponents

Like Becker, Hillman writes to purge the reader of all healthy-mindedness. If Hades is the *finis* and *telos*, then psychotherapy as soul making must refuse all goals of cure, adjustment, happiness, and growth. These are all heroic fantasies of the ego, moralistic imports from "earth's surface." But unlike those who wish to strip psychotherapy of all its links with medicine, who view "mental illness" as a product of social labeling, Hillman keeps "pathology" or rather, "pathologizing" as a central motif of therapy, while he removes both the medical hope of cure for it and the humanistic one of growth beyond it. From Hades, the shades expect no reincarnation or resurrection. Hillman, like Becker, can legitimately see himself as the preserver of the original dark wisdom of the founders of depth psychology. Both authors cry out against those who for several generations have worked to dilute, soften, and brighten the real legacies of Freud and Jung. As with Becker, whether the reader can respond to this vision depends less upon arguments or evidence, and much more upon a personal identification with Hillman's own "persona."

Again, like Becker, Hillman repudiates the hope and the imagery of the ethical naturalist. Harmony with the earth, natural cycles, and growth are not what "soul" is about. "Nature" Hillman insists, is not a given, but itself "one of the fantasies of soul and itself an imaginal topography" (Hillman 1979:72). Therefore, in one step Hillman undermines both ethical naturalism and the intensified "gnostic" opposition between nature and spirit championed by Becker. Neither are universal "givens." Hillman goes on to insist that earth and underworld are two different "places." In his language, Demeter loses Persephone to Hades. Kübler-Ross figures as a personification of Demeter, one might imagine. A maternal presence, assisting the terminally ill toward a "natural" and peaceful death, she ends by abandoning death's reality altogether. As Hillman would see it, Demeter loses Persephone to Hades, but Hades is simply not part of our ego-centered landscape.

Hillman knows that not only ethical naturalism, but many other powerful currents in Western thought oppose his soulish yearning for Hades. Among them is "Christianism," the ideology that insists every descent to the underworld must be a victorious harrowing of hell, followed by a glorious resurrection. Christianism turns the dark but basically nonthreatening realm of shades into a place of burning and torment, then claims that Christ can "annul it through his resurrected victory over death" (Hillman 1979:85). Hillman finds the ego at work in this model of Christ, so that, as hell, the underworld's death becomes a "last enemy." At minimum, the theme of vicarious sacrifice makes our own personal descent into the underworld superfluous. Christ did it, once and for all; therefore, we are exempt from entering the dark realm of death.

Hillman finds in this an instance of symbolism used for purposes of defense. He warns that "Every resurrection fantasy of theology may be a defense against death, every rebirth fantasy in psychology a defense against depth" (Hillman 1979:90). In the original Jungian context, death and rebirth went together, but this is too easily co-opted into an ego-oriented quest for cure, growth, and wholeness. Hillman finds visions of ascended spirit a poor exchange for the loss of soul. In case one imagines that Hillman is simply engaging in caricature here, the heavy use of the "last enemy" phrase, along with Beckerian-style reliance on "horror" and "terror" in some fairly recent Christian writings about death, is of a piece with this portrait. Christianism rests on a fear of soul and its kind of death, which is then transferred into an exaggerated terror of biological death. Against such an ideology Hillman protests, and within this struggle themes like "the radical dominion of death" receive their peculiar significance.

Nevertheless, even the sympathetic reader of *The Dream and the Underworld* may marvel at how Hillman can make a goal such as "the Resurrection of Death" sound so appealing. Set side-by-side with Freud's theme of *Ananke* and the renunciation of illusion, it seems a glamorous, romantic aim. One reason why Hillman can so whole-heartedly advocate Hades, and get away with it, is that virtually all public images of mass death and ordinary violence are consigned by him to the sphere of the ego. Auschwitz, Hiroshima, and Jonestown, not to mention more day-to-day street crime, are events of earth's surface, grisly mementos of the ego's unlimited passion for literal killing. They have no connection with soul whatsoever. Thus to sink down to the underworld, to die out of life and into soul, avoids any contamination from those brutal images of mass death. The violence of Hades is illustrated by the rape of Persephone, not by ordinary muggings and sexual assaults. At this point we may ask if some of Hillman's uses become a screen to protect us from the empirical actualities of violence, and from the tragic intertwining of death and violence in many situations. In this, Hillman comes close to Kübler-Ross' equation of death and "peace," although he might find this parallel distasteful.

Why is Hillman so sure that Auschwitz and Hiroshima are not soulish images as well as literal events? For that matter, why cannot literal death serve to conduct us into the realm of Hades, Gods, and soul? Like "the moon" of AIDS for autobiographer Monette, physical death creates a place of exile from "life," a mythic space from which to see earth's surface. To blame the heroic ego for all literal death, illness, and killing is to lighten the burden placed on psychic death-language, to lighten it beyond credibility. Hillman is not being fair in his apprehension of death's presence. His selection of imagery betrays a distinct bias, and perhaps in spite of his assertion that the Gods are psychic, not ontological, powers, the Greek pantheon functions to set severe limits upon what Hillman can say about death. Perhaps it is irrelevant that back in historical, literal Greece, the incessant warfare among city-states brought about the decline of Greek civic culture, and with it the rise of later yearnings for "the One beyond the many," and the style of philosophical monotheism that Hillman deplores.

Like Becker, Hillman takes the isolation of the individual as given. Although internal plurality reigns, his worldview makes no allowance for a plurality of souls. Family, community, and nation are all consigned to earth's surface, severed from inner life by the power of Hillman's own imaginal landscape. These realities remain thoroughly outside the proper range of a truly psychological perspective until they are transformed into underworld images. Just as Becker ontologizes a specific historically conditioned style of selfhood by jumping into the language of "universal human nature" so quickly, Hillman's surface/underworld imagery eternalizes an isolation of the inner self that just as clearly seems a product of a certain specific historical situation.

Hillman's project aims at overcoming the "balance" model of the Jungian legacy, with its dualism of ego and unconscious. Yet his dualism of ego and soul, surface and underworld, thus ends by retaining this original Jungian motif, and tearing apart our experience. Although he reintroduces death into psychic life, he does so by redividing psychic life from ordinary life. Of course, a true Hillmanian reply would see this complaint as a sign of the ego's insistence on "integration" and "unity" no matter what the cost. But a psychology of death ought to be prepared for twentieth-century images of death, including the very worst images of death, and be able to trace their impact upon soul.

Yet perhaps a deeper, more lasting problem for Hillman is that ego and soul are simply too few terms; they echo the Jungian "balance" principle that reduces all psychic forces to sets of polar opposites. What about "spirit" as a third and separate possibility, functioning as a genuine alternative, to

counter both "heroic ego" and the powers of soul? Why is
Hillman so convinced that underworld and earth's surface are
the only two locales in the psychic landscape? This is where
Christianism might give way to Christianity, whose imagery
always included additional forces and agencies, as well as
"places" for inner events to happen. Even if we take Hillman's
caution against quick jumps into resurrection, rebirth, and new
life very seriously, there is no need for us to eliminate such language. In fact, at best, Hillman's reappropriation of mythic discourse for psychology can open such categories up for the post-
Hillmanian interpreter, in a way not possible before. In
Hillman's mythic re-visioning of psychology's terrain, we find
a new approach to a psychological reading of Christian imagery
of death.

Robert Lifton

The most comprehensive, balanced, and integrated psychological theory of death's roles and meanings is that of Robert
J. Lifton. In *The Broken Connection*, he offers his solution to
the issue discussed by Becker and Hillman: can psychology find
room for death, and so acknowledge its presence throughout
human life? Lifton differs from them in his direct inclusion of
culture and history as factors in their own right, not automatically reducible to psychological forces. His use of the Freudian
and existentialist legacies is mediated by the ego-psychological
theories of Erik Erikson. Lifton's outlook upon human beings
appears considerably more "healthy-minded" than either
Becker's or Hillman's. Where Becker sees nothing but tormented paradox and Hillman only pathologizing, Lifton finds
both conflict and resolution, suffering and renewal, death and
immortality. Nevertheless, Lifton's moral outrage at contemporary culture's distortions of death goes at least as deep as
theirs. The difference is in the ground for his ethical vision of
humanity.

Lifton begins his study of death and its meanings with a
rejection of both Freud's "death instinct" and the common post-
Freudian view that death is unsymbolizable ("In the unconscious death is never possible in regard to ourselves"). Lifton
believes the idea of an "instinct" to be a confused intrusion of
a biological force into a psychological theory. As we have seen

from our look at *Beyond the Pleasure Principle*, he is probably
right here. Yet from this he does not conclude that the body
will be merely an external, accidental factor in human identity.
Lifton always finds the body as an element in human identity
and the lifecycle; he is no dualist in Becker's style. For Lifton,
the body is mediated and experienced in terms of psyche and
culture, a fact that the language of "instincts" thoroughly
obscures. Every vision of embodiment is already psychic; what
we experience as "the body" cannot be severed from human
capacity to symbolize.

As for the mind's supposed incapacity to symbolize death,
this is simply inaccurate. Freud himself, Lifton notes, was preoccupied with death fears, and did not interpret them as disguised castration anxieties (Lifton 1979:47ff.). Lifton notes how
this version of Freudianism dominates the American scene,
because it falsely legitimizes our cultural inability to symbolize death. Our own society may find death "unimaginable," and
we have misread Freud so as to justify this. Moreover, we have
denigrated or misunderstood past cultures' attempts to symbolize death, automatically labeling these as defenses against
death's terror.

Death and Immortality Symbolism

Lifton now introduces the main thesis of his psychology of
death: a better understanding of death symbolism yields a
more comprehensive sense of its power for a deeper vision of
life. Lifton sees "the symbolizing process around death and
immortality as the individual's experience of participation in
some form of collective life-continuity."

> Images which suggest immortality reflect a compelling and
> universal inner quest for continuous symbolic relationship to
> what has gone before and what will continue after our finite
> individual lives. . . . The struggle toward, or experience of a
> sense of immortality is in itself neither compensatory nor "irra-
> tional" but an appropriate symbolization of our biological and
> historical connectedness. (Lifton 1979:17)

We have here three important claims that dominate the rest
of *The Broken Connection*. First, when one speaks of humans
psychologically, one should never omit our capacity as symbol-

izing beings. "Human nature" so defined is never stuck within what suffices to understand nonhuman organisms, and Lifton is able to treat spiritual and cultural capacities as if these were primary to our definition as a species. In this way, he supports exactly the position Freud explicitly denied when he refused to allow for a "progressive" instinct as an explanation for such achievements. Nor, as in some of the more simplistic versions of ethical naturalism, can "nature" be turned into a benevolent force pitted against culture.

Second, Lifton's nonsuspicious approach to symbols includes particularly symbols of immortality. No longer are these prime examples of "benevolent illusions." So deeply has depth psychology become associated with the "hermeneutic of suspicion" as a cultural stance, that it is hard even for Hillman to let go of this attitude in regard to such symbolism. Jungian when it comes to most images, he balks at approving fantasies of resurrection and rebirth.

Third, the autonomous individual is replaced as the center of meaning by a view of humanity as interrelated. Thus, for Lifton the individual's own death should not be confused with "the end of everything." The whole purpose of immortality symbolism is to help apprehend and acknowledge those continuities and connections within nature, history, and the cosmos, that link each individual self to all other selves.

MODES OF SYMBOLIC IMMORTALITY

Lifton identifies five "modes of symbolic immortality," patterns of symbolism. The first, "biological," is expressed in the hope to live on in one's children. This has always been the most popular way that human beings imagine their own continuity. Lifton's appreciative stance toward this hope has been shared by few psychologists. Lifton insists that the underlying wish for continuity is a valid one. We are not *causa sui*, "the fathers of ourselves." This is not a tragedy but a built-in feature of the human condition that gives affirmation to parenthood. Lifton's vision here resembles that of one of the autobiographers, Joan Gould, for whom the "spirals" of interrelated generations form the very texture of human life, and give meaning to individual deaths.

A second mode of symbolic immortality is labeled by Lifton "theological." He downplays belief in an afterlife per se, and

concentrates on the thought that "The common thread in all
great religions is the spiritual quest and realization of the hero-
founder that enables him to confront and transcend death and
to provide a model for generations of believers to do the same"
(Lifton 1979:20). Thus we see Lifton retaining some distance
from traditional religious beliefs about "survival," yet attempting to approach such traditions' ideas appreciatively. This is
clearly a different reading of religious "immortality" than
Kübler-Ross' caterpillar-into-butterfly imagery, in which personal survival of physical death is the sole focus.

The third mode of symbolic immortality is "creative." This
requires connectedness with the future through some lasting
cultural accomplishment. We may think of giant artistic or scientific achievements here, but one can also imagine persons
participating in this mode through self-identification with a
major cultural institution. For scholars, ideally, this mode of
"creative" symbolic immortality should be particularly salient.
Yet a colleague once confessed that his private hope was to
write an article that someone would read fifteen years after his
death—hardly the kind of reliance upon this mode that Lifton
envisioned! Nor did the autobiographies in Chapter 1 show
that Americans place much faith in this mode, in spite of the
active participants in cultural institutions noted among the
subjects of those works.

"Nature" provides the fourth mode for symbolizing connectedness with a world that will live on after my individual death.
Lifton, who relies on Japanese examples throughout *The
Broken Connection* to compensate for the Western bias of most
psychological studies, notes that in Japan, continuities in
nature have been given great spiritual significance. "The state
may collapse but the mountains and rivers remain" (Lifton
1979:22) goes one Japanese proverb. This is a different use of
"nature" than in Western versions of ethical naturalism. In the
latter, "nature" legitimates individual death, but does not offer
strong images of continuity. Once again, Lifton is clear that
"nature" is a symbolic concept, not just a "raw given."

The fifth but most basic and significant mode of symbolic
immortality Lifton labels "transcendence." This is an altered
state of consciousness, a breakthrough for a sense of abundant
life in the midst of death. Transcendence is the foundation for
all four other modes (Lifton 1979:24). It liberates the individ-

ual into ultimacy, splendor surpassing what were thought to be the boundaries of the universe. It is the Liftonian equivalent to that moment in Becker's thought when the self, faced with the wonder and mystery of the cosmos, "sees God and dies." Paradoxically, it is in the moment of transcendence that the self feels fully alive. Because Lifton is not hostile to embodiment, he is willing to include sexual union as one of the potential vehicles for transcendence, alongside mystical states. Where Lifton differs from many recent advocates of "transcendence" is that he sadly recognizes how it alone is not sufficient to guarantee a sense of immortality. It must be communicated in terms of some intellectually, emotionally, and culturally meaningful sustaining framework. Pure, naked transcendence will not have more than private and temporary effectiveness. For this reason, transcendence has in the past invariably been linked to one of the other four modes of symbolic immortality.

If "immortality" symbolism is humanly meaningful in these ways, then so is the other pole of connection between life and death. Lifton believes that death as well as immortality can be symbolized: "Death is indeed essentially a negation—the epitome of all negations—but that does not mean that the mind has no way of 'representing' death, of constructing its versions of death" (Lifton 1979:48). In fact, each individual learns to symbolize death, in analogies drawn from other experiences. Just as death is the opposite or negation of life, so each "experiential cluster" of death-imagery is actually a polarity of life/death symbols (Lifton 1979:53).

EXPERIENTIAL CLUSTERS OF DEATH-IMAGERY

Three such experiential clusters are discussed by Lifton, all arising out of early childhood experience. The first is connectedness-separation. As in Bowlby's work, cited by Lifton (Lifton 1979:54–55), the child experiences both relationships and separations, then builds an image of death as abandonment and life as relatedness. Birth, of course, is the primordial "separation" upon which all others may be patterned, yet Lifton does not make much of this idea. In his treatment of infantile separation anxiety, he healthy-mindedly asserts that a normal child can acknowledge separation, and permit a certain amount of it. Only an abnormally vulnerable child finds it virtually intolerable. The child can then use the individual experience of loss

and separation as a personal foundation upon which to build a
vision of death and immortality from whatever cultural symbolism is available. Such symbolism will draw much of its
power from its hidden link with these childhood experiences. It
is intriguing to note that virtually everything Kübler-Ross has
to say about dying and death as anticipated loss falls under the
umbrella of this imagery.

The second experiential cluster of imagery is of integrity-dis-
integration (Lifton 1979:57). This includes the fear of death as
annihilation, but also anxiety over mutilation, dismemberment, and wounding. This imagery-cluster has attracted the
major share of psychoanalytic attention, Lifton notes. In a
sense the "castration connection" of the Freudian legacy
emphasizes these same basic fears. Death is equated with a
direct attack upon the body's integrity. As in the case of separation, Lifton feels that a healthy form of embodiment includes
a sense of "finitude, limitation and boundary" (Lifton 1979:63);
therefore, disintegration experiences are assimilated by the
child, rather than merely denied. Here we may see Becker as
an example of a thinker preoccupied with just this "experiential cluster" of death-imagery, and refusing Lifton's reconciliation of vulnerability with selfhood. At a different level, Jung's
fascination with alchemical imagery of dismemberment reveals
the subtle ways this pattern of imagery can be transmitted into
cultural modes. Several steps removed from childhood fantasies of mutilation and annihilation, the alchemists' interpretation of "death" as the violent destruction of the metals they
worked, let such imagery flourish.

A third cluster of images is believed by Lifton to be the most
neglected of the trio. Movement-stasis is the polarity between
being alive as motion, versus death as sleep, stillness, or
enclosedness. It is often noted how children assume that death,
like sleep, is a reversible condition (Lifton 1979:64). Once
again, Lifton stresses the "normality" both of stasis as an element in life, and of practices that seem to intensify it, such as
the swaddling of babies. Just as Kübler-Ross exemplifies a
model of death based upon separation, and Becker one based
on disintegration, so Hillman's Hades is preeminently the
realm of stasis.

Lifton's reformulation of some Freudian themes allows us to
wonder if these patterns of imagery are linked to gender. Such

links would be very indirect and deliteralized compared to Freud's focus on castration. Is the focus on women as relationship-oriented correlated in this culture to a preference for the imagery of death as isolation and loss? Is the violence associated with the disintegration and annihilation imagery more typical of male experience? The testimony of the autobiographies of Chapter 1 is extremely ambivalent here, as the physical ravages of some illnesses make "mutilation" a very literal and real possibility for both men and women sufferers. Against any simplistic sex linking of these patterns of imagery is the fact that all must be integrated through available cultural expressions. If the latter rely on one experiential cluster, or are radically depleted, then both women and men will share the consequences.

Lifton leans most heavily on connectedness-separation, not just in his explicit discussion, but throughout his book, and most directly in his title. Because he ties the question of death-symbolization in with childhood experience and social learning, he has provided a framework that permits us to ask about gender. Nor does his theory presuppose a certain style of death-denial right from the start. Preferring polarities to absolute oppositions, Lifton tries to show how people have in fact linked death to life in a variety of ways, drawing upon these three symbolic patterns.

Lifton then traces the development and elaboration of these three clusters of imagery throughout the life-span of the individual. He notes how initiation rituals can be characterized as "carefully staged death immersions culminating in honorable survival and earned rebirth" (Lifton 1979:74). Their message is that one must "'know death' in order to become a powerful and responsible sexual adult" (Lifton 1979:77). Our lack of a cultural equivalent to these initiations is noted. Not human nature, but specific cultural obstacles, make this "knowledge of death" unobtainable.

The Nuclear Image

Up to this point, what one finds in *The Broken Connection* is a powerful, comprehensive, and psychologically enriching theory about the roles of death and immortality in human existence. But it is only in the final and perhaps most controver-

sial section of the book that the fully "mythic" element in
Lifton's psychology of death emerges. Because Lifton refuses to
locate the contemporary terror of death in "universal human
nature," he turns to twentieth-century history to explain and
account for it. Especially since 1945, since Hiroshima, humanity has lived on the brink of catastrophic world destruction. A
nuclear war would ruin all continuities: children, work, rivers,
and mountains would no longer survive. There may be no
taken-for-granted future but only the death of everyone and
everything.

More precisely, the image of such a total annihilation pervades and darkens our capacity to exist in connection with
death. World War III is not "history"; it is, however, an imaginal possibility whose plausibility is both rooted in history and
threatens to undermine it. Because nuclear war is an image,
not yet an event, it is not exactly relevant to Lifton's argument
to debate whether a nuclear war would have to be "total," and
if not, whether a "limited" war could be survived and by whom.
The image of total annihilation remains unavoidable. The same
is true for any of the several scenarios of ecological catastrophe
that have arisen more recently. Their exact scientific plausibility is of course an important factor, but Lifton's theory helps
account for their psychological impact at another level.

According to Lifton, "As death imagery comes to take the
shape of total annihilation or extinction, religious symbolism
becomes both more sought after and more inadequate" (Lifton
1979:339). A well-populated heaven is no consolation for the
vision of a poisoned and ruined earth. An exaggerated reliance
on pure transcendence, the fifth mode of symbolic immortality,
stripped of all links to cultural ideals and shared beliefs, has
tried to fill the gap. Such quests for transcendence in the end
isolate the individual, and exacerbate one's sense of alienation
from history and community. The result of this "totalism" of
death-imagery is that all images of connectedness are endangered, or rendered inadequate. Language and imagination simply fail. Lifton quotes Loren Eiseley: "To perpetuate this final
act of malice seems somehow disproportionate, beyond
endurance. It is like tampering with the secret purposes of the
universe itself, and involving not just men but life in the final
holocaust—an act of petulant, deliberate blasphemy" (Lifton
1979:344). The final holocaust, the ultimate "No" to vitality,

continuity, and meaning: Lifton does not create this mythic image, but he must encounter it in all its starkness, dread, and limiting force.

In the face of this unimaginable and unsymbolizable possibility, Lifton identifies a villain—not a psychic agency such as the "heroic ego," but an ideology that he calls "nuclearism." He describes it as "the passionate embrace of nuclear weapons as a solution to death anxiety and a way of restoring a lost sense of immortality" (Lifton 1979:369). As a hope for ultimate resolution of death-anxiety, it is a false and idolatrous faith. It "involves a search for grace and glory in which technical-scientific transcendence, apocalyptic destruction, national power, personal salvation and committed individual identity all become psychically bound up with the bomb" (Lifton 1979:376).

Nuclearism is the religion of Hillman's heroic ego, a dangerous and vicious idolatry that substitutes triumph over death through technology for the difficult and ambiguous human connection with death. One aspect of nuclearism is its faith in technology, in this case atomic weapons. A second and even more sinister aspect of this psychological condition is its embrace of the apocalyptic myths of past eras. In Lifton's eyes, such myths invite us to assure ourselves that a new heaven and a new earth automatically emerge from the ruins of the old. They assure us that God's purposes might well be served by the final, deliberate blasphemy. They also promise invulnerability for the righteous, and the purification of evil through mass destruction. Although the image of total annihilation negates such promises—the good and the evil all perish together—the apocalyptic framework creates a mind set that cannot admit itself as equally vulnerable to mass destruction.

Because of Lifton's passionate concern for the threat of mass annihilation, we can better understand his advocacy of the more basic, biological mode of symbolic immortality. The hope for continuities, for something—children, nature, works of culture—to survive into the future, has become a precarious one. Previous generations could rely on theological beliefs, but there was always the presumption that human life as a cycle of generations would also continue. Without that, today we have a different priority. In a sense, Lifton's version of ethical naturalism emerges at a more ultimate, symbolic level as a trust in

life, in the cycle of generations, in the capacity of human beings
to integrate death-experiences.

Particularly in the figure of the survivor, rather than the
martyr or hero, Lifton finds the prototype of twentieth-century
humanity's best response to nuclearism and other global
threats of mass annihilation. In the experience of survivors,
"Renewal involves a . . . measure of annihilation along with
imagery of vitality beyond the death immersion" (Lifton
1979:392). Lifton's own earlier work with Hiroshima survivors
and Vietnam veterans leads him to such paradigms. Unlike the
martyr, whose culturally approved death in the name of ideals
validates nonbiological continuities, the survivor has chosen
life. But this life will be touched by death, and perhaps irrevocably contaminated by it. Here again, we have a stress on symbolizing capacities rather than biological categories in themselves, but "survival" becomes a valued link with the realm of
nature, of rivers and mountains, as well as to other persons. Is
this kind of imagery enough to counter that of total annihilation? Will its naturalism suffice to integrate the horrible vision
of the death of everyone? Lifton appears to believe so, but this
is certainly open to question.

It is clearly Lifton's theory, of all those examined so far, that
seems to encompass the widest range of human experience.
Without forsaking the language and legacy of depth psychology, Lifton shows how to reconnect depth, death, and soul with
ordinary life, history, and religious meanings. Lifton tries to
affirm the connectedness of all these, so that biological life and
inner personhood are no longer set against each other. There
is no room in his theory for the exaggerated split between spirit
and body, or soul and ego, developed by Becker and Hillman,
respectively. Lifton finds in our current unprecedented situation no solution through such dualisms, but only in their
renunciation. His hope is to seek the connectedness between
humanity and nature, soul and earth, life and death. Insofar
as his psychological theory attempts to reunite these possibilities, he has contributed to a psychology of death that holds
promise for integration with Christian thought and practice.

But is Lifton's emphasis on "connections" too sure of itself?
Are there indeed no intrinsic, perennial disconnections within
human existence? Or can we admit, in the words of Simone
Weil, that here below, nature is "irremediably wounded" and

therefore no vision of full integration of death such as Lifton promises *ought* to succeed? Surely, too, although "the nuclear image" undoubtedly has had an impact upon the contemporary capacity to symbolize death and immortality, it seems a mistaken literalism to claim that our culture's problems with death and its denial began in 1945. In other words, the presence of nuclear weapons is less a matter of strict cause for the problem than Lifton's formulation would have it. Nevertheless, by setting out any connection to world history, we can appreciate the massiveness, the seriousness, and the intransigence of the problem as Lifton defines its scope. Even if at the individual level, "transcendence" would do, neither this nor the other modes of traditional immortality can in themselves be guaranteed to encompass the possibility of worldwide death, that final petulant blasphemy. To explore the roles of death in human existence requires that this level of death-imagery be included.

5

Psychology's
Farther
Reaches

The legacies of Freud and Jung live on in Becker, Hillman, and Lifton. Together these thinkers provide alternatives to the naturalism of Kübler-Ross and much contemporary thanatology. All of the depth psychological theories manage to convey the complexity and paradoxical quality of human beings' relation to death. Far from making dying into a "natural" and unproblematic process, they try to demonstrate how radically tortured humans are by the presence of death, not only at the "end" but throughout our lives. Even Lifton, whose belief in resolution to this presence of death we found compelling, is aware that for us, death is never merely "nature."

All of these theorists must raise with Freud the question, "Do organisms die for *internal* reasons?" Even when this is transposed into *human* terms and categories, it remains a vivid reminder of what a psychological theory of death must include. If death is a continuous psychological fact, then how does it become such? How, if at all, is it included within a total life-world? If, as Becker insists, denial is almost inescapable, then although the body may die for internal reasons, the self never will submit to this death. Or perhaps, in an act of self-annihilation that may also become self-transcendence, it may "see God and die."

Is death to be paired with rebirth or resurrection, as a pattern of initiatory symbolism necessary for human development? This is the stance shared by Jung and Lifton. To split death symbolism from immortality is to play false to the psyche's capacity for hope and change, they would both claim. For Lifton the reality of human connections to the future and the next generation is expressed through such imagery. In this death/rebirth initiatory sequence, to know death, to enter a "death-experience" is to begin a process needed for growth. A psychology of death that is not at least potentially a psychology of symbolic immortality will be truncated and misleading, they could agree. In contrast, neither Freud nor Hillman (let alone Becker!) would agree with this relatively optimistic stance. For Freud, a "progressive instinct" operating alongside the death instinct was a fiction, and Hillman too applied a hermeneutic of suspicion to all "resurrection" language, seeing it as a refusal of the true destiny of soul. All would agree, however, that "death" needs to be somewhere in the experience, that a symbolism of transformation requires this deep moment of negation, separation, destruction for it to be ultimately powerful. All of them would find the natural transition from caterpillar to butterfly less than satisfactory, since this image in fact denies that the "death" of the organism is a reality.

As we maintained, all of our theorists venture into the realm of "myth" in order to encounter death as psychological reality. Yet all retain identity as depth psychologists, thinking within the *"logos"* of psyche. Hillman and Freud disagree over the placing of that *"logos"* and its relation to natural science. Yet all shrink from a psychology that becomes a direct adjunct to religion. Even Becker, the least clear on this question, will not want to annex Freud imperialistically into the "Augustinian-Lutheran tradition" without qualification. Freud may, in Becker's eyes, be a continuer of that tradition, but without merely aping it. As for Hillman, he is most eloquent that although the *logos* of psyche includes "Gods" and a certain religious dimension, it is not his goal to establish a new form of worship. In fact, he criticizes Jung for reliance upon the monotheism of the Self-archetype, for continuing in disguised form the Protestant heritage of his culture. Once the issue of myth is faced as unavoidable, the question of which myth or whose myth is also unavoidable.

Death in Transpersonal Psychology

Before we turn to the other body of thought on the topic of death, perspectives drawn directly from Christianity, we should pause to consider more carefully this unusual placing of psychological theory as somewhere between science and myth, nature and soul. One way to discern the location of depth psychology of the sort we considered is to look briefly at some forms of "psychology" that have entirely crossed over the boundary, and seem at home only in the realm of religion. These psychologies may much better be labeled "alternative spiritualities," directly prescriptive of spiritual visions and embracing a "religious" language with no qualifications. In a sense, their appearance marks the collapse of the gap between psychology and religion that both we and our theorists assumed. Whereas the "mythic" dimension of depth psychology was and remains muted, in these other thinkers it is blatant.

"Transpersonal psychology" is a term coined by Charles Tart in the 1970s. Perhaps "spiritual psychology" would have been more appropriate, since as we saw, there are important elements in both Freud's and Jung's theories that are distinctly "transpersonal." One way to characterize this movement is to see it as an extension of the "third force" of humanistic psychology, concerned especially with altered states of consciousness and "farther reaches of human nature" (Maslow 1971). Another definition sees this model of psychology as a rediscovery of the "psychological" theory and practice of spiritual systems, especially non-Western systems. So, for example, one may speak of a "Buddhist psychology," and read traditional meditative texts not as expositions of a religion, but as reflections on the nature of mind and consciousness. (Given the traditional vocabulary of philosophical Buddhism, this may be a particularly feasible example.) Many interested in such projects hope to chart a universal "map" of altered states of consciousness, or find universal techniques through which to reach such states.

It appears impossible to use this road, and arrive at any nonarbitrary and generally compelling definition of "spiritual"

as opposed to "transpersonal" as opposed to "religious."
Although religion does appear to most thinkers to include an
institutional component not necessary to the other terms,
debates about where the "transpersonal" ends and where the
"spiritual" begins will continue interminably due to problems
in defining such extremely global, amorphous concepts. What
to an outsider looks to be a transparently "religious" system of
interpreting human experiences, a system functioning in ways
that exactly parallel Christianity as a system of personal guidance will be vigorously defended as a "psychology" by its advocates. That all these systems may require a degree of faith or
commitment, that all of them claim to be validated through
"experience," and that all depend upon spiritual discernment
seem apparent. For some of them, the claim to stand in the
Western scientific, psychological tradition has become completely expendable.

Examples of such "transpersonal psychologies" that focus
explicitly on dying and death include the work of Stanislav
Grof in the 1970s, Stephen Levine, and others fascinated with
near-death experiences. Grof, whose original work was carried
out with LSD given as a "psychic amplifier," develops a model
of "psychic levels" in *Realms of the Human Unconscious* (1976)
and then revises it in *The Human Encounter with Death* (1977)
The first work is quasi-Jungian, and depends upon a series of
four hierarchical levels of psychic functioning. One of these is
related to "birth" as psychic, a spiritual as well as a physical
event. The ultimate, deepest level is of "transpersonal" archetypal phenomena, but unlike Jung Grof insists that the final
ontological reality is that of the Void or Emptiness. This
apophatic beyond-all-images spirituality is quite normative for
most transpersonalists, setting their ontologies directly on a
collision course with Hillman's diatribes against Western
image-phobia.

Grof and Halifax's *Human Encounter with Death* focuses
upon imagery, however. This work describes LSD therapy with
terminally ill persons. The "posthumous journey of the soul"
found in many mythologies is, the authors believe, a pictorial
representation of a psychic transformation brought about
through awareness of death's nearness. Scenarios of after-
death states are actually reports of altered states of consciousness among the living, in anticipation of death (Grof and

Halifax 1977:158–89). The authors are less interested in the specific details of any of the mythological "journeys" than in the entire theme of postdeath or near-death experience. Moreover, a certain form of reductionism reigns here. There is no commitment to the practices—meditation, for example—which each traditional "itinerary" presupposed as preparation for the traveler, nor is there belief in the ontology or cosmology presupposed by the authors of religious texts.

These neglects are rectified in the work of Levine. *Who Dies? An Investigation of Conscious Living and Conscious Dying* (1982) might be described as an American Buddhist revisioning of Kübler-Ross. A Buddhist passion for the illusory nature of ordinary selfhood and reality is combined with a great amount of practical advice on care and counseling with the dying. Levine very sensibly advises against reading "The Tibetan Book of the Dead" to one's dying relatives, if they are ordinary Americans who do not share Grof and Halifax's spirituality. To encounter death is to encounter the precariousness of identity as we normally experience and assume it. To press into the "who" of dying is to dissolve and renounce our ordinary self-awareness. The emotional tone of this work is in some ways as somber as Becker, yet filled as well with the (traditional Buddhist) hope for bliss as well as emptiness. What it does *not* offer is the promise of caterpillar into butterfly, for everyone, as a guarantee. "After death" is less important than awareness of the death of who each of us has really been.

Yet this goal is itself corruptible or co-optible into the slickest self-help format. Just as Kübler-Ross borders upon writing inspirational literature, so too the visions of Grof and Halifax and Levine can become reduced to "helpful techniques." A dreadful example of this, showing the liability of transpersonal psychology as it becomes popularized alternative spirituality, can be seen in the claims made by Anya Foos-Graber in *Deathing: An Intelligent Alternative for the Final Moments of Life*: "This deliberate approach toward the death moment can enable people to attain higher levels of consciousness, by whatever routings, so that they can reach out to meet the final light even as it approaches them, just as one accelerates before shifting gears in a car to achieve a smooth transition" (Foos-Graber 1984:12). The emphasis on technique, on "easy-to-follow steps," goes hand in hand with the exorbitant promises of spiritual fulfillment provided the reader follows the book's suggestions exactly. If, for Freud, science goes hand in hand with resignation to *Ananke*, to somber acknowledgment of limits, it is ironic that the trappings of science as "technique" have been enlisted to serve the goal of welcoming death as "the final light."

Near-Death Experiences

Still another area in which transpersonal psychology has shown great interest is in the study of near-death experiences. Unlike Grof and Halifax, who translate postdeath into near-death scenarios, contemporary persons are more than likely to interpret "near-death" altered states of consciousness into anticipations of a "postdeath" condition. Raymond Moody, Kenneth Ring, and others, including Kübler-Ross, who have become fascinated with this topic generally wish us to understand such experiences as signs of the mysterious, uncharted human potential for self-transcendence, linked to the hope for survival of physical death. The experiences themselves, which were schematized in Moody's *Life after Life,* include many components that are indeed very mysterious. Persons lying unconscious, in wrecked cars or on operating tables, see and hear events occurring around them, and can report details of these with remarkable accuracy. Certain standard imagery—a dark tunnel with a light at its end, a "being of light," and a glimpse of a landscape transfigured and beautiful—all figure in contemporary accounts (Moody 1975:30–64). The claim that this is "universal" imagery, and not a product of our cultural expectations and beliefs, is quite debatable, and has been seriously challenged by historian Carol Zaleski. Insofar as anyone takes these narratives as definite promises of individual survival (Kübler-Ross surely does) they function to support a caterpillar-into-butterfly belief system.

At this point, however, it seems we have crossed over from a psychological theory about death and near-death into the realm of alternative New Age spirituality. Advocacy is more direct, experiences are valued as definite "proofs" of a worldview, and the ontological claims built upon those experiences resemble those of religious traditions, comprehensive and cosmological. Although there may indeed be qualitative differences among the various exponents of this spirituality (I for one prefer Grof,

Halifax, and Levine to Foos-Graber and Moody) they all operate within a hermeneutic of restoration, in which what is being
"restored" is a full spiritual vision. Whether this vision is
Buddhist, monistic-mystical, or other, they do exactly what
Hillman disclaimed for his own work: they seek to establish
new forms of worship, foregoing all distinction between the psyche's *logos* and that of religion.

How does the flowering of this new spirituality fit within the
contours of the American cultural-religious landscape? When
we recall the tentativeness and subjectivism of the autobiographers in finding meaning-frameworks for death, it is no sur-
prise that almost any system of meanings that provides a
coherent "pathway" to encounter death will have some positive
reception. A gap or vacancy surely existed in contemporary
American culture, filled first by Kübler-Ross but then later by
others such as Levine and Foos-Graber, offering "self-help" to
the bewildered and suffering. Curiously, although many of the
autobiographical narratives depict "good deaths," there is a
lack of the ecstatic or paranormal in these that contrasts with
the expectations raised by some of the transpersonalists. Many
of the individual protagonists do indeed discover "who dies" but
in ways that correspond with their ordinary identities, with
how they had lived when healthy. If indeed these persons
engaged in out-of-the-body adventures or predeath "journeys of
the soul" to other realms, we do not hear about this aspect of
their experiences. This is not to say such things never occur "in
real life." But, to judge by the sample of American autobiographies discussed in Chapter 1, they do not regularly become
reorganizing forces in individuals' selfhood during the final
stage of life. Denial and "unconscious" approaches to death are
far more frequent. Which, of course, is just why self-help in this
area is desperately needed, authors of inspirational volumes
will claim.

A Dialogue of Perspectives

The existence of transpersonal psychologies of death and
dying may help us situate our own dialogue of perspectives
more carefully. Psychological perspectives such as those of the
Freudian and Jungian legacies can serve as interpreters of religious texts, as both Freud and Jung energetically and contro-

versially demonstrated. Or spokespersons of religious traditions can critically interpret these psychological theories as car-
riers of a worldview, or a vision of human nature that can be
contrasted to that of the tradition. Both of these approaches
assume two separate partners in a dialogue. Moreover, both
partners may share the need for "myth," but rely upon it for
different goals and use it in different ways. There may indeed
be a *logos* of psyche that stands separate from the *logos* of religious discourse.

This model of a dialogue does not require an eventual "integration" in the sense of assimilation of one partner by the
other, nor a blending of both into a third entity. Both remain
theoretical perspectives, answerable to their own norms of
truth. The merger transpersonal psychology proposes is a more
clearcut "integration" and unification of perspectives, into one.
But this one appears so close to a new form of religion, that it
is unconvincing as a solution to the terms of the problem as
originally posed. To "integrate" the perspective of Freud with
that of Foos-Graber is as difficult as to "integrate" Freud with
the thought of Paul the apostle.

The contribution of transpersonal psychologies of dying is
significant for us, however, in at least one respect. The idea of
reading religious texts, not to demean their meanings by reductionism but to allow texts and authors credit for substantial
psychological insight, is a breakthrough. Jung's very reverent
approach to alchemy as precursor to psychotherapy anticipated
this, but it is from the claim (if not the actual method) of
transpersonal psychology that we can learn to overcome the
simple opposition between psychologist-interpreter and religious believer. It is certainly false to read the New Testament
as "psychology" in the contemporary sense. But it is just as
false to deny to its authors a measure of psychological insight,
and awareness of their own emotional and cognitive foundations. This step calls into question the hegemony of Western
twentieth-century modes of understanding death, self, and the
sacred—exactly the stance of receptivity to alternative perspectives needed in our efforts.

As we turn to examine the perspectives drawn from Christian
faith, those of the biblical writers, spiritual guides, and theologians, we should bear in mind that these are not apsychological.
Just as psychologists needed "myth" to encounter death, so reli-

gious thinkers have needed "psyche" and have journeyed into its landscape, even as they set forth to discover the landscape of faith. The dialogue image requires awareness that both partners may speak several different languages, more or less consciously. In this sense, transpersonal psychologists may have something to contribute to our project, insofar as many of them respect the psychological insight of spiritual traditions, recognizing these as something more than "benevolent illusion" at work. If silence, repression, and ignorance mark the modern, "psychological" era's response to death, then authentic knowledge of death may be sought in the testimonies of the past.

For Christians, the "past" in the sense of the theological tradition is never discardable. Nor is it revered because it is "the past" but because then, there, in certain times and places, God acted definitively, bringing into existence new and eternal possibilities for humanity. Not just any past—Tibetan, Native American, and the like—but the past of the people of Israel, the past of Jesus Christ and the early church, is the past that counts, that structures a landscape of faith for us. Into this landscape, we now prepare to take our first steps.

6

Death
in Christian Theology
Today

In this chapter, we begin our exploration of Christian perspectives on death. I emphasize the plural "perspectives," for there is no one single insight upon the subject that comprehends adequately all that Christian revelation contains. Moreover, this diversity of approaches, beginning with the biblical authors, is to be treasured. It has made possible the appropriation of Christian images and hopes by diverse cultures, eras, and types of persons. Some positions and attitudes have been ruled out very firmly by the tradition, some images were never and could never have been used to shape Christians' expectations. But even within such limits, there exists a range of starting points, central ideas, and symbols. Death, as Pelikan noted in the little work cited in our introduction, is one of those topics upon which Christian intellectuals have always pondered, and there has been room for them to envision it in a variety of "shapes." There is no one "biblical" perspective, nor has a mandated later official church position ever closed off redefinitions or reformulations.

Theological Foundations

I will take a particular stance on certain theological issues, recognizing that there are alternatives. For a start, I propose that what Christianity has to say about death and dying is tied more or less directly to its central narrative, that of the incarnation, death, and resurrection of Jesus Christ. Because this narrative is unique to Christianity, what this religion has to say about death will also be unique. There will, nevertheless, be a great amount of overlap and similarity of imagery between Christianity and other religions; the same core of basic symbolism is available to all human beings. Specific uses of this imagery within Christianity will be guided by the narrative about Jesus' redemptive death. Buddhists, Muslims, and others share the basic stock of potential images, but do not share with Christians this central narrative.

Such a position means that theologies that are "Christocentric" will be given preference over those that are "theocentric." At least in regard to this topic, there is less warrant to speak of a "Judeo-Christian tradition" than might be right in regard to other issues. Judaism has its own resources through which to comprehend and make space for death, but these do not include Christianity's central narrative. Still less is there justification for a "universal theology" or a perspective drawn from a supposed amalgam of all major religious traditions. Not only does this create many problems of theological method, but it denies right from the start the uniqueness of each tradition's central narrative or story, by reducing all to a non-narrative, highly abstract religious-philosophical core.

Within Christianity itself, there has been much debate over the sources of authority and the methods appropriate for theology. Should theologians begin from the Bible, from Christian tradition, or from "experience"? What is the relation between doctrine and biblical texts? Between traditional formulations and today's apprehensions of divine reality? How much status should be given to "secular" thought-forms, including those of depth psychology? Recalling that Christian intellectuals have always borrowed from whatever cultural systems of thought were available to them and have never been content to repeat the biblical texts without commentary or expansion on them, the problem should not be formulated so as to involve an absolute opposition between the Bible and other modes of thought, or between traditional authority and "experience." On the other hand, at least in regard to death, the testimony of the twentieth century is primarily that of ignorance and silence; we have good reason not to elevate our "experience" to the status of judge over the past and its resources. A receptive and humble willingness to be open to and guided by the images from biblical authors is intrinsic to our own method.

In this chapter, we will set the stage for a close examination of those images, with a summarized overview of twentieth-century theological and pastoral psychological perspectives on death. Theology as a scholarly discipline reflects the faith of the church at any particular time; it is not itself "revelation." Nor, alas, has it always reflected the faith of *all* of the church, since academic theology as a calling is open to only a small minority. For this reason, some today wish to consider "theologizing" an activity of which all are capable, and in which most Christians participate consciously or unconsciously. The woman who explained the sudden death of her seventeen-year-old son by stating, "God took him, so that he would be saved from further sin," is in this sense "doing theology." So are some of the autobiographers of Chapter 1, even if they lack the academic training of professional theologians. Although such a usage expresses a laudable inclusiveness, however, the fact remains that "theology" as a discipline with a history, method, and set of problems of its own cannot be ignored or by-passed. Many of those who wish to do so, and begin instead from their "experience," run the risk of repeating the problems of the past unwittingly, or incorporating into the category of "experience" perspectives of contemporary culture at odds with the deepest insights of Christian faith.

In summarizing twentieth-century theological thought on death, one theme will emerge quickly: personal death has not been a central theological theme in these writings. Even those that seem to focus on death, often do so with a different underlying agenda in mind. Sometimes these writings are more preoccupied with a confrontation with Marxism or existentialism than with death. In other instances, the agenda is to purge Christian thought of all traces of "Platonism," and that whatever gets said about death is placed in the service of this goal. Finally, the "death" that seems to have played the major role in this body of writings is that of Western European cultural forms, shattered early in this century by two World Wars. The struggle to redefine Christian hope, the nature of God, and suffering that underlies many of these theologies, cannot be understood apart from this historical context.

In contrast, the pastoral care literature is by its nature concerned with the personal, the small-scale, the individual's dying. Yet much of this can be seen as the Christian chaplain's or pastor's appropriation of Kübler-Ross and the ethical naturalist approach to dying. In some cases, it is an uncritical appropriation, in others more selective. There is very little connection between the theological writings and those by pastoral caregivers; themes of great centrality to the theologians rarely make an appearance at all in the latter writers.

We will look at three distinct themes within theological writing: renewal of interest in eschatology; concern over "immortality" and "resurrection"—or the battle between supposedly "Platonic" and "Hebraic" forms of thought; and the motif of divine suffering. It seems that much of what theology has had to say about death can be viewed through these three categories of idea. Although many of the writers whose works I will mention are among the finest and most sophisticated thinkers within the Christian tradition of this century, it is often helpful to turn to more simplistic examples that express these same themes. There are also writers who do not share in the common agenda, who discuss the same topics freed from a particular set of assumptions held by the rest. On this topic, categories such as "Protestant" and "Catholic" or "liberal" and "conservative" are less relevant than commonly presupposed. Perhaps because death has been less of a central concern than other issues, it has also remained relatively less politicized by such divisions.

Eschatology as Central to the Gospel

In pre-twentieth-century Christian systematic theology, eschatology was the doctrine that referred to "last things"—to death, judgment, heaven, and hell. It was one section out of many, and not a centrally significant section. This is as true for Schleiermacher, the father of Protestant liberalism, as for his orthodox opponents. In contrast, for a good deal of twentieth-century theology, eschatology appears as a center-stage concern. The term, however, no longer means a set of beliefs about the final judgment. It now can be used in adjectival form as a synonym for the "ultimate" dimension of all human relations to God. Or it can retain some tie with temporality, for example, in the idea of the future as the horizon for divine activity. But whether this means what we may call "the historical future" very much depends upon the particular thinker and how that individual chooses to use this term. (Until recently, of course, the nature of academic theology restricted it as a vocation to men, a fact that may or may not have any bearing on its preoccupations.)

Eschatology Rediscovered

"Eschatology" was rediscovered by Protestant biblical scholarship at around the turn of the century. Readers of Albert Schweitzer's classic *The Quest for the Historical Jesus* will recall that although he discards all the more "liberal" and acceptable reconstructions, Schweitzer's own "Jesus of history" is a thoroughgoing apocalyptic visionary, who firmly expects the end of the world and the dramatic takeover of history by God. When this does not happen of its own, Schweitzer believes, Jesus "lays hold of the wheel of the world to set it moving on that last revolution which is to bring all ordinary history to a close. It refuses to turn, and He throws Himself upon it. Then it does turn, and crushes Him" (Schweitzer 1945 [1906]:368–69).

Although almost no biblical scholars hold this view today, it is significant that such an extreme position was suggested. Schweitzer's account requires response at two levels: Is it appropriate text interpretation? How can we now integrate this apocalyptic eschatology into theology? Is the entire framework for New Testament faith built upon the hope for a catastrophic end of history, marked by an immanent "day of Christ"? This *parousia,* or return of the risen Jesus in glory, never occurred in the expected form, according to Schweitzer and others who share his ideas. If so, how did those who believed in it accept its delay? And what do such beliefs have to say about the foundations of Christian faith for persons today? Is the apocalyptic-eschatological belief system of the New Testament church a framework we can abandon and disregard, or does it tell us something substantive about humanity's relation with God through Christ? Schweitzer answers this question by picking the first option. "The Spirit of Jesus" is what Christians relate to now; the relation between this Christ-Spirit and the Jesus of history, poor apocalyptic-driven victim, is tenuous and accidental (Schweitzer 1945 [1906]:399).

This is a conclusion few twentieth-century theologians are willing to accept, especially if they take eschatology seriously. The Jesus of history must be "the same" as the Christ of the church. Moreover, if eschatology, in the form of hopeful concern for an "end" to history, dominated early Christian expectation, and not just Jesus' own preaching, then any convenient division between Jesus and "the Spirit of Christ" Schweitzer or others might make is faultily construed. It is not just the faith of Jesus, but of Paul, of the author of the Fourth Gospel—and of almost all contributors to the New Testament and the congregations for whom it was written. "Eschatology" was not one doctrine out of many for them; it was the matrix within which all their beliefs held together. Whether this is true as an empirical statement about first-century Christians, it has definitely influenced much contemporary Christian rethinking of the role of death and afterlife in the total structure of faith.

How does the concern for "the eschatological dimension" of that faith affect Christian thinking about death? First and most central, it pulls attention toward God, toward divine sovereignty and activity as the source and locus of ultimacy. Within the original eschatological-apocalyptic scenario, one element (but only one) of the "day of the Lord" or "the last day" was to be a general resurrection of all the dead. This hope was firmly tied to a faith in God's justice, his life-giving capacity to create again what he had created once before, and to an entire cosmic renewal. The end—in the sense of the goal as well as the "last" thing—is God. This final and ultimate triumph of God places virtually every other event of any kind in a relative position. Among the events so included are the deaths of individuals, including my own death.

Hope and Death: Brunner's View

Christian theologians in the twentieth century who write on eschatology insist upon this order of priorities. The titles of their works are revealing: *Eternal Hope, The Hope of Glory, In the End God, On the Way to the Future,* and *A Theology of*

Hope. In all of the above books, the "hope" is referred to God and God's intentions for the future consummation of his own rule, of justice and peace and renewal. Although the authors disagree on how to interpret "future," all insist on it as *God's* future. They also disagree over whether categories such as "wrath" and "judgment" have any role to play within this divinely ordered future. In contrast, all of the above authors agree that *my* death and *my* immortality are relatively unimportant elements in the total hope, and have no independent meaning apart from God and God's final purposes for creation.

This is not to say that individual death plays absolutely no role in these theologies. But its role is small and restricted. In what I believe to be the best of this genre, Emil Brunner's *Eternal Hope* (1954), individual and collective hope are linked together, just as are individual and collective death. For Brunner, the "eternal" quality of this hope signifies that it transcends time and history, and cannot be fulfilled within either. This is an example of someone reading biblical "eschatology" as if it could be extracted from the context of chronological "last-ness" altogether. Brunner raises the question: Why not an "eschatological" hope within history, presumably as envisioned by Marxism or other modern ideologies of human progress? Brunner, using an existentialist vocabulary, examines the Bible as the source for Christian response to such alternatives. For Brunner, the "mythic" dimension of the biblical language stands, more or less, and can be used to point the way to more philosophically informed reflection. Thus, the answer he gives to the question, "Why not a hope within history?" takes the admittedly mythic theme of "the Antichrist" seriously. The coming of Antichrist signifies, in this theology, that Christians cannot read history as "progress." It will never be solely the progress of God's kingdom, for it is equally plausible to see it as the progress of the kingdom of evil. History itself remains inherently ambiguous.

This is why, for Brunner, "eternal" does not equate with "future" in any chronological sense. Christianity during the liberal era mistakenly became confused with the hope for historical progress. The Bible does not reveal a God who puts such faith in human improvement. In one of the most vivid passages of the book, Brunner sees that the chronological future of the earth, and in fact the entire physical universe, may be destruction or disintegration:

> It is only with difficulty that we can adjust ourselves to the
> thought that humanity must have an end, just like the individual man, who must inescapably die. When we are confronted
> with this outlook it is only then that we perceive how deeply
> rooted in us all is some form of the belief in progress and how
> hard it is for us to renounce it. (Brunner 1954:152–53)

Only then can we, having renounced such hope, put our trust in the eternal hope, the hope of God. Because the latter is completely atemporal, those who die now and those who die in the projected final destruction of the physical globe, will all enter God's hope "simultaneously."

Brunner also keeps the category of judgment, not only that of historical negativity. Is the eternal hope a universal hope, or is it dependent in some mysterious way upon our "Yes" to God's purposes? Do some persons end by being defined as objects of divine wrath, or do all share in the eternal hope of God's love? Or, in more common language, will some of us end up forever damned, in hell, separated from God? The biblical language certainly includes an element of judgment, of wrath, of negative, unhopeful despairing destiny for some. It also is so focused upon the purposes of God and divine intentions that to rule out "election" in favor of "free will" is to distort the proper balance. So Brunner keeps the symmetrical dualistic sheep/goats model of eternal existence (as in Matt. 25) and the hope for universal fulfillment in paradox, refusing to sketch out a scenario in which God becomes purely "all in all" or "everything for everyone" (1 Cor. 15:28).

American readers of this technical and abstract treatment will be puzzled when at the close, Brunner confesses that the death of his son in a railway accident prompted its writing. We miss the Kübler-Rossian focus upon individual dying, upon emotions and personal anxiety almost altogether. Yet what Brunner is doing is what Ernest Becker saw as the perennial function for religion: not "consolation" so much as placing human conflict upon the widest possible cosmic stage. In this way, the swallowing up of personal death by general eschatology makes perfect sense, for Brunner's vision of the stage is appropriately immense and comprehensive.

Other Theological Accounts of Hope and Death

In contrast to Brunner, several other works that treat the same theme appear one-sided or defective in methodology. Dale Moody's *Hope of Glory* (1964) offers a conservative coverage; unlike Brunner, he makes no attempt to link biblical imagery to contemporary thought-forms, existentialist or otherwise. All of the eschatological materials are taken seriously, quasi-historically. Unlike Brunner, Moody does not want to substitute "eternal atemporal" for "last" things. Within Moody's treatment, death is both destruction and departure; he replicates Lifton's first two clusters of imagery, disintegration and separation. Yet once again, the primary focus is not upon individual death but upon the totality of the hoped-for eschatological future.

Another treatment of exactly the same topic, this time from the liberal point of view, is John A. T. Robinson's *In the End God* (Robinson 1968). This is a much more popular book than either Brunner's or Moody's, and also more representative of the 1960s enthusiasm for "secular" thought-forms. Robinson adopts Rudolph Bultmann's famous "demythologizing" program, to purge Christianity of leftover prescientific thought-forms. This approach requires that all references to the historical future, to judgment, and even to individual death be dropped. *In the End God* means that Christianity holds to an entirely universal, cosmic, and inclusive vision of divinely sanctioned fulfillment for humanity. God is to be all in all. Because biblical eschatology is, in Robinson's eyes, universal and cosmic in scope, any concern with individual death is a sign of selfish individualism on our part. This verdict enables him to ignore virtually all of the "death-language" of the New Testament. Such an argument reappears from time to time in Christian writings; no wonder Kübler-Ross' work filled a vacant niche, especially in an individualistic culture where our own deaths do matter to us!

Another work on the same topic is Hans Schwartz' *On the Way to the Future* (1979). This book attempts to be inclusive and comparative; Christian eschatological expectations are compared to Marxist, existentialist, and other views of what "future" will mean. One senses that this confrontation with various "futures" at the political and collective level is the spur not only to this work but to many of the genre. Nevertheless, within his task of responding to these non-Christian alternative future hopes, Schwartz finds it important to stress the totality of death. This implies a corresponding "complete newness" of resurrection, a theme we will examine shortly; but once again the focus is well off individual death. Schwartz, like Moody but unlike Robinson, keeps the sheep/goats model of a dual eschatological future, and finds the "all in all" scenario one of several blind alleys for theology and Christians to take. The others include treating the eschatological expected future so literally that one can set dates for its coming, and belief in purgatory.

A much more profound and influential book, *The Theology of Hope* (1965) by Jürgen Moltmann, tries to make of eschatology *the* key to Christian faith. Moltmann wishes to make history and the future the spheres of God's activity, and explicitly repudiates an atemporal model of "eternity" such as that held by Brunner. Moltmann's "thoroughgoing eschatological perspective" attempts to turn Christians' attention back into history and political life, away from "Platonized" and otherworldly hopes. The church should be an "Exodus church" on the road toward a future within history. Consequently, in this work death is not a topic at all, nor are the traditional subthemes of eschatology addressed explicitly. For example, there is no reference, however demythologized, to the Antichrist theme so critical to Brunner's critique of historizing eschatological expectations. Moltmann is an excellent example of the problems that redefining terms create; how seriously, how literally, or how chronologically he takes the "temporal" dimension to eschatology is very difficult to determine. Moreover, this work could just as easily be seen as an example of the "anti-Platonism" agenda that dominates other twentieth-century theological writers.

In a much more philosophical vein, John Hick's *Death and Eternal Life* (1975) would appear to include "death" more centrally within its scope. In one sense it does, as Hick reviews all the various literature on "survival" after death. But the work properly belongs within the genre of theologies of eschatology. Hick sees that there is an ultimate *telos* to divine purpose, and this is indeed an "apocatastisis," an "all in all" consummation including everyone and everything. But there is also, Hick believes, a need for a "par-eschatology," a not-quite ultimate reality within which problems of justice and rehabilitation will be worked out. *Death and Eternal Life* tries to provide just that, drawing upon Hindu,

Christian, and philosophical speculation. The final result would infuriate both Brunner and Moltmann, since it combines both a faith in human "progress" and a quasi-"Platonist" vision of how this might be achieved. In Hick's scheme, we have a fresh version of a set of beliefs once ascribed to Origen (d. 265); embodiment within this life becomes a way-station on the road toward spiritual perfection. The latter includes perhaps multiple embodiments (reincarnation) and almost certainly multiple existences within various spiritual realms for the spirit on the way toward its own future *telos*. Thus "eternity" is not strictly atemporal here, although it is definitely transworldly and transmaterial. On the other hand, death itself ceases to be destruction or departure. It is so swallowed up into both eschatology and par-eschatology that, as in so many of these other works, there is little that addresses its presence within this life now.

Still another effort that takes the pathway of comprehensiveness is Hans Küng's *Eternal Life?* (1984). Like Schwartz, he surveys what every major thinker or discipline has had to say upon the subject of death and its survival. Küng is particularly aware of critiques of traditional belief in immortality, such as those of Feuerbach and Freud, which accuse religion of fostering "otherworldliness" at the expense of liberation within this life. Küng's work, like that of Robinson earlier, shows selective enthusiasm for some "secular" thought-forms, and lacks a way to determine which, if any, are really relevant to the task of the theologian. Simply to cite such perspectives is not to address their import for Christian theological method.

What all of these works have in common is that they subordinate the issue of death, even of Christ's death, to the theme of eschatology. In a few, individual death is deliberately set aside; in others it is "taken up" into hope for a generalized future. It is fair to see all of these works as theocentric rather than Christocentric. But there is also a peculiar impersonality to them worth mentioning. All of these *might* have grown out of personal experience with death, as Brunner's apparently did. But more likely, many of them grew out of their authors' personal encounter with Marxism, critical theory, or other twentieth-century thinking about the future of human society. How does the *eternal* hope treated by Christian eschatology touch upon our faith in these other hopes? This is an entirely legitimate question, but it is not aimed directly at the issue of personal death.

Just for a contrast, we might mention a much earlier and still excellent work entitled *And the Life Everlasting* (1933) by John Baillie. This book on the surface covers much the same ground as Küng's, for instance. But it also includes what we have called "personal death" and therefore individual post-death existence into its scope, without letting this become entirely overshadowed by the "cosmic" dimensions of eschatology. For Baillie, the answers to the Freudian-Feuerbachian critique of belief in immortality are no great problem. We genuinely would wish for the immortality of others whom we love, a nonselfish and altruistic hope. Moreover, the earliest and most widespread views of after-death existence, including that found among the ancient Hebrews, are hardly "wishful" in tone; to descend to Sheol was never the object of any religious "hope." For Baillie, hope for an individualized "life everlasting" is an entirely legitimate element within Christianity:

> But if God is the God of individuals, if individuals can enter into fellowship with Him, if individuals are precious in His sight, then our hope in God necessarily becomes a hope for the individual. The argument is unanswerable; and is indeed the only unanswerable argument for immortality that has ever been given. . . . If the individual can commune with God, then he must matter to God; and if he matters to God, he must share God's eternity. (Baillie 1933:137)

Such arguments are only "unanswerable" to those who share these premises. Moltmann and others would maintain that when individuals are given such high priority and severed from communities and collectivities, we already have an interpretation of the gospel that does not take certain features of biblical eschatology into account. How much do individuals matter, within the scope of the biblical vision? Baillie's altruistic hope of immortality for loved ones therefore also vanishes as a serious consideration. To the later theologians, this level of hope fails to satisfy the quest for cosmic universalism. Perhaps it smacks of sentimentalism, measured against the eschatologies of Brunner, Moody, and Moltmann. Unfortunately, this quest leaves a vacant niche in the space Baillie could fill, a niche reminiscent not only of Kübler-Ross, but of the "memorialized" dead loved ones within the autobiographical narratives. Theologians look to God's future, the largest possible stage upon which to set the human drama. But that drama itself may have vanished or become truncated and abstracted in the process.

Resurrection and Immortality

The rediscovery of "eschatology" as a category of New Testament thought was tied to an agenda of purgation. As this became part of theology, biblical scholarship, and Christian reflection, it became formulated as the hope to cleanse Christianity, in thought and practice, from its long captivity to certain philosophical and cultural traditions. These were perceived as inhibiting reception and understanding of the authentic gospel. Within much Protestant and some Roman Catholic theology, this agenda takes on the task of restoring Christianity to its "Hebraic" roots, in contrast to the "Greek" or "Platonizing" influences that infiltrated the early church. Within the scope of this particular twentieth-century dichotomy, "Hebraic" is always a "plus" and "Greek" is equally always a "minus." This itself represents something of a reversal from an earlier era, when the Judaic background was perceived as "primitive" and parochial, a limitation that may originally have impeded the spread and comprehension of Christianity's real message.

Twentieth-century theological users of the dichotomy place on the "Hebraic" side the Old Testament, particularly its historical narratives; history as the sphere of God's activity; and embodiment as an intrinsic and necessary dimension to personhood. The "Hebraic" worldview is adequate to the biblical doctrine of creation, and to persons who must relate to God as whole, unified beings. On the "Greek" side go those Church Fathers who "spiritualized" and "Platonized" the gospel, such as Clement and Origen; a static and atemporal view of God's relation to the world; and contempt for the body at the expense of the soul.[1] "Hebraic" thought is holistic; "Greek" thought is dualistic and oppressively hierarchical.

1. Although one would expect that "Platonism" would have its origins in Plato's thought, those who use this term pejoratively equate it with intense revulsion toward the body and physical beauty. While for Plato the contemplation of visible beauty could lead to contemplation of the higher and supersensible beauty of the soul, twentieth-century opponents of "Platonism" rarely notice this in making their case against "Platonic dualism."

In regard to our topic, the two options are resurrection (the "Hebraic" version of postdeath existence) or "immortality" (the fate of the soul according to Greek wisdom). The first requires some form of embodiment, while the second eschews it. The vigor with which this dichotomy is often expressed has convinced me that it represents a deeply felt contemporary protest on behalf of certain vital concerns. This can be maintained in spite of its dubious relevance to the world of the Bible, or of ancient Christianity. A recent, thorough treatment of the literature on this issue by John Cooper (Cooper 1989) reinforces this suspicion that the dichotomy projects contemporary concerns back into the past.

According to those who rely upon this dichotomy, biblical eschatology originally dealt with hope for the future renewal of *this* earth. The establishment of justice and peace, the fruitfulness of nature, and the peaceful cycle of human generations were all part of such a hope. Nothing could have been more foreign to ancient Hebraic expectations than the hope for an atemporal heaven, removed from matter. Thus, the resurrection of the body was the appropriate correlate for the human mode of being in the eschatological era. Full personhood demands embodiment, and there is nothing evil in the body per se. With this emphasis, what can be said about death will dramatically shift from certain traditional Christian expectations, and although some possibilities are opened up, others are closed down. As for the focus upon history, we have already mentioned how works such as Moltmann's *Theology of Hope* want to employ the "thoroughgoing eschatological perspective": to wrench Christianity away from exactly the kind of individualized, atemporalized ethos reflected so well in the Baillie quotation. God is less concerned with my private loves and losses than with politics, social transformation, and large-scale history. This same set of priorities dominates contemporary Latin American liberation theologies, especially since in that part of the world the discourse of "eternity" has masked church involvement in oppressive political structures.

Cullman's Dichotomy

Perhaps the most outspoken and simplistic instance of the resurrection/immortality, Hebraic/Greek dichotomy is also one of the most revealing and influential: Oscar Cullman's "Immortality of the Soul or Resurrection of the Dead?" For Cullman, it is simply obvious that these two are not just different, but opposite and incompatible possibilities. For Socrates, representing the "Greek" outlook, immortality of the soul was a natural possibility, a predictable hope. Hence his death was peaceful, sublime, fully accepted—because it was no real ending, destruction, or loss whatsoever. In contrast, the Hebraic worldview to which Jesus subscribed saw death as a "horror," a "terror." It was God's enemy; therefore "to die means to be utterly forsaken" (Cullman 1965:16). There could be no such thing as a good death. Death was the complete negation of the person, for Hebraic thought did not divide us into "soul" and "body." Thus, in this worldview, persons really do *die*, and death is a catastrophe.

Cullman's dramatic climax comes in this contrast between the deaths of Socrates and Jesus. Jesus, unlike Socrates, feared his own death and wept when facing it. "Jesus is afraid, though not as a coward would be. . . . He is afraid in the face of death itself. Death for him is not something divine: it is something dreadful" (Cullman 1965:15). In Gethsemane, Jesus anticipates nothing less horrible than complete separation from God, and complete victory for God's enemy, death. He weeps because he is a realist about death's horror. Cullman, like Becker, relies on terms such as "terror" and "horror," although in this case, the New Testament texts he interprets do not directly supply them.

Against this background, the resurrection was something completely new, completely miraculous, and also completely "embodied." Only as a result of the resurrection can Christians face "the last enemy" with hope and confidence. For Cullman admits that in the meditations of Paul facing his own possible death, one does find an equanimity resembling that of Socrates. Nevertheless, death remains an utter evil; not just the last enemy, but perhaps, in this presentation, the only enemy. Nor is there any doubt that Cullman means biological death; remember that one's person and one's body are inseparable in "Hebraic" thought. Perhaps we have in Cullman's retelling of the Passion narrative what Hillman would see as the epitome of "Christianism."

Cullman is also haunted by the criticism so frequently leveled at popular Christianity, that it promotes "wish-fulfillment" at the expense of reality. He blames this problem on "Platonism's" invasion of popular Christianity. "Platonism" has dominated its expectations, and so gives plenty of excuse for Christianity's opponents to label such hopes as "illusion." Cullman would surely label Baillie, Hick, and Brunner (not to mention Kübler-Ross' caterpillar-to-butterfly hope) as exponents of this "Greek" substitute for authentic Christianity.

When "resurrection" is substituted for "immortality" in this fashion, one faces once again the whole issue of how eschatology relates to ordinary time. For Paul in 1 Corinthians 15, the resurrection of Jesus is past, but that of everyone else ahead, on that day when God will become "everything for everyone" and death, the last enemy, will be put forever under his feet. But what of the interim? What is the status of those who die in Christ now? They "sleep"—but although this is clearly a form of existence, it is an unfulfilled existence; they are on hold, so to speak, until the last day. The consequence is puzzling: no one, except Jesus himself, is truly awake and resurrected prior to the eschatological end. This, of course, is simply not what Christians have traditionally expected, either for their loved ones or themselves. If Cullman were right, however, it is what they ought to have expected. Anything else, in this age of the world, is Platonic, benevolent illusion.

We should separate two Cullman themes at this point: death as pure negativity, and the person as necessarily embodied. In one way, almost all Christian thinkers agree that death is a "minus" term, and that terms such as "destruction" or "loss" or "negation" are well suited to it. But Cullman is not supporting a view of the individual who matters to God and whom God makes "immortal" to compensate for bodily death; this Baillie idea sounds more like Socrates. Cullman's chief focus is that death is necessarily the absolute enemy of God. Yet missing from this interpretation is any notion of death as punishment for sin. Jesus' weeping was therefore not tied to the theme of atonement for sin, vicarious expiation, or sacrifice. It was terror of death, divorced from these particular meanings. In short, the "judicial" framework within which much of the traditional Pauline and theological language functioned is not evoked by a twentieth-century thinker intent on making death as negative as possible. No more than in Kübler-Ross are such metaphors used to comprehend why death is so terrible, such an enemy.

Other Theological Examples

Cullman's dichotomy, although oversimplified and challenged by biblical scholars, has had a life of its own. At least two sophisticated and provocative writers, working outside Christian "theology" proper, have relied on it indirectly to analyze contemporary experience. Milton Gatch, in *Death: Meaning and Mortality in Christian Thought and Contemporary Culture*, is able to employ the dichotomy so as to interpret the interiorized, "otherworldly" hope of Tolstoy's "Death of Ivan Ilych" as a modern variant of the "Greek" immortality motif (Gatch 1969:172–76). In contrast, Camus' *The Plague* exemplifies "resurrection"—not because its author holds any hope for a "postdeath" existence, but because Camus, unwitting heir to the "Hebraic" vision, writes of human solidarity and communal renewal in the face of death (Gatch 1969:176–81). Gatch personally rejects any form of "postdeath" individual survival, yet finds the basic dichotomy meaningful to us today.

Still another use of this Cullmanian dichotomy, more indirect than Gatch's, is Edith Wyschogrod's opposition between the "authenticity paradigm" for individual death, and that which takes the social nature of selfhood seriously. In *Spirit in Ashes: Hegel, Heidegger and Man-Made Mass Death* (Wyschogrod 1985) she regards this dichotomy as an outcome of philosophical reflection on the Holocaust, which (according to Wyschogrod) calls into question the individualized, privatized, and transcendent selfhood of the traditional "authenticity paradigm"—the equivalent of Cullman's "Greek" model of immortality (Wsychogrod 1985:2–6). Mass death reveals the sociality and vulnerability of the self to history; death is fully experienced as negation of the self, as in Cullman's "Hebraic" pattern. Both Wyschogrod and Gatch manage to salvage the profound contemporary relevance of these two alternatives. They, unlike Cullman, capture the tragic dimension in both models, in the midst of their preference for the "Hebraic."

Curiously, when biblical scholars challenge Cullman's presentation, and particularly the idea of death as God's enemy, they usually preserve his other assumptions. For instance,

Lloyd Bailey, Sr.'s *Biblical Perspectives on Death* entirely accepts the second Cullman thesis, the necessity of embodiment for personhood. Versus Cullman, Bailey claims that the ancient Hebrews did distinguish between a "good death" and a "bad death," and that overall for them, mortality was not a major "terror" at all (Bailey 1979:48-52). Bailey's treatment of the New Testament and his own constructive suggestions, however, reveal how firmly the "Hebraic" sense of embodiment shapes his interpretation. It is impossible for us to accept the idea of "resurrection," he claims, and today we know that death is "natural" for all embodied beings. This does not make death a "good" but if we take embodiment seriously, we will find mortality as its inevitable correlate. This, Bailey believes, is the authentic Hebraic view of death, to which Christians should return; we should not cling to later formulas that promote denial (Bailey 1979:109–10).

The person as necessarily embodied thus proves a more central contention than that of death as enemy: this is also the case in another quasi-theological study of ancient materials, Margaret Miles' *Fullness of Life* (1981). Miles examines the ancient church writers whom Cullman and others have castigated as "Platonists" and body-haters. She finds that contempt toward the body was not the authentic Christian teaching. Although body and soul were distinguished and the soul was believed to be "higher," the person as a totality was the subject of the ascetic ascent toward God. Therefore, although their language sounds more like Socrates, the ancient Christians' allegiance is toward embodied personhood. An "incarnational" outlook upon bodies and matter predominated after all.

When "embodiment" itself becomes a plus term, postdeath existence becomes hard to imagine, let alone defend philosophically (Cooper 1989:54ff.). Moreover, any sense of the body as fragile, weak, vulnerable, and occasionally disgusting is eclipsed, or quickly labeled as Platonic or gnostic-ascetic. That bodies can be impaired, imperfect, and ugly seems to have been deliberately forgotten. Admittedly, to stress embodiment can become a way to integrate such awareness of limits into one's sense of personhood, but it is curious how little attention is given to this problem. By contrast, depth psychology has taken up this theme, and as we saw, is very sensitive to the ambiguities and paradoxes of embodiment. Becker, Hillman, and even

Lifton would criticize as shallow much of the theological enthusiasm for embodiment.

Contrasting Alternatives

What of writers who are less swayed by the Greek-Hebraic dichotomy, or who deny its validity altogether? It is perhaps at this point that two Roman Catholic contributions should be introduced, to serve as vivid contrasts to this exclusive stress on history and embodiment. Ladislas Boros, in *The Moment of Truth*, constructs an entire theology focused upon "the moment of death," a moment defined as outside time, as one when an "eternal decision" is made by the soul for or against God. Such a moment summarizes a life lived within time, but is also a "last chance" for repentance (Boros 1969:84). Boros' idea shows that "Platonism" is alive and well, for his "moment" is atemporal and his self an entirely disembodied being, living out the authenticity paradigm rejected by Wyschogrod. One can well see Tolstoy's Ivan Ilych's dying moment as a prime literary illustration of Boros' motif. Of course, an additional theological criticism of this idea is that through the narrow gap of the "last chance," the moment of truth, will creep virtually everyone, regardless of the quality of life. In other words, Boros' atemporal "moment" looks like still one more strategy to resolve the paradox of God's universal love for humanity and individuals' freedom to reject such love.

A far more profound theology of death and after-death is that of Karl Rahner. Rahner, unlike Cullman and so many others, simply accepts as given the traditional Roman Catholic dogmatic definition of death as "the separation of body and soul" (Rahner 1958). But because the person is embodied soul and a unified being, the soul itself is *not* untouched by death (as Cullman's Socrates believed). What happens to the soul as it loses its own body? It gains a new, "pan-cosmic" relation to all of matter (Rahner 1958:20–22). It dies to an individual embodiment, and lives in God and through all material reality. In this mysterious fashion, Rahner preserves a dualistic view of the person, while maintaining that death is a total event. Neither "Hebraic" nor "Greek" alone can capture this paradox.

Rahner, unlike Cullman, is also able to find death an active event, rather than a "horror" or "catastrophe" that falls upon

us from outside. Death is therefore linked to human freedom
in a positive way; we do not merely drop into death, but turn
toward it as free beings and make it an act of our being. This
idea, radically different from Cullman's "last enemy" theology,
enables Rahner to see in the death of the martyr the prototypi-
cal Christian death. For the martyr, more clearly than for most
of us, death is a freely chosen act of love (Ochs 1969:68).
Therefore, as positive act, death is curiously more connected to
"history" for Rahner than for Cullman. This history is first and
foremost the total history of that self who dies—perhaps one
more expression of the "authenticity paradigm." In fact,
Wyschogrod would probably find that Rahner's idea of death as
a free act, however appealing, is no more than a romantic
expression of individual transcendence in a world now dominated by mass death. Like Lifton, Wyschogrod discards the
martyr as the paradigm twentieth-century figure, and prefers
the survivor.

We may ask to what extent the twentieth-century theological rediscovery of the "embodied person" is a proper interpretation of Christianity as "incarnational." Is it not better labeled
"ethical naturalism" baptized, made superficially Christian? All
of the thinkers we have examined would deny this; "nature" is
not a sufficient category for human life or death. None would
view death as merely a biological event, as naturalism does. On
the other hand, the easy choice is to turn "death" into "last
enemy" in such a way as to keep it external, a hostile intrusive
force against which God and we ourselves must struggle. This
is why Cullman reads like such an excellent example of
Hillman's "Christianism." Yet other trends within Christian
theology go in a very different direction, plunging into a vision
of divine suffering and death that radically challenges the more
simplistic implications of the Cullman dichotomy. Alternative
paths remain, but these are no longer so clearly marked as
were those of the thinkers who follow the "Hebraic versus
Greek" agenda.

Christ's Death and Divine Suffering

The traditional attributes of God stress transcendence of
suffering, evil, limitation, and dependency. God exists beyond
time, space, change, pain, and neediness. The theological terms

for this are aseity—self-sufficiency of being—and impassibility—
freedom from being harmed or affected by evil. Such a God exists
in a nonspatial realm, "dwelling in light inaccessible from before
time and forever" to cite the elegant words of the Episcopal *Book
of Common Prayer* (Episcopal Church 1979:373). This is not
Hillman's "Gods of the soul," of course: these dwell in an equally
atemporal Hades. The God "above" (identified by Hillman with
the heroic ego) is the God "beyond." This is the familiar Western
monotheistic conception of the divine.

It is familiar, but is it Christian? Is this truly the way
Christians ought to speak of God? *The Book of Common Prayer*
goes on to recite the entire history of fall and redemption,
stressing how God became accessible to humankind: "in your
mercy you came to our help." Traditionally, the involvement of
God through Christ in redemption and deliverance from death
was seen as compatible with a view of the divine as entirely
"beyond." There seemed to be, as in this particular liturgical
expression, no necessary opposition between the two poles of
aseity and involvement. Yet by the late twentieth century,
many theologians recognize that the God who loves us enough
to come to our help, could not be a God unaffected by suffering,
pain, and death. Such a God is "for us" in innermost character,
not "for himself" and beyond all relatedness. Traditional teaching on divine aseity and impassibility seems to contradict God's
full involvement in the drama of redemption. Incarnation was
not an isolated, "out of character" event for the God of
Christianity. This God had been "involved" and affected right
from the beginning. (Because the "personal" language is so
intrinsic to this portrayal, I will continue to refer to God as
"he," although the Divine of utter aseitic transcendence might
just as well be referred to as "it.")

The issues involved are so theologically central that it is surprising how quietly "impassibility" has been rejected by contemporary thinkers, in contrast to the militant and vigorous
attack on supposed "Platonism." It appears that the underlying quest is for a God whose involvement is with us, in our
pain and experiences of suffering and oppression (McWilliams
1980). The opposite appears be a God too remote to feel with
us, a God who floats above the realm of suffering. What in the
past might have seemed a tribute to divine glory, now appears
closer to divine heartlessness.

Why so? Perhaps the major influence here lies in that same experience of mass suffering and abusive coercive power in twentieth-century history, marked by Wyschogrod as a watershed for other reasons. In the light of this historical catastrophe, traditional power language ascribed to God made him too much like a cosmic Hitler or Stalin, too close to being the enemy of persons and freedom everywhere. Therefore God as "weak and powerless in the world," in the words of Dietrich Bonhoeffer (Bonhoeffer 1967:196), seemed more real, more truly divine. Traditional views of divine providence also turned God into "the executioner," whereas God as fellow-sufferer along with creation preserved him and us from turning the doctrine of divine sovereignty into masochistic glorification of power. "Only a God who can suffer can help" amid situations of mass suffering and injustice. A God who remains "in light inaccessible" is no help at all.

Theologies of Divine Suffering

This theme, set forth and repeated in some of the finest religious writings of our century, is overtly Christological. "The Cross of Christ as the Foundation and Criticism of Christian Theology" is the subtitle of Jürgen Moltmann's *The Crucified God* (Moltmann 1974), and this phrase could serve as a banner under which gathers a range of religious thinkers. The death of Jesus is the way God's full participation in human suffering and death is enacted; to make the cross central repudiates forever any definition of God as a being immune to pain. Here, the death of Jesus is not his defeat by an enemy, but his complete and final act of solidarity in the human condition of mortality and oppression. And, as already indicated, this could not have been a once-and-once-only kind of solidarity; it reveals more clearly the permanent character of God as a participant in the pain and alienation of creation.

Yet it is one of the most bitter ironies of twentieth-century religious thought that the clearest, starkest expression of this idea is not found in a theology text, nor even in the writing of a Christian. It is from Elie Wiesel's *Night*, an autobiographical narrative of imprisonment in Nazi concentration camps, that one can find the most vivid discovery of the reality of divine suffering. One particular scene in this work has been a source for theological meditation on the presence and absence of the divine in a world dominated by death and evil. Wiesel describes how in the camp, three prisoners were to be hung while the rest of the camp inmates were forced to watch their deaths. Two were adults, the third a boy with a face like a "sad-eyed angel." As the boy dies a gruesome, prolonged, agonizing death, the author and his fellow-prisoners must look him full in the face. Wiesel hears a man ask:

> "Where is God? Where is He?"
> And I heard a voice within me answer him: "Where is He? Here He is—He is hanging here on this gallows." (Wiesel 1969 [1958]:76)

The "Christological" element of this scene is noted by François Mauriac in the foreword to *Night* (Wiesel 1969 [1958]:10); it makes real the divine suffering that Christianity had treated for so long as abstract theological truth, or as mythic scenario. Here it becomes literal historical event once again—it moves onto earth's surface (as Hillman would say)— and yet becomes a new kind of theological truth. God is no longer "in charge" of the horrors of history, but right in their midst, as innocent victim.

Wiesel's discernment of God as "hanging here on this gallows" is paralleled by others' insights. Simone Weil was a young woman of Jewish background and radical political interests, who became, almost in spite of herself, a Christian mystic. A refugee from Hitler's Europe, she too rejected the link between divine being and contemporary expressions of power. In her essay on the love of God and affliction, Weil speaks about "affliction" as the extension of physical or moral suffering that kills the soul. Martyrs bore pain bravely and triumphantly; Christ was afflicted (Weil 1973 [1951]:125). What makes this different from Cullman's dichotomy of Socrates/Christ? For Weil, the latter's affliction can also be attributed to God. Christ's separation from God permeates the divine itself. "This infinite distance between God and God, this supreme tearing apart, this agony beyond all others, this marvel of love, is the crucifixion. Nothing can be further from God than that which has been made accursed" (Weil 1973

[1951]:123–24). Hence, in our relation to God, affliction is also the key: "He whose soul remains ever turned toward God though the nail pierces it finds himself nailed to the very center of the universe. It is the true center; it is not in the middle; it is beyond space and time; it is God" (Weil 1973 [1951]:135).

To translate these spiritual insights into theological language, some thinkers draw upon the Lutheran opposition between a "theology of the cross" and a "theology of glory." Whatever these terms meant for Luther, for twentieth-century interpreters they have come to bear the weight of history as read by Moltmann, Wiesel, and Weil. A theology of glory is one that emphasizes both divine power and what we call "realized eschatology"—God's reign and triumph over evil in the *now*. In contrast, a theology of the cross emphasizes divine involvement in the unredeemed world. In this outlook, even postresurrection, it remains an unredeemed world. A theology of the cross makes God's self-negation and self-emptying the cornerstone for an entire religious vision. There is no enthusiasm for "history" in many of these thinkers; history as the realm of Antichrist probably fits this portrait most accurately.

An interesting example of this use of Lutheran tradition is Kazoh Kitamori's *Theology of the Pain of God*. This work by a Japanese Christian was first published during or right after World War II, and in this country in 1965. Its thesis is that God's wrath overcome by God's love is God's pain, and that this pain, centrally visible in the cross, lies at the heart of God. God's pain is related to Luther's theme of the "hidden God"; our own pain will be healed when it is taken up within this hidden God. Kitamori's reliance on Lutheran categories accounts for his use of "wrath" in relation to pain (Kitamori 1965 [1958]:109). Divine wrath is simply not a major twentieth-century theological focus, and none of the other thinkers discussed in this section connect it with the theme of divine suffering.

Suffering, by Dorothy Soelle, is another powerful work dedicated to oppose "Christian masochism," the worship of power at the expense of both justice and self. Soelle borrows from Weil, yet tries to balance what may have been Weil's own "masochism" with an activist concern on behalf of sufferers. Too frequently in the past, "divine pain" and mystical participation in it have produced a stance of social passivity in the face of evil. Partly for this reason, Thomas Muntzer, not Luther, is her

Reformation hero; yet Muntzer's dichotomy between "a honey-sweet Christ" and a "bitter Christ" duplicates—as she presents it—Kitamori's use of Luther's dichotomy (Soelle 1975:127–29). In each case, the "negative" category is for Christians the true one; the other is a murderous illusion. The honey-sweet Christ of glory denies the reality of suffering, for his too-realized eschatology leaves no room for anyone's pain.

Moltmann's Theology of Death in God

Jürgen Moltmann's *The Crucified God*, with its focus on the cross of Christ as foundation and criticism, is the most systematic exploration of this theme. The cross is a foundation because this is who God is for us; it is a criticism because the crucified God should function as a standard against which to judge all theologies that depend on some other image of God. Moltmann even criticizes Christians' use of the very term "God," for as Trinitarians "God" for us is never simply "one." In fact, to understand the cross, one needs at least two persons in the Trinity: Father and Son. The Son dies, and the Father suffers loss and separation, experiencing what Weil calls "this supreme tearing apart" within "God" himself.

This point about the Trinity may sound abstract in the extreme. Nevertheless, it reveals how a focus on divine suffering provides a new home for death-imagery. Moltmann is perfectly aware that the ancient church rejected as heresy the view known as "patripassionalism." This was the belief that the Father suffered death on the cross as Jesus of Nazareth. Retrospectively, the energy used to reject any such view seems due more to Platonic squeamishness about God's link to embodiment, than to other theological necessity. Yet there is something missing from the claim that "He is hanging here on this gallows," if by that one implies that God "died." Does God cease as transcendent, becoming so fully incarnate and immanent that no trace of the divine as "other" than Christ remains?

In contrast to the ancient heresy, Moltmann keeps two separate "Persons" in view. Yet he connects them both to death. "In the death of the Son, death comes upon God himself, and the Father suffers the death of his Son in his love for forsaken man" (Moltmann 1974:192). This avoids the consequence of ancient patripassionalism's version of "the death of God."

"Jesus' death cannot be understood 'as the death of God,' but only as death *in* God" (Moltmann 1974:207). Trinitarian theology does not exempt the Father from suffering; in this sense "patripassionalism" is no heresy. But the Father's suffering is not identical to that of the Son, and "death in God" unites both Persons. In speaking this way, Moltmann also avoids a version of the atonement that makes the Father into the Son's executioner, for the repayment of the debt owed by sinful humanity. The relation between Father and Son is liberated from imagery of transaction for which suffering becomes payment rendered. The Father in that imagery remained entirely exempt from pain, whereas in Moltmann's revision he too is "afflicted" in the drama of salvation.

A word should be said of the "family" imagery so central to this theological vision. For Moltmann, the terms "Father" and "Son" suddenly spring to life as important elements in the total crucifixion-event. Not only did Jesus select "Abba" as his term for God, signifying the maximum of love, intimacy, and power, but "Son" is the reciprocal designation for his own being as truly "the Word made flesh." At the crucifixion, "God" becomes both murdered child and grieving parent, and it is these designations that have endured at the highest level of theological formulation. In contrast, Lord and vassal or Master and servant, while appropriate up to a point, do not do justice to the tie of intense love and grief implied in the family titles. Those who find the male gender as used for both Persons problematic, should recognize that the loss of family imagery most proposed changes require will exert a cost that may exceed the benefits.

What happens in this vision of divine "death" to the correlate motif of resurrection? Moltmann does not chop off all "resurrection" language just because there is "death in God." The crucified God is also the risen God (unlike for Weil, whose writings are almost devoid of references to resurrection). Still, no doctrine of resurrection should prevent us from seeing the unredeemed nature of the world as it is. For Moltmann, the unique and valid contribution of Judaism continues to be its insistence on just this reality, as over against a Christianity far too committed to a theology of glory and triumphalism. The more important truth for Moltmann is that God continues to be present with those who suffer, enmeshed within their pain and their struggles for liberation.

Jesus' particular death is not irrelevant to those struggles. One feature of this death emphasized by Moltmann is its character as "judicial murder." It is extremely important for Moltmann's position that God's involvement in human suffering should take the form of victimization at the hands of political and religious authorities. These forms of human activity, law and religion, are humanity's highest achievements. It is precisely in politics and religion that human sinfulness abounds, that our murderous hatred against God and his creation is exercised under the most effective disguises. Jesus' death was absolutely legal, and was religiously sanctioned; it was not a mistake, or the result of disobedience to human law. A Jesus who had been mugged by bandits, or died of a heart attack, would never have suffered so directly at the hands of human institutionalized oppression; his solidarity with other sufferers from oppression would have been incomplete. Moltmann does not state these alternatives in quite so many words, but it is virtually impossible to separate Jesus' mode of death from its meaning. And too often Christian theology has rebuilt God so that its image of the divine resembles Jesus' executioners more than it does their victim.

Judicial murder: this phrase severs Jesus' dying from the category of "natural death," which is appropriate to grasp its meaning. True, Jesus did not die triumphantly like the Christian martyrs who became Rahner's model. Nor did he die peacefully, like Cullman's Socrates. But in its character as "judicial murder," as legal execution, Jesus' death was far more like both Socrates' and the martyrs' than Cullman would admit. Socrates too died at the hands of legitimate political and religious authority, and the scenes Plato offers of his dying are filled with anguished pleas of his friends to escape, answered by Socrates' own sense of obedience to fallible human law. Cullman, preoccupied with biological death as "the enemy" omits this dimension of both deaths entirely, never raising the question of why two such "unnatural" and political deaths have dominated the Western imagination.

Not only the mode through which Jesus met his death, but also the how of his dying, seems critical to Moltmann's portrayal of the crucified God. Wiesel's sad-eyed angel is absolutely silent in the face of his executioners, although his fellow-victims defiantly shout, "Long live liberty!" just before their deaths.

Moltmann's key text is Mark's Gospel, and especially the last cry recorded there: "My God, my God, why have you forsaken me?" (Mark 15:34). Whether Jesus actually quoted from Psalm 22, or only shrieked in agony, it is this sense of absolute distance and desolation, the abandonment of God by God, that marks in language what "death in God" signifies. Here, Moltmann's selectivity in reading biblical texts is as evident as Cullman's. Luke's and John's Passion narratives, which are radically different in tone, are dismissed from Moltmann's vision. As with the case of "Hebraic" versus "Greek," the choice among Gospels is more likely to reflect contemporary preoccupations than to be based solely on empirical historical criteria.

Another area where Moltmann seems one-sided in his focus upon Christ's death is that one might not glean from *The Crucified God* how lifestyle and mode of death belong together. John Galvin notes that we must accept the Gospels' assurances that "Jesus faced death as he lived. Jesus integrated his approaching death into his eschatological self-understanding and his life of 'pro-existence.' . . . Since Jesus' way of life led to the cross, either both are salvific or neither is" (Galvin 1986:247, 251). This approach puts less of a burden on Jesus' last moments. Jesus did not run afoul of political and religious authorities just at the very end of his life; nor was he surprised by his arrest, death, and sufferings. Moltmann and the others whose ideas reflect the theme of divine suffering do not deny the lifestyle and deathstyle link, but the form these theologies of divine suffering take does not always make it clear. Or, to state this in Moltmann's own phrase, if there were "death in God" at the cross, then it was prefigured and implicitly present in Jesus the Son's entire incarnate existence.

It is clear from this selection of religious writings that the theme of divine suffering is a productive resource for Christian thinking about death. Rahner's idea of death as a free act, mentioned in the close of the previous section, seems more appropriate when one examines the literature of divine suffering, for death now is taken up into God's freedom. For God, if not for each of us, death is indeed a free act rather than a "fate." For Christ, death and dying and life activity are all linked together, revelations of divine suffering and redemption. Moreover, if some form of "death-experience" is considered an intrinsic element in human existence, as it is for Becker,

Hillman, and Lifton, then this same may hold true for divine existence too. One might almost say that what Moltmann, Kitamori, and Weil present is such a "death-experience" suffered by the Father and Son. And so, although God is not dead, there is indeed according to these thinkers "death in God."

Death and Dying in Pastoral Psychology

We now turn from theology to a more practical area of religious reflection. Pastoral care is a major task for North American Christian clergy, and this activity has generated a vast quantity of psychological writings on the subject of death and dying. This literature is aimed at pastors who do counseling, and who need to be informed on the latest therapeutic techniques and methods. Consequently, the majority of such writings are less theological than psychotherapeutic in outlook; perhaps the assumption is that pastors already know enough theology but need "practical tools" to do their work. If so, the result is often a theologically vapid approach to pastoral tasks. Or, in some cases, theologies are proposed or assumed that do not coincide with those advocated by the thinkers surveyed earlier in this chapter. Moreover, since psychotherapies carry along with them certain ethical and spiritual content, there is a risk of double or conflicting messages. When this happens, we have an unfortunate blend of "Kübler-Ross for chaplains," ethical naturalism falsely baptized and re-presented as pastoral care.

Nevertheless, there has been a growing reaction against uncritical absorption of psychological theories by religious professionals. Many of those who had previously endorsed unlimited borrowing from Carl Rogers and other secular psychotherapists are now more cautious. This reaction is stated clearly by Don Browning and Samuel Southard. Browning believes the church should provide moral teachings, clear norms for Christian life. Within such a structure, counseling may function as a remedial activity, but secular counseling norms such as "self-acceptance" are insufficient substitutes for Christian ethics. Unfortunately, too often they have become just that. Southard is more focused upon theology; he notes that during the rise of pastoral counseling in the 1950s, ministers worried about imposing their moral and religious views on clients. Today, they sense the need for theological frameworks in order

to do psychological counseling as pastors, rather than as duplicates of secular psychotherapists.

This concern helps to organize a presentation, sampling the
vast pastoral psychology literature on death and dying. We
begin with works that really do seem most vulnerable to the
Browning–Southard criticism, that seem content to duplicate
Kübler-Ross and secular thanatology. Then we will examine
others that deliberately try to move beyond this stance.
Finally, as contrast to the literature written exclusively for
pastors, we will close with a look at two excellent Christian
inspirational writings. These are closer in genre to the autobiographies of Chapter 1, while more informed by theological
insights than much of the pastoral psychology materials.

Pastoral Appropriations of Psychology

By the above criterion of explicit Christian moral-theologi-
cal context, *Death and Ministry: Pastoral Care for the Dying
and Bereaved* (1975) falls within the category of "Kübler-Ross
for pastors." Of the thirty-six contributions, few contain anything to introduce theological concerns in a substantive way.
Even the "theological" section of the book emphasizes how
Christianity is compatible with "acceptance of death," as this
is now defined psychologically. Traditional belief in an afterlife
of any kind is neither important nor intrinsic to faith. The min-
ister is advised to be "present," to listen, not to impose personal
views or commitments on others (exactly Southard's characterization of pastoral care in the 1950s). What makes the pastor's
counseling different from that of any other support person?
Why could not a hospice volunteer, a social worker, or a nurse
perform these same functions? What unique resources does the
pastor have to offer the dying person? And should the pastor
simply accept the terms of the modern death-and-dying movement, and fit expectations within its norms? No such questions
are raised here.

Another example of this approach is Wayne Oates' *Pastoral
Care and Counseling in Grief and Separation* (1976). Here, too,
Kübler-Ross provides the basic framework, supplemented by
Gestalt therapy for the "technique" to work with problems of grief,
mourning, and other separations within a group church context.
Oates emphasizes expression of feelings, support from others who

have "made it through" separation and loss, and a nonjudgmental empathetic pastoral presence. Once again, the theological content is largely negative; the church has aided denial of death. This is exactly the outlook Browning and Southard protest; pastoral presence and nonjudgmental empathy are not substitutes for cognitive content and more specific guidance.

The theme of "pastoral presence" also plays a large role in a work considerably more theological and sophisticated: Charles Gerkin's *Crisis Experience in Modern Life: Theory and Theology for Pastoral Care* (1979). Gerkin thinks that belief in divine providence, sustaining individuals through crisis, is no longer viable for most persons today. He proposes instead a theology of hope, of God's future-oriented action, as a substitute; he explicitly relies on Moltmann here. What sustains the individual sufferer in the present? Gerkin opts for what he calls an "incarnational" model of pastoral care, in which the pastor incarnates Christ as present in the crisis. In other words, the theology adopts an "unrealized eschatology," yet the pastor's personal care compensates for this and comes to symbolize "realized eschatology."

This theological dimension lets Gerkin criticize how modern persons live with infinite expectations and ignore or deny their finite limits. This makes all forms of suffering, and especially death, extremely difficult for us to integrate. He vividly contrasts the Moltmannian Christ, who dies in pain and abandonment, to the "heroic humanism" he finds in so much of the secular death and dying literature, held out as a model (Gerkin 1979:101). This excellent critique of some of the idealized hopes for "acceptance" current in secular theories shows how theology need not always remain at the most abstract and "unpractical" level.

A word should be said about the motif of the pastor's "incarnational" presence, as the one who represents Christ for the parishioner. A great many writings in this genre repeat this idea. Yet in the Reformation theological and church traditions, there are certain limits on how heavily the role of clergy can be accented. First, there is the traditional Lutheran teaching on "the priesthood of all believers." If the pastor can be "Christ" for me, then that is fundamentally because we can all be "Christs" for each other. Second, there is little warrant for making any one person or role into a "sacramental presence," in the sense of a special intermediary between God and ordinary persons. No one save Christ can take on the role of "mediator." How then does the heavy stress on the unique role of the pastor not conflict at some level with these traditional Protestant motifs? Has the pastor as "presence" the capacity to replace "divine providence," as Gerkin seems to hope?

Distinctive Religious Resources in Pastoral Care

We may contrast the works already mentioned with several that explicitly incorporate distinctive religious resources into pastoral care for the dying. What can the pastor provide that is different from other support persons? What are the special roles of the pastor, once it is established that presence, listening, acceptance, and the like are aspects of ministry? William Hulme's *Pastoral Care and Counseling Using the Unique Resources of the Christian Tradition* (1981) tries to answer these questions. These resources include Scripture, prayer, and faith. The chapter on death and resurrection emphasizes hope, including the hope for eternal life. Unlike the contributors to the Bane volume, Hulme finds such a belief once again a central rather than peripheral teaching. Curiously, his case example of Christian hope sounds almost exactly like Kübler-Ross' interview on "acceptance": "I . . . told the Lord that I was ready either way. I want to live, but I am also ready to die" (Hulme 1981:78).

A more interesting work that attempts the same task is Thomas Oden's *Pastoral Theology: Essentials of Ministry* (1983). Oden, a vigorous advocate of the Browning–Southard critique of American pastoral psychology approaches, resolved to write a theology of pastoral care that systematically avoided all twentieth-century psychological theories! He draws instead from the Church Fathers, Richard Baxter, the seventeenth-century pastoral expert, and many others to describe what the ministry to the sick, the dying, and the poor ought to include. When he comes to the section on dying, he emphasizes the awe and ultimacy of death, not its psychological "acceptance." There is also a discussion of the rites for dying, absent from much contemporary pastoral care literature. Even more unusual is his section on theodicy for pastoral practice, which deals with the problem of suffering as a cognitive, theological issue. Although expression of feelings and pastoral presence are important, suffering poses questions that remain valid in the realm of thought. The church has pondered these questions extensively; Oden reviews twelve separate theological motifs of comfort intended for sufferers (Oden 1983:223–44). It behooves the pastor to become familiar with these answers, and be able to communicate them to others.

An interesting contrast to both Oden and the prevailing psychological outlook he criticizes can be found in a work written earlier in the twentieth century, yet dealing with the same topic. Richard Cabot and Russell Dicks' *Art of Ministering to the Sick* was first published in 1936. It contains no explicit psychological theory, yet virtually all of the "raw data" Kübler-Ross discovered are present. The book excellently documents the special needs, complaints, and circumstances of the sick, the humiliating frustrations of hospital routine, and the like. The spiritual outlook is liberal Protestant, almost Emersonian, yet realism and ambiguity are preserved in the authors' awareness of their own limits. Their equivalent to "acceptance" is "dying nobly," but this is not exactly the "heroic humanism" criticized by Gerkin. The ideal attitude is identical to that cited in the case histories of both Kübler-Ross and Hulme: "It is all right. Whether I get well or whether I die, it is all right" (Cabot and Dicks 1951 [1936]:299). When dying hospital patients can say those words, they have achieved what faith can accomplish. Cabot and Dicks also, unlike the more contemporary psychologically oriented authors, feel comfortable discussing prayer and its use with the sick. What makes this book worth reading is that although it is over fifty years old, it is just as helpful to pastors as anything more recent, in respect to practical advice. Why did psychological theory have to rediscover the insights about dying that it contains? Those in disagreement with the authors' theology will at least admit that *The Art of Ministering to the Sick*, along with its practical emphasis, contains more theology with which to disagree than do the majority of more contemporary writings.

Still another version of pastoral care, also in contrast to the dominance of psychological perspectives, is provided by Norman Autton's *Pastoral Care of the Dying* (1966). Writing out of sacramental Anglicanism, Autton too ignores psychological theory, and focuses upon the liturgical-sacramental role of the priest. He reviews both medieval and early modern "art of

dying" literature, about which we will have more to say ourselves, then discusses the contemporary hospital. One meets
all of Kübler-Ross' data, but without her framework or psychological vocabulary. Autton's emphasis on survival of death as
intrinsic to Christian faith and his sacramental interest make
this work sound very "traditional" compared to all of the
American ones, even Cabot and Dicks. A whole section of *The
Pastoral Care of the Dying* is based upon liturgies found within
the *Book of Common Prayer*, under the heading "Ministration
at the Time of Death." Perhaps the Anglican, like the Roman
Catholic, has such resources to hand in a way that most
Protestant pastors do not. A pastor steeped in Moltmann, however, would find the particular theological ideas embedded in
"Ministration at the Time of Death" problematic; they are
based upon very traditional and ancient sources, and reflect
the outlook of those.

Suppose Gerkin's assessment is correct, and Americans
today do not accept traditional beliefs in divine providence or
the meaningfulness of suffering the way Christians once did.
One may say to pastors, "Here are the resources; use them!"
but what if pastors and laypersons alike simply find these
incredible, oppressive, or useless? It is one thing to complain
that "Kübler-Ross for pastors" is theologically empty; it is
another to fill the void with what Cullman would describe as
Platonism, or Soelle as "worship of the executioner." Any adequate answer to these questions involves one immediately and
inevitably in severe debates about the nature of the church, its
ministry, its norms of belief and practice. For the most part,
pastoral psychology literature such as that we have examined
so far is not adept at resolving these. Still, a work such as
Oden's reminds us that pastoral activities take place within
the framework of an institution with certain beliefs and boundaries, with a history of its own, with an identity apart from its
locus in North American culture. If its resources are not flaw-
less, then they are at least unlikely to duplicate our culture's
biases and blind spots.

Inspirational Writings

All of the above materials, without exception, are addressed
primarily to pastors and chaplains. They are not aimed directly
at the dying, or their families. But are there writings on death

and dying aimed to provide comfort, hope, or understanding for Christians touched by death? The answer may lie in the autobiographies we discovered in Chapter 1, part of whose function was inspiration and "self-help" for others in crisis. Yet in addition to those examined earlier, two quasi-autobiographical works stand out for their theological clarity, emotional honesty, and spiritual sensitivity. Strictly speaking, these are not works on "pastoral care," but they could provide what even the pastor's "incarnational presence" might not be able to effect.

The first is C. S. Lewis' *Grief Observed*. This work was originally published anonymously during its author's lifetime; it was reprinted under his own name after his death. *A Grief Observed* consists of Lewis' private notebooks following the death of his wife. Thus it fits well within the autobiographical genre. Lewis documents psychological reactions, and also repeatedly asks, "Where is God?" "Talk to me about the truth of religion and I'll listen gladly. Talk to me about the duty of religion and I'll listen submissively. But don't come talking to me about the consolation of religion or I shall suspect that you don't understand" (Lewis 1976 [1963]:28).

Lewis enters the problem of "theodicy" existentially, and experiments with a variety of answers to it, including the horrible possibility that God is a "cosmic sadist." Like Soelle, he refuses to worship the executioner. He eventually recognizes that "My idea of God is not a divine idea. It has to be shattered time after time. He shatters it himself" (Lewis 1976 [1963]:76). Only then can he renew his relationship with God, and—in a mysterious way—with his dead wife. He is able to let go of her and yet find her again. In the process he has learned that "bereavement is a universal and integral part of our experience of love. . . . It is not a truncation of the process but one of its phases" (Lewis 1976 [1963]:58–59). Within the natural realm of existence, this must be faced, so that a genuinely new and eternal phase can begin. In the book, this is symbolized by a final quote from Dante's *Divine Comedy*: "She turned back to the Eternal Fountain" (Lewis 1976 [1963]:89); death is for the dead as well as the living a real separation from this life, as well as entrance into the life of God.

A Grief Observed teaches about death and separation as Christians can experience and reflect upon them. It avoids

entirely the idea that religion automatically consoles, that
Christian hope leaves no room for bitterness or loneliness or
grief. It avoids both the denial of death, and denial of an eschatological future. Especially given the critique of psychotherapy
as a substitute for theological emphasis, Lewis' discussion of
theodicy is significant; it implements Oden's agenda in a way
that the average reader can appreciate.

The second work, Henri Nouwen's *Letter of Consolation*, is
Christocentric more than it is theodicy-centered. Nouwen's
mother in Holland has died; he writes to his elderly father both
to share his grief and to console. In the process, he reflects upon
the way Christians should relate to death. He begins with the
task, "to befriend death" (Nouwen 1982:29), a phrase that he
(ironically) borrows from James Hillman. For Nouwen, befriending death means to explore its meaning, integrating it into the
totality of our experience, and so relate to death "as a familiar
guest instead of a threatening stranger" (Nouwen 1982:31).

What follows is theologically sophisticated inspirational literature. Nouwen's road to "befriending death" leads not
through Kübler-Ross, but to an intense immersion in Christ's
passion, death, and resurrection, culminating in Holy Week
spent in a monastery. Through liturgical participation and
interior identification, Christ's death and our deaths become
meshed. Through Christ's death, our death is transformed
"from a totally absurd end to all that gives life its meaning into
an event that liberates us and those whom we love" (Nouwen
1982:59). This Christological death is never used to denigrate
Christians' ties to others or the natural world. In fact, if
Christ's death was a death for others, the same can become
true of all deaths. Nouwen stresses interconnections among
persons more forcefully than most of the psychologically oriented literature dares to do.

But although Nouwen tries to "befriend death," and partici-
pates via liturgy in Christ's own death, a new theme emerges.
In spite of the need to integrate death into his ongoing life, in
spite of the strong antidenial thrust of his outlook, he comes at
last to a position strikingly unlike "befriending." What makes
death so particularly painful for Christians is that there is an
essential antipathy between God and death. "Something that I
could not see as clearly before is now becoming more visible to
me. It is that death does not belong to God. God did not create

death. God does not want death. God does not desire death for us. In God there is no death" (Nouwen 1982:75).

Has Nouwen suddenly embraced Cullman, for whom death is and remains the enemy, a terror and horror? Much more likely, is this passage explicitly, specifically directed against Moltmann, who deliberately uses the phrase "death in God" to declare that God crucified is the only authentic God known in the gospel? If so, Nouwen sets up a different boundary for how "death-language" can properly be used by Christians. One cannot make "death" an ultimate category in the way Moltmann wants. The most "ultimate" thing to say about death is that it is *not* in God.

Perhaps discussion of Nouwen's remarkable little book belongs in the previous, theological sections of this chapter. *A Letter of Consolation* demonstrates how some of the themes from the theological perspectives can be integrated with pastoral care, with the practical task of consolation. Although Nouwen is a pastor and writing as one, he is not presenting himself as an "incarnational presence" for his father; although his life and identity are tied to the sacraments, what animates this identification is not so much his professional role as his interior link with Christ crucified and risen. No amount of psychological theory can, of course, answer for us the unsettled and unsettling question, whether it is possible to speak truly of "death in God." But such a question is one that the majority of pastoral psychology writers seem not yet ready to ask, let alone answer. What is clear is that so long as much of the pastoral care literature either avoids the call for "theological counsel," or embraces past resources rather unselectively, a question such as this will remain obscured. And the dilemma of death's role within the totality of faith will probably not be profoundly addressed.

7

Biblical Resources: The Roles of Death in the Landscape of Faith

We now turn to the perspectives foundational to Christianity, and to the sources that stand as authoritative for theological and pastoral reflection. In our own analysis, we will enter what may be called "the landscape of faith," our metaphor for the vision of reality, God, and the human condition that is presented by these sources. This is what theologian Karl Barth referred to as "the strange new world of the Bible," and in contrast to all of the contemporary sources, it will appear both strange and new. When we ask, "What are the roles of death within this landscape of faith?" we open ourselves to points of view not identical to those even of the twentieth-century theological writers, let alone that of ethical naturalism. Although we will occasionally draw upon the depth psychological theories to bring this "strange new world" into focus, in the world of the Bible, the individual psyche, the intended center of depth psychology, plays an unfamiliar role. It is within this world, this landscape, that familiar theological statements such as "The last enemy is death" take on their meaning. Hence it is especially important where this world places such pronouncements, which have come to serve as slogans entirely divorced from their original context.

Through the Lens of Christ

We must first overcome the common prejudice that the Bible provides one unambiguous sustained understanding that can function as "the Christian view of death." This is simply not the case. Death is not the subject of any direct, extended treatment, even though references to it pervade the New Testament. Moreover, however many references to death there are, and however central it becomes as an image, death enters into Christianity not for its own sake, but in the wake of other concerns. In this respect, I believe twentieth-century theology has been on the mark, at least insofar as it subsumes death under themes such as eschatology or crucifixion.

A correlate to this is that religious thought has always been free to "fill in" the narratives, images, and scattered reflections of the Bible with more systematic treatments. Many of these required the categories of philosophical thought-forms, from Platonism to existentialism. The stage is set for a dialogue with depth psychological thought, provided we do not begin by assuming that the latter can fully and adequately "translate" all of the biblical insights into its own terms. But we can never rest content by merely repeating quotes from Scripture, on the false assumption that this method guarantees a genuinely "biblical" view of death. Biblical thought and imagery call out for further reflection; Christian tradition has always recognized this. Psychology is but one possible mode of thought for carrying on this task.

The Bible is more heterogeneous than many persons who wish to establish "the biblical view" allow. I believe we may solidly reject Cullman's belief that "death as enemy" is *the* view of Scripture, and the only view that needs to be considered authentically Christian or "Hebraic." On the other hand, an opposite extreme of laissez-faire pluralism is equally unsatisfactory. As Christians read the Bible, we read it as a totality, and trace in its pages the adventures of God the redeemer of his people, and through them, of the entire creation. God delivers from slavery and enemies in the Hebrew Scriptures, and God in Christ delivers from sin, the flesh, the devil, and death in the era of the New Covenant. It is through Christ that most of us come to hear these adventures, and it is through him that the earlier materials become focused for us. Not everything in the Old Testament is a promise to be fulfilled in the New, but we read the Bible through the lens of Christ. I do not find this a restriction on our comprehension of it, but an acknowledgment of Christ as the one who "opens the Scriptures" for us. Of course, this view of Scripture as thematically unified, and as "opened" by Christ, is itself a theological assumption, not an empirical observation. It is, however, an assumption that Paul and the other early witnesses all share. It makes the process of canon formation an appropriate and meaningful, rather than arbitrary event, even if its details rest upon historical contingencies.

With our focus on Christ, then God as redeemer, deliverer, and savior is just as fundamental as God the creator. To grasp what the Christian landscape looks like, we must turn first to the central narratives of redemption, and to the Passion narratives in particular. The primacy of story or narrative is a better way to express what theologians and biblical scholars have generally called "salvation history." Christian faith has a narrative cast to it, and that narrative dramatically depends upon the death of the protagonist. When we accept this theological priority, then we also recognize that questions such as "Did God intend death?" and "Is death natural?" cannot be the starting places for Christian reflection. They receive answers, if at all, only in the light cast by the central narrative of Christ— his life, death, and resurrection. Moltmann's idea that the cross of Christ serves as foundation and criticism for Christian thought implies this priority. Even if general questions about humans and death may be our first questions, the biblical landscape sets them in a subordinate place.

Another primary theological motif is that we are linked to Christ through identification with him, most especially through participation in his death. This is expressed both experientially and sacramentally. Diverse sources within the New Testament converge on this theme. It permeates the Pauline writings. It is expressed by the Fourth Gospel's injunction to "Abide in me." Another version is the promise that through Christ we have "become partakers of the divine nature" (2 Pet. 1:4). The language of "discipleship" and following, so intrinsic to the Synoptic Gospels, also supports this. "What happened to

152 Death in the Midst of Life

Christ, happens to Christians" (Schnackenburg 1964:157) in
this form of identification.

When this theme is understood, one form of "Christianism"
is eliminated. Whatever the meaning of "substitution" theories
of the atonement, the motif of substitution cannot be used to
destroy the profound participation or identification with Christ.
Moreover, the idea of "vicarious" sacrifice cannot serve to
exempt us from connection to death. "Because Jesus died, we
don't have to" is a severe distortion of the biblical witness.

We will examine in depth the model of identity upon which
this "participation" rests. It provides a key to the biblical landscape's way to link individual and collective death. It also challenges the individualism of contemporary psychology and culture
in a manner that parallels some but not all of Lifton's concerns.
Out of this will emerge the full complexity of biblical "death-
imagery" as a way to grasp spiritual transformation. Such
imagery is profound and deeply ambiguous. Finally, we will ask,
"What of resurrection?" for in the biblical landscape no one
would deny that this accompanies death at almost every turn.

Jesus' Dying and Death

If the cross is the center of theological reflection, the narrative of Jesus' dying and death dominates the four New
Testament Gospels. If "participation" in Christ is one of the
major themes of Christian spirituality, then both Jesus' life
and dying are of direct concern to Christians. Christ does not
start to be savior at his death when, as vicarious sacrifice for
us, his death becomes effective for our salvation. If the Christ
we know is "no longer after the flesh" but is the resurrected
Christ, then this is still the man who wandered around
Palestine and was executed outside Jerusalem one Friday
afternoon. The central role belongs to Christ, not to "death."

Yet within the role given to Christ, his own death plays such
an overwhelming part that it casts its shadow over all the participation and identification language. If what happened to
Christ happens to Christians, then dying and death are central
events in this process. Although Paul does not dwell on the
narrative details of Christ's dying, it is still important that
Christ "hung on a tree" and therefore died accursed. For Paul,
no less than for Mark or Luke, Christ could not have lived and

died any old way; the mode and how of his death were important (Beker 1980:182).

The Passion Narratives: Central Themes

When we turn to the Gospel narratives of the Passion, we
find both variations of detail and much essential unity. We
may decide that one account is more "authentic" than the others, or that all contain important if independent and nonre-
ducible material. Since it lies beyond the scope of this project
to debate the issue of historical priority, I should point out that
some of the arguments used by scholars seem guided more by
theological preferences than by historical evidence. Moltmann
and Cullman both prefer Mark's narrative, with its heightened
focus on abandonment or the "terror" of death, rather than
Luke's, where Jesus retains connection to both his Father and
those around him. In John's narrative, Jesus' sense of control,
of inner triumph, seems to mitigate against the twentieth century's desire to see God as "weak," as vulnerable victim in the
world. The ancient church wisely decided to include all four
narratives, and eventually discouraged efforts to synthesize
them into one consistent yet depleted narrative. The result is
that, although Jesus' death has been seen as a model for com-
prehending death's meaning, or even for a "good death," the
plurality of narratives leaves room for much variation.

Nevertheless, several central features of these narratives
are key motifs for any Christian interpretation of death. The
sense of Christ's death as a free act, a voluntary act of obedience to the will of the Father, and thus an act integrated
totally into a life of obedience, is one such motif. Jesus' death
was not just anticipated by him, but was intended, self-chosen
in that he could have avoided execution, and knew it. No matter what language we use, we will never depart from a Christ
whose incarnation was an incarnation-toward-death. To consider death as external event, added on to a life already self-
contained without it, simply does not fit the portrait of the
Gospels, nor the Christology of the other New Testament documents. Nor can we imagine a Jesus surprised by his death,
unaware of it as a possibility until it suddenly comes upon him.
Attempts to attribute all the "Passion predictions" to the era of

the early church have been convincingly refuted by current biblical scholarship (Galvin 1986:246–47).

The sense of awareness of impending death is conveyed in many ways. In addition to specific predictions of his suffering and death, the scenes of the last supper effectively consummate this sense of immanent death. "I shall not drink again of the fruit of the vine until that day when I drink it new in the kingdom of God" (Mark 14:25). Distribution of bread and wine is Jesus' method to prefigure, even rehearse his own death, to convey a sense of its meaning to his disciples as a final legacy to them. The long discourse in John's Gospel that substitutes for the bread and wine serves a parallel function. It is Jesus' recapitulation of the meaning of his life, and a legacy to them, in the form of a promise that he will not leave them permanently. "Abide in me, and I in you" (John 15:4), he tells them, while in the other narratives this is enacted within the rite of the meal.

Yet the prayer in the garden of Gethsemane stands as a sign that death, even when anticipated, is negation and destruction. It is with this prayer that we enter Cullman territory. Does the plea to the Father to "take this cup from me" allow us to construe a more externalized relation to death as enemy? Is Jesus truly afraid of death's "horror"? In a sense, yes, if by that one means that Jesus' acceptance of the Father's will does not equate with acceptance of death as a "good." But insofar as terms such as "horror" are not native to the texts and suggest exactly the externalized and accidental approach of death that nothing else in the narrative supports, then the answer is no.[1] Mark's narrative of Gethsemane is read by Cullman as if its protagonist were Becker's heroic death-denying self, or Hillman's heroic ego, convinced of his own immortality until the sudden shock of mortality and vulnerability intrudes. But

1. Although the text of Mark 14:33–34 is usually translated to express "sorrow" and "anguish" or "amazement" in the sense of shock and dismay, one commentator does prefer "horror" for verse 33 (see Hendriksen 1975:586). "Greatly distressed and troubled," however, more directly echoes the language of the psalms (Juel 1990:196; Anderson 1976:319). Curiously, another commentator refers to Jesus' "experience of shuddering horror" while not directly translating the text in this way (Lane 1974:516). What all could agree upon is that at this point in the narrative, "Evil now . . . attacks from within" (Best 1965:94). Whether that evil be fear, sin, or death, the sense of inward struggle predominates.

this ignores the point that Jesus' character is consistent from life into dying to death, consistent both at the level of narrative and theologically (Galvin 1986:247). The emphasis in the Gethsemane scene is on death as freely chosen, an act of the self (Rahner's motif), not on death as catastrophe.

A second feature of Jesus' death, noticed and stressed by Moltmann, is its political dimension. The different New Testament sources vary in how they identify Jesus' opponents. Paul was not interested in Pilate or the Sanhedrin, but in "the rulers of this age," spiritual powers whose human representatives arrested and condemned Christ (1 Cor. 2:8). The drama of opposition between evil forces, construed under the image of "rule" and "power," and God in Christ is central to Paul's presentation of the gospel. The idea of Jesus put to death by "powers" rather than by "nature" is crucial. In the narratives of Jesus' trial and condemnation, each author seems intent to retell the story in a slightly different way, yet to include all human "rulers of this age" in the process.

The result is that what we can continue to call "political" or even "military" images are incorporated into the narratives and into the theology. As "judicial murder" Jesus' death calls for the language of law, judgment, and political conflict: "Having canceled the bond which stood against us with its legal demands; this he set aside, nailing it to the cross. He disarmed the principalities and powers and made a public example of them, triumphing over them in him" (Col. 2:14–15). However far this is from the preferences for divine weakness that characterize Weil's or Moltmann's thought, it is much farther from twentieth-century ethical naturalism's desire to exclude all "political" categories in regard to death. As victim of human institutions, especially religious and legal structures, Jesus is one with the other victims of history. As victor, he "disarms" those spiritual forces that oppress humanity. These "powers" are truly God's enemies, more directly and unequivocably than biological death.

The Passion Narratives: Abandonment and Pain

When we turn our attention to the details of the Passion narratives, we find that Jesus' death is marked by abandonment and physical pain. Whatever the actual physical mutila-

tions inflicted by crucifixion, the authors of the narratives do
not dwell on these. Nevertheless, the actual mode of death
lends itself to imagery of dismemberment, disintegration, and
mutilation—unlike death by poisoning (this, however, was not
Cullman's point about Socrates). It is, however, abandonment
and separation that appear more theologically significant.
Here, of course, variations in the narratives become important.
Mark and Matthew insist that Jesus was abandoned by all his
male followers, and especially stress cowardice and betrayal on
Peter's part. A few of Jesus' female followers stand off to the
side of the drama, helpless and passive (Mark 15:40). Jesus'
final hours find him totally dependent upon the kindness of
strangers, amid an environment of cruelty and mockery. The
few small acts that are done for him accomplish nothing, and
his last words are misunderstood. The consummation of this
isolation, abandonment, and despair is his cry, "My God, my
God, why hast thou forsaken me?" It is entirely illegitimate to
imagine a small, inner voice that reassures: "No, I've not. I'm
still here." On this score, Moltmann and the others are correct:
Mark's narrative, at least, supports the split within God, just
as the temple curtain is rent at Jesus' death. It is this "split"
that reveals the nature of God in Christ, to the centurion who
witnesses the death, and cries out, "Truly this man was the
Son of God!" (Mark 15:38–39).

In Luke's narrative, Jesus continues his ministry right up to
the end. He consoles the weeping women of Jerusalem, and
even the thief who dies next to him. In this thief, we find
acknowledgment of how "judicial" categories may play a further role in composing a portrait of Christian death. The thief
admits that he and his fellow-criminal deserve death, while
Jesus is innocent (Luke 23:40–41). This is a narrative root for
the theological motif of death as punishment. Jesus, mean-
while, remains in communion with God, forgives his executioners, and commits his spirit into the loving hands of the Father.
We need not argue that this version is a "defense" against a
horrible disgraceful death, a theological whitewash of Mark's
more authentic narrative. But abandonment and separation
are less total.

Nor is there a sense of despair and abandonment in John's
narrative. Although the other disciples flee, Jesus' "beloved disciple" and his mother continue to "abide in him." In arranging

for an adoption of disciple by mother, and vice versa (John 19:26–27), Jesus is bequeathing his own identity by adoption to the church, establishing a link to its next generation. Connection is maintained at the divine as well as the human level. "It is finished" is a cry of triumph, not despair. Jesus dies here as he had lived, entirely at one with the Father. After his death, even his mutilated body provides a legacy for his future followers, for out of the wound in his side flow blood and water—a probable sacramental reference (Brown 1970:951–52; Bultmann 1951:vol. 1, 142).

Are these two Gospels evidence for the early church's timidity, its reluctance to affirm the infinite split of "death in God"? Or are they authentic perceptions of certain limits to separation themes, to abandonment as an absolute unambiguous theological motif? The third and fourth Gospels tell the story in ways that convey how, ultimately, God does not entirely abandon Jesus, and even at the moment of death there is no triumph of despair. This at minimum prevents one peculiar misreading of the total narrative. It is not the case that the Father abandoned Jesus the Son at his death, then changed his mind and effected the Son's resurrection as demonstration of this change. Insofar as the resurrection is portrayed as a "reversal" by those such as Cullman who stress death's totality (as did many of the theologians whose works were reviewed in Chapter 6), we must be careful not to fall into that kind of language of what gets "reversed" and by whom.

All four narratives clearly testify that Jesus' death was followed by entombment. "Died and was buried" signifies an "all-the-way" into death (Schnackenburg 1964:34). If there is any role at all for what Lifton characterizes as "stasis" imagery, of sleep or enclosure, it might come only in the state of burial. Although the death of Socrates seems to rely upon such imagery—is this why Cullman found it false?—on this point the two deaths diverge greatly. Moreover, any references to Jesus' descent to Hades, to deliver the dead imprisoned there, require some form of activity even within the condition of death.

Jesus' death was total. There is absolutely no hint that something within him remained unaffected or uncontaminated by death. When Jesus embraced death, he did so as a unified, whole individual. All of the contemporary theological writers acknowledge this. Even Rahner's revision of the traditional body/soul language is so interesting precisely because it accepts this totality of death. For Rahner, the soul goes through it too, dying to its tie with one particular body and entering into a pan-cosmic relation with the entire world. An image of transformation less drastic, and one that takes death less seriously, is inadequate and inappropriate, if one bases one's image of death upon the Passion narratives.

This sense of the totality of Jesus' death makes possible a stress on resurrection as "total newness." Insofar as resurrection is not a "natural fate" and not a case of caterpillar into butterfly, this is all to the good. On the other hand, the resurrected Christ is still "the same person" as the Christ who died. There is continuity of memory and—in an extremely ambiguous way—continuity of physical appearance. Some of the "resurrection appearance" stories tell how Jesus' real identity was at first hidden to those who encountered him (Luke 24:13–31). The most paradoxical case is that in John's Gospel, in which Christ remains wounded, and so almost more "embodied" than he had seemed in life (John 20:27). Is this a case where "flesh and blood" did indeed "inherit the kingdom of God"? Or does it perhaps show that, in the poignant words of Weil, here below, nature is "irremediably wounded" (Weil 1973 [1951]:123)? It is principally the fourth evangelist's way to insist that Christ's death and glorification are inseparable.

Christ's death, understood this way, becomes a model of death, and a model for our deaths. Christ's death is appropriable—by Paul, by others, by each Christian. I believe that this makes it the primary starting point for a Christian theology of death. Its imagery has certainly guided Christians in their reflections upon death. The variations in the narratives' details should spur us to reflect upon our presuppositions and biases in reading texts. Within the narratives, we might, if we tried, find support for Becker, Lifton, and probably Hillman, not to mention a wide range of theologies. But if we accept their imagery, their portraits of this most central death, it will reshape our evaluations of what is "natural" or "normal" by contemporary criteria. By recentering ourselves upon Christ's death, we return to a central source for locating death within the landscape of faith.

Individual and Collective Death

"What happened to Christ happens to the Christian" (Schnackenburg 1964:157). We have noted this sense of "participation" or "identification," which very directly includes immersion in Christ's death. What model of identity enables the biblical writers to envision Christian life in these terms? How is such "participation" possible? In the technical language of biblical scholarship, this link to Christ depends upon an ancient understanding of "corporate personality" (Silberman 1969:26). In this view, an individual's basic identity lies in enmeshment within a larger whole, a family or tribe or nation. Such a model of personhood seems to be the norm in many traditional societies. Within this framework, a founder "is not only an individual person, but comprehends in himself the whole community that is associated with and derives from him" (Schnackenburg 1964:114). Actions performed "in the name of" this founder serve to establish the connection, a collective identity within which statements such as "You are all one in Christ Jesus" make perfect sense. Through baptism, a Christian "puts on Christ," and finds a true identity in Christ. We will see some of the ramifications of this for personal spirituality later.

"Christ" is by far the most central "corporate identity" in the New Testament. He is "the new man," the man from heaven who replaces Adam, the man from earth. But significantly, the importance of other biblical persons seems also to depend upon this conception. Peter in the Gospels and Acts is not just an individual disciple of Jesus, but is "Mr. Church." Mary for both Luke and John is "Ms. Faithful Israel," as well as an individual woman. We will begin to understand the roles of death in the landscape of faith only when we recognize how different this form of identity is from that presupposed by our culture with its "authenticity paradigm" of death focused exclusively on the individual.

This conception also sheds new light on a common observation—namely, how few and sparse are the references to death and afterlife in Hebrew Scriptures. These persons may or may not have accepted death as a "natural" event; it is unlikely that they consistently found it "the enemy" of God, and there is an absence of preoccupation about it in their writings. Nevertheless, it is a great mistake to say that death does not play any role at all in these writings. For a people immersed in "corporate identity" the death that counted was their possible death as a people, the annihilation of "Israel" as a nation and a community. This possibility dominates the prophetic and historical writings. The great drama of national destruction, exile, and return is an expression of corporate death and rebirth, within which death-imagery becomes symbolically appropriate. The vision of Ezekiel, who sees the dry bones arise and become "a mighty army" (Chapter 37), is an instance of death-imagery applied to collective, national experience.[2]

What happens in the New Testament to this "collective" or "communal" motif? What role, if any, is there for "collective" death based upon a model of "corporate personality" in Christ? Historically, by the early Christian era, within Judaism as well as in the wider Hellenistic world, there appears to have been a breakdown of traditional, taken-for-granted forms of "corporate identity" such as those based upon family or village membership. But instead of simply vanishing, perhaps the forms and specific types of communities shifted, so as to open up new possibilities for participation in "corporate personalities" other than those of the past.

At the level of theological reflection, we may find the New Testament holds onto at least some measure of the "corporate

2. These generalizations about the dominance of collective over individual death in the writings of ancient Israel assume the perspective of the biblical writers—not necessarily that of the original protagonists. Stories such as that of "the witch of Endor" who on Saul's command raised up the shade of Samuel the prophet (1 Sam. 28:8–14) draw upon folklore that remained peripheral to the major preoccupations of the Old Testament writers. For the latter, the real point of the story is to validate David's succession to the throne by showing how utterly unfit Saul was to rule. Kingship outweighs individual death as a central concern. The same pattern occurs in the story of Elijah's raising to life of the widow's dead son (1 Kings 17:17–24). The original story of the prophet's miracle is integrated into a narrative whose focus is the "death" of the northern kingdom, and the evil of its kings and worship. Still another example is Hezekiah's illness and miraculous recovery (Isa. 38–39). The king's near-death prefigures the ruin and death of his nation; his recovery is presented as a one-man prefiguration of the entire nation's restoration, the theme of the chapters that follow (40–55). Kings obviously "represent" their kingdoms and subjects, according to the logic of "corporate personality." However psychologically interesting the story of Hezekiah may be for us, its inclusion suggests that in the eyes of the biblical writers, he became "Mr. Jerusalem" in an especially vivid manner while sick.

personality" idea. We may ask how the traditional use of "death" for collective destruction, defeat, and exile fares in the era of the New Testament and for the community founded by Christ. There are at least two answers to this question that should be rejected almost immediately, because both impede an adequate understanding of the roles of death in the *Christian* faith. The first, and most common, misconception is that just as redemption is individualized, so death in Christianity becomes purely individual, personal death. Therefore references to "collective" death and resurrection are simply left behind. We may recall Baillie's insistence that "the individual matters to God," and that this is the foundation for Christian hope in "the life everlasting." It is too easy to divide up the two covenants so as to make the first a matter of collective redemption, and the latter one in which the individual and the individual alone "matters" to God. Much of the antagonism against alleged "Platonism" that we found among theological writers was also a protest against the privatizing of Christianity for the sake of a more communal vision of redemption. But if salvation extends to the collective dimension of human existence, what about death?

A second mistake is to allow for this collective dimension to Christian faith, but to let "death"- and "life"-language work more simplistically at the collective level, than at the individual level. As we recall, certain theological writers on eschatology—most noticeably Robinson—wanted a future in which God's cosmic triumph and universal reality would be "all in all"; no shadow of death at the collective level would be retained (although this same author had no qualms about letting individual death stand!). Most frequently, some vision of "progress within history" conveyed this hope. In contrast, Brunner ingeniously relied upon the mythic figure of the Antichrist in order to sever Christian hopes from any hope of progress within history, and indeed from any vision of "life" without death for humanity as a species. The eschatological imagery of the Bible comes closer to portrayal of a universal death and resurrection that touches everyone and everything, with a "new heaven and a new earth" (Rev. 21:1) as the final outcome beyond the death of the old.

Does the church, as Christ's body, repeat in its own existence his fate, in order to become more fully the body of the crucified

God? Does the Antichrist signify that not only progress within history, but even progress within the church is not a given and unquestionable hope for Christians? Here, we need not opt for those schemes of multiple dispensations, of historical agendas for tribulation and apostasy that have perplexed, intrigued, and (I believe) confused so many persons. "False historicization" might be another pathway to take in regard to this topic. On the other hand, it appears arbitrary just to ignore what appear to be images of collective death, in favor of a thoroughly individualized eschatology. However, even those who attempt to rethink eschatology generally focus upon the "cosmic" and universal dimensions of God's reign, giving less thought to how to integrate the language of destruction and betrayal that makes its appearance in these same texts.

If both of these approaches are defective, we are left with the problem of how much space, if any, can be found for "collective death" in Christian faith. Christ's death as an individual personal death has replaced the language of national death in Christianity's primary vision. Christ may represent his entire people, and indeed all of humanity as he died on the cross; this does not change the fact that his death personifies and individualizes death as no general belief in the solidarity of individual and larger group could. For this reason, individualism of a certain type is built into a faith that rests upon the life and death of an individual. Christ is the message and not the messenger, and he is the vehicle through whom all further reflection upon death is conveyed. No amount of rehabilitation for the communal, "peoplehood" dimensions of Christianity, however necessary, will refute that essential individual focus at the level of Jesus the Christ. This focus may have opened the door to Neo-Platonism, to an unbiblical preoccupation with the soul at the expense of both body and community, and to all the evils that Moltmann, Cullman, and others find problematic. But the topic of death is one where the individual focus of Christianity ought not to be swallowed up in reaction against this tradition.

Nevertheless, the logic of corporate personality states that in Christ, we are all members of his body, and this body undergoes suffering, death, and resurrection. As Christ is the "first fruits" of the dead (1 Cor. 15:20) so the church is also, in him, in relation to death and the dead. The church qua community has been brought from death to life, and in that sense is the conveyer and expression of new and eternal life. Yet it does not leave death behind, so much as it incorporates it, sharing in Christ's predeath sufferings. It is sometimes the community of those who mourn, but who will one day laugh. None of this is easy to express, for given the focus upon the individual in our culture and in traditional theology, it may be that any use of collective "death-language" in regard to the church is almost incomprehensible. Still, for those eager to recapture the communal and universal dimensions of eschatology, this dimension of the biblical death-language should be included, rather than excluded as an "over and done with" element in the biblical landscape of faith.

What role does "wrath" play in this ultimate, eschatological landscape? Theological writers surveyed in Chapter 6 were divided as to whether any such concept belonged in a properly focused Christian eschatology. At the same time, we have noted how political and legal categories were central to any narrative of Jesus' death, and so to a model of "Christian death" emerging from this. But what of Jesus as himself the final judge, no longer victim of human injustice? What of the theme that links death—whether biological or spiritual or both—to "punishment"? Not even Cullman, with his repeated use of "horror" and "terror," could find room for this theme. Even at the individual level, it has vanished from much twentieth-century religious thought, and at the collective level it is absent as well.

In contrast, the biblical authors do presuppose such imagery, and even Paul's hope for a day of Christ when God will be "all in all" (1 Cor 15:28 NIV) or "everything to everyone" (RSV) does not totally eliminate all references to divine wrath. Yet we may contrast Paul's relativization of this idea with the later vision of the end as "day of wrath," in which the negative element dominates. It is incorrect to find the early church awaiting "the end of the world," or its destruction. They awaited instead the glorious return of Christ, on the day when the whole creation would achieve the "glorious liberty" for which God had destined it. A new creation, by the logic of "unrealized eschatology," requires a death of the old. But that was not the major emphasis of early Christianity. To the extent to which "wrath" and destruction play some role here, it is to be one of cleansing—not meaningless anger, but divine purgation of all reality.

It is at this point, if not much sooner, that our own unique historical relation to mass destruction makes this imagery so vivid and so near to us—and yet, so problematic. We will examine, at the close of this work, what the future of "collective death" imagery of this sort should be, in the light of Lifton's theory of "nuclearism" and the contemporary world's peculiar and horrible nearness to total annihilation as an imaginal possibility. Yet we should mention now, in the context of this initial introduction of "corporate personality," and the forms of collective identity it makes available, that Lifton alone of the psychological thinkers seems prepared to accept correctives to the modern focus on the individual as the sole locus and source of meanings. "For we are all one in Christ Jesus" requires persons to consider that the deepest roots of their selfhood reside not within the physical boundaries of their own skins, but "elsewhere." Such individuals will not equate their deaths with "the end of everything," and will abide within connections and collectivities in a way unknown to the self enshrined by Becker, for example, or the self of Wyschogrod's "authenticity paradigm." Yet what some of the autobiographers and other thinkers strive for—a model of selfhood that does justice to connections among generations, and across the boundaries of individualities—is seemingly a foundation for the self of the strange new world of biblical faith.

Death-Language in New Testament Spirituality

We take for granted as we read the New Testament the presence of abundant references to death. We find them particularly in Paul's letters, at the core of his personal interior appropriation of Christ as the "I" who now lives within him: "We are afflicted in every way, but not crushed . . . always carrying in the body the death of Jesus, so that the life of Jesus may also be manifested in our bodies. For while we live we are always being given up to death for Jesus' sake. . . . So death is at work in us, but life in you" (2 Cor. 4:8, 10–12).

In this section, we will examine the ins and outs of this "death-imagery"; I will stress its pervasiveness and complexity, focusing upon Paul's usages. When we can read the New Testament as opening for us an entire spiritual landscape, dominated by the central presence of Christ's cross and resurrection, how does the imagery of death become part of the very texture of individual Christian existence? Although several of the psychological theorists write about some form of "death-experience" as necessary for personal transformation, we need to see exactly how this looks within the context of the Bible's "strange new world."

Symbolic and Literal Meanings

To suggest just how complex and ambivalent this reliance upon death-imagery really is, imagine Cullman and Hillman placed in opposition to each other over the meaning of "death." For Cullman, "death" is pure negation, means biological death, and connotes violence, estrangement, and "horror." In total contrast, Hillman links "death" to depth, and the unconscious to a nonrepressive, nonviolent, non-ego-centered mode of personal functioning. Via this unusual route, death becomes a positive rather than a negative term. Which, if either, of these views is "Christian"?

Curiously, the answer may be "both"! The reader of the New Testament can find both these functions, or ones very like them, ascribed to "death-language" in a manner that most of us find difficult to follow. Simultaneously, Christians are said to have passed "from death to life," and yet to be "dead" themselves. Although "death" in itself is a negative term, in appropriate contexts it is said to be the state of those saved by Christ, and therefore on the "plus" side of redemption: "For he who has died is freed from sin" (Rom. 6:7). If the New Testament's imagery were as one-dimensional as either Cullman or Hillman, this ambivalent usage would not appear. Moreover, it would always be absolutely clear whether biological death or some "death-equivalent" were intended by the writers.

The New Testament's language of "death" will teach contemporary readers to mistrust the simple equation of death with the chronological end of biological life. Death as spiritual reality reaches beyond the physical, biological condition we now restrictedly call "death." We today may permit symbolic meanings for "death," but assume these to be secondary derivations from a more basic and biological meaning. In short, as in other areas of imagery, most of us are materialists and naturalists.

But in contrast, the New Testament writers and their early readers did not hold our theory of imagery, did not so clearly prefer physical to what we label "symbolic" meanings. Although they too divide reality, they split it into "earth" and "heaven," or sometimes "natural" and "spiritual." Yet we may say that *both* sides of these dichotomies to them are literal and symbolic realities. Therefore, there is no exact identity between New Testament categories of "natural," "carnal," and "earth" and *our* use of "physical," "natural," and "biological." Often that which is described as "carnal" or "fleshly" is anything but "material"; we would describe it as "psychic" or "emotional." A great deal of attention has already been given to the New Testament (particularly Pauline) use of the term "body" (Bultmann 1951; Stacey 1956; Gundry 1976; Jewett 1971). From this, it is apparent how "body" rarely means what we now, given our "naturalistic" theory of symbolism, assume it to mean.[3]

Another way to express this is to see that the New Testament authors know more about symbolism than we do, as well as more about death. These two advantages are related. They wrote for persons who could probably follow complex and ambiguous patterns of imagery better than most of us. Some arguments built upon such imagery may have been hard to follow even by Paul's contemporaries, although perhaps not because they depend upon imagery to so great an extent. But imagine average contemporary readers faced with the text of the letter to the Ephesians for the very first time. What would they make of the rapid transition from "you were dead" to "God raised us up with Christ" into the discussion of the two groups now joined through the cross, "by which he put to death their hostility" (Eph. 2:16 NIV)? No wonder it has been easier to render such language by compressing it into a few more simple theological statements, of which "Death is the last enemy" and "To die is gain" are only two.

To avoid this is to let the death-language be heard. The depth psychological theories help to highlight how some immersion in "death" or some activity of the self rendered as

3. These arguments, recently summarized by John Cooper (1989:147–71) hinge on whether the Greek *sōma* comes closer to meaning a human "inner essence" (*tous*, a self) or an outer manifestation in space of a self who can be construed as potentially separable from its *sōma*. Bultmann (1951:194) takes the first position, while Gundry (1976:184ff.) takes the second.

"putting to death" the sinful past and its ways, finds a place at the heart of New Testament spirituality. Christianity appears not only centered upon Christ's death, but intent on duplicating and appropriating its imagery in regard to ongoing existence, especially at the level of individual transformation. What happened to Christ will indeed become what happens to Christians. Some death-immersion, some experience of participation in an equivalent to death, is located in the initiation rite of baptism. But baptism is a once-and-for-all experience, unrepeatable by anyone. What is remarkable is how the kind of death-immersion experience permeates the Pauline language about Christian postbaptismal living.

Those who, following Cullman, want only "life" and consign death to absolute opposition to God, cannot find room for such language. The original injunction of the Hebrew Scriptures— "I have set before you life and death, blessings and curse; therefore choose life" (Deut. 30:19)—is insufficient to accommodate to the complexity of the New Testament spiritual path. For the very choice that appears to be "life" will lead to "death," and the choice of a certain kind of "death" is in reality the entrance into "life." Continuously Christians are to pass from death into life, by putting to death their old selves, while at the same time they have already died and their new and real selves are hidden with God. Moreover, precisely these evocative and mysterious usages for "death" are integrated into reflections and injunctions upon a wide range of practical problems faced by Christians. Thus death-imagery lies at the heart of much New Testament spirituality, not just its central narrative or its eschatology.

The Body

To what extent do any of these meanings include biological death? Or are they all what we call "spiritual," all "symbolic"? Yes, they are all spiritual, in the sense that Paul and the other authors are all concerned for the spirit or inward person in relation to God. But not all "death" references are disembodied, or irrelevant to one's physical death. The body is very much a participant and not a spectator in this language. "But if Christ is in you, although your bodies are dead because of sin, your spirits are alive because of righteousness. If the Spirit of him who raised Jesus from the dead dwells in you, he who raised Christ Jesus from the dead will give life to your mortal bodies also through his Spirit which dwells in you" (Rom. 8:10–11). What is "the body" here? Is it a sheer physical material entity, that which, being of "flesh and blood," cannot inherit the kingdom of God? Yet the sheer physical material entity is also en-Spirited, given life even now, although it is still "mortal" and not the "glorious" and imperishable body of the resurrection. So our bodies/selves are dead yet alive-from-the-Spirit, the perfect vehicles for the paradox of unrealized yet realized biblical eschatology.

Moreover, as Christ's death was total, so Christ's raising from the dead will have impact at all levels. If Christ's death had only been part-way, or only affected one accidental aspect of his being, then this imagery simply could not work the way it does. It is therefore too simple to say that although Christ's death was total, physical, ours is "symbolic." That is *not* what the above passage implies. Our embodiment is drawn into the process of "death to the old self" and "being brought from death to life," so that the "mortal body's" vulnerability can be seen as a sign of both. The body's weakness, about which the Pauline letters speak so frequently, is an expression of its "being-toward-death" and its association with sin. But it is also "being-brought-from-death" or "being-made-alive" and its vulnerability is a sign of God's gracious promise to bestow complete, resurrected new life upon it (Beker 1980:223). As is the case for the Freudian tradition, the body is a psychic-spiritual reality in its very materiality.

Curiously, the dualism of a Becker, for whom the body verges upon becoming merely "alien casing" that traps the spirit inside, also seems appropriate for some of the other Pauline language. Paul can appear just as dualistic when he writes about civil war within the person, the battle between flesh and spirit, "members" and inner man (Rom. 7:22–23). Yet this battle is carried out as if both sides were agencies, with intentions and aims, rather than as if one were merely inert matter. The body is not only the battleground, but also divided. It wages war against itself, in a manner analogous to Freud's battle of twin embodied inner instincts. It is never merely spectator, nor is it strictly "alien" to me.

Such language is extremely unpopular today, as we saw, among theological writers. In their revulsion against the "dualism" of "Platonism's" body/soul split many thinkers appealed back to the earlier "Hebraic," allegedly nondualistic thought of the Old Testament. This, it was claimed, treats the person "holistically," as a unity. But once again, the New Testament is more complex in its use of imagery than our thought-patterns can accommodate. Paul treats Christ's death "holistically." Christ died "once for all," totally. Paul never hints that this death was less than complete. Unlike the "civil war" within the body, between members and inner man, "death" language comprehends the old person as a totality. "We know that our old self was crucified with him so that the sinful body might be destroyed" (Rom. 6:6). Not just its members, but the body as a totality! Death-language, like the language of incorporation and participation, functions "holistically" whatever its particular application. It has an unrestricted aspect to it, perhaps more so than we ourselves can accept, with our convenient disjunction between literal and symbolic meanings.

Clusters of Death-Imagery

Is it possible to distinguish types of death-imagery used by exponents of Pauline spirituality? Here, as when we surveyed the Passion narratives, Lifton's idea of "experiential clusters" is most helpful in grasping the connotations of such imagery. Of these, it seems that disintegration, with its focus upon bodily mutilation, is most intrinsically appropriate for imaging death as crucifixion. Although as we saw, theologically the most important dimension of Jesus' death was its meaning as separation, from God and within God, "crucifixion" at the level of New Testament spirituality does not rely principally upon this. Separation language is reserved for pre-Christian existence. We were then "dead in our sins," and therefore separated from God (strangers and alienated, in the terms of Eph. 2:12). But now we are connected to God and joined to God's people. True, Christian life requires certain separations, such as a break from the past, or from sin. But the "death" that describes these is one that heavily relies upon other imagery.

By far the most poignant and dramatic death-language is that tied to disintegration. Christ's death on the cross was violent and gruesome. It is never linked to "sleep" by the same Paul who is willing to use "fallen asleep" as a euphemism for the dead elsewhere in his writings. Paul's own adventures included repeated physically mutilating sufferings which he could view as his personal sharing in Christ's own sufferings. And, insofar as Christian spirituality depends upon this imagery of death and suffering drawn from the crucifixion, so "putting to death" one's sinful nature and habits becomes directly tied to the civil war within the body, referred to already. It is not merely withering away, sinking into stasis, or even "departure" and loss. It is a direct, gruesome mutilation.

In Colossians, the death of the old self in baptism is explicitly linked to Christ's death understood as circumcision, one "made without hands" (Col. 2:11–13). Christ's death as a circumcision turns the part into the totality, a stripping away of an entire body rather than a small piece of skin. This reference to participation in mutilating death is immediately followed by the reverse and more positive image: "And you, who were dead in trespasses and the uncircumcision of your flesh, God made alive together with him." Interestingly, this reference to Christ's death as a circumcision is addressed to those fascinated by ascetic practices, and perhaps drawn to physical circumcision as an expression of human triumph over "the power of the flesh" (Keck 1979:85). The author, whether Paul or someone else writing in his name, clearly sees this impulse as "the flesh" in the sense of psychological pride. The letter nowhere denies the value of ascetic practices in themselves, but recognizes how too often they, like ordinary circumcision, are "made by hands," by the human ego. In contrast, bodily disintegration such as Christ experienced is for Christians the true circumcision, performed by God upon the total individual who shares in Christ's death.

A further word should be said about the "civil war" imagery of spiritual-psychic-embodied conflict. Not only are the forces involved "inner," such as "inner man" versus "members," but the "warfare" language also connects with other, more cosmic and external opposition. As we saw in the discussion of the Passion narratives, political and military imagery is unavoidable, and is elaborated in the Pauline materials as well. Insofar as the New Testament uses warfare imagery, it includes those "powers and principalities" that lie "outside" the body and its unruly members. The death-language of Christian spirituality, of "putting to death" in oneself all that still lives of sin and "flesh," is also a language of military conquest. It is Christ and not the ego who conquers, and if "we are more than conquerors" it is because we belong totally to Christ, as he belongs to God.

Nowhere does the New Testament promise that evil will simply "wither away" or that personal transformation can occur without some violence, the rejection of some possibilities, the struggle against forces within and outside the self. At this level, there is no hope held out that everything can be united or "integrated" as it stands. Distaste for military imagery, or for the idea that some elements of existence cannot be "accepted" or even "healed" but can only be struggled against, may run very deep in some of us. But such imagery stands as one element within the totality of death-imagery for the early Christian community. In the New Testament, the necessity for this language is never argued; at this level a kind of dualism is taken for granted. Hence, transformation is perceived by Paul and the other writers not only as "healing" but also under the imagery of battle and athletic contest. Jesus is "Prince of Peace," yet he came to bring a spiritual sword, and this language appears to be intrinsic to the New Testament's message about him.

As for these "powers," they seem to be the primary enemies of Christ, mentioned far more frequently as opponents than "death." "Elementary principles" Paul sometimes calls them, or "the rulers of this age." The language about them, unlike the New Testament death-language, is never placed on the "plus" side, the side of redemption, and the Christian's relation to them is one of unmitigated hostility. What we today make of this imagery of evil spiritual forces is an interesting question. We ought to retain its political connotations. Perhaps we should also recover its impersonal quality; it is less a matter of individual abusive rulers, and more a system of injustice and abuse of power. Walter Wink (Wink 1984, 1986) takes this direction, and also allows that these have some constructive yet subordinate role to play in the total picture of reality. Wink's portrayal of these as elements in the New Testament landscape of faith may be too positive, too balanced (Wink 1984:100). Perhaps, as Nouwen discovered, there are limits to how far one can "befriend" certain realities, whether death or "powers." Traditionally, Christians have found that they need to retain a sense of an evil too evil for redemption, too hostile to God, and too destructive of the self to be befriended, tamed, and "integrated" into the redeemed creation.

But this evil is not death, at least not biological death. Whatever death as negation may mean in the New Testament, the prevalence of death-imagery and death-language there reveals the striking capacity for meshing life and death, dying to self and living to God, at many levels of experience. Far from being an unthinkable reality that must invariably be repressed or denied, death for Christians becomes a figure for a range of struggles, conflicts, transitions, and violent renunciations. This language is used "existentially"; it is linked to Christ's death and is the sign of our participation in his nature and destiny. To that final destiny, "resurrection," we now turn.

Resurrection-Imagery

Throughout this work, dominated by focus upon "death," we have had to refer this again and again to patterns of polarity and dualism. Freud, for example, retained a "dualism" of instincts, and so postulated a "life instinct" to counter the forces of the death instinct. Lifton argued that human beings learn death-equivalents by pairing these with symbols of vitality, as in "separation/connection." It would betray the entire spirit of the New Testament if one were to omit the "vital" opposite to death it too postulates. We must, in short, not fail to include an acknowledgment of "resurrection" as the New Testament's "opposite" and response to death. To move from death to life is, for the early Christian authors, to move into new, transformed, and "spiritual" life, into resurrection life. In the sequence of the Passion narratives, this was the final stage in what happened to Jesus.

Resurrection and Narrative

Each Gospel includes its own set of specific episodes, both of "appearances" and of the empty tomb. In none is "the resurrection" itself an event recorded on-stage, so to speak. The reader sees its effects and results, not the actual "raising up." Since the same motive that makes biblical scholars and theologians wary that too much "realized" eschatology can operate in our appre-

hension of those narratives from the Gospels, one may emphasize the indirect, hidden, and tentative quality of these resurrection "appearances." Also, of course, a well-known theological
debate, set off by Bultmann's "demythologizing" agenda, centered on whether *any* "event" such as traditionally implied in
the term "resurrection" is a possibility for modern people's faith.
The confused nature of this debate is apparent, because several
intertwined theological motifs all converged in this challenge to
traditional formulations. The "prescientific" and "mythological"
nature of traditional doctrines was one of them. Another was
the aforementioned suspicion of too much "glorification" in our
understanding of Christian faith. Tied to this was a distinctively Lutheran argument that, to make "the resurrection" into
an objective historical event would be to make it a "work," or to
lessen its value for faith (Bultmann 1961:40–42).

At the level of narrative, the resurrection is intrinsic to the
story as story. Even if the ending of Mark's Gospel has been lost,
or the real ending comes as the frightened women rush from the
empty tomb rather than with the traditional last twelve verses
(Farmer 1974:109), some ending "beyond" the death and burial
of Jesus is needed. All four Gospels do give this an elusive quality—by showing Jesus as at first unrecognized, for example, even
by those who had been close to him. Yet to overstress this
appears to be part of twentieth-century reluctance to press the
language of "glorified" existence, in the face of an overwhelming
awareness of divine suffering. Typically, Simone Weil notes how
the wounds on the risen Christ show how "here below" nature
remains "irremediably wounded," and it is this and not the joy of
triumph over death that has made the greatest impact among the
religious thinkers we surveyed. To the extent that this can
become a positive obstacle to apprehension of the texts' own focus
of concern, we may label it the diametrical opposite of Hillman's
"Christianism." Not only in regard to the authenticity of the
Gospel narratives, but also with reference to Paul, this same bias
against "resurrection now" language and imagery appears.

Pauline language relies on the imagery of death and resurrection with Christ, following the principle that what happened
to Christ happens or will happen to the Christian. Death and
resurrection are paired in almost all of the Pauline references
we have already cited. It is in the light of Christ's resurrection
that all human problems, not just biological death, become

potentially envisioned under the aspect of a "death" from which there is a liberation. The crucified God is always a resurrected God as well. The New Testament definitely wishes "resurrection" to stand as the other side in death's polarity.

Now and Future

But is resurrection as "event" in the lives of Christians happening now, or only reserved for "then," at the eschatological last day? It is less clear that for the New Testament's landscape, "resurrection" is always an appropriate image for us, as those who participate in Christ's death. Language that applies "resurrection" in any way to the Christian now risks minimizing the reality of ongoing suffering. It smacks of a "theology of glory" that betrays the theology of the cross. A theology of "resurrection now" also seems—so the argument goes—to validate the status quo to a degree that a more "unrealized" eschatology does not (Beker 1980:225–26). The cross, not the resurrection, according to Moltmann, can function as a "critique" of an unredeemed world.

When this concern is applied back to the interpretation of New Testament texts, it becomes conflated with a textual-historical issue: the authorship of certain letters traditionally ascribed to Paul. Are the epistles to Colossians and Ephesians written by another hand, non-Pauline, and theologically inferior to those from the authentic Paul? Is this a reason for their seemingly more "conservative" ethical outlook? These two writings hold that "resurrection" applies now to the state of the baptized Christian. Whereas Romans 6, in a passage saturated with death-language, states that "We shall certainly be united with him in a resurrection like his" (v. 5)—note the future tense—in Colossians it is already upon us: "You were buried with him in baptism, in which you were also raised with him through faith" (Col. 2:12). In Ephesians, God "made us alive together with Christ . . . and raised us up with him, and made us sit with him in the heavenly places in Christ Jesus" (Eph. 2:5–6). Is this shift in language a later, more "triumphalist" misinterpretation of Paul's incorporation imagery (Fuller 1976:21–23; Beker 1980:213ff.), or is Paul writing in response to different problems (Schnackenburg 1964:71)? Is the question one of theological preference, or textual analysis?

Both sets of materials know Christ's resurrection as something that has already happened. Can Christians appropriate its spiritual power, and therefore live from it now, while in their mortal bodies? The clear answer from the Pauline letters is yes; it happened already to Christ, and as imagery it is available to all who share in his death. But Paul was forced to resist what one can call the full "spiritualization" of this term. In 1 Corinthians 15, it is clear he refused to discard the Jewish apocalyptic hope for a general resurrection of the dead, for some replacement of mortal and perishable with immortal and imperishable embodiment. This is yet to come; no substitute that leaves out or ignores the body and its continued vulnerability is going to satisfy a Paul who awaits the complete victory of Christ (Beker 1980:233). Paul will not settle only for a "resurrection" of the pure spirit, as his opponents seem to do. It should be stressed again that only in the context of this total vision of redeemed and glorified creation does the phrase "the last enemy" get applied to death. To isolate this and locate it solely within the confines of this life, is to deny what Paul himself hoped for, namely, the totality and completion of God's triumph.

For Paul, this is exactly the context where ambivalence over the body as weak and vulnerable and the site of sin becomes most apparent. If flesh and blood cannot inherit the kingdom of God, the resurrection body will be a "spiritual body," bearing the same relationship to current bodies as Christ does to Adam. No amount of expert exegesis will turn this imagery and allegory into a philosophically coherent argument, and the term "spiritual body" sticks out as among the most enigmatic in the New Testament (Cooper 1989:153–54). Even for Paul, who himself had an experience of ecstatic, transcendent disembodiment such as we might now classify along with other "near-death" experiences (2 Cor. 12:2–5), the terms of resurrection embodiment remain mysterious and unavailable except through analogies.

Scholars agree that the apostle's own ecstatic experience was never meant by him to become normative as an expression of "resurrection" life within all Christians (Schnackenburg 1964:182–83). Paul indirectly tells of "a man" "caught up to the third heaven . . . whether in the body or out of the body I do not know." Whatever the meaning of this experience—puzzling to Paul himself, let alone to readers—it is not the way to explicate what the "resurrected" status of the Christian might mean now, as in those passages where "resurrection" and "being seated with Christ in the heavenly places" is applied to all Christians in their current existence (Eph. 2:6; Col. 2:12).

What then does this language mean? Like the death-language, it has a totality about it. Take the following vivid passage:

> If then you have been raised with Christ, seek the things that are above, where Christ is, seated at the right hand of God. Set your minds on things that are above, not on things that are on earth. For you have died and your life is hid with Christ in God. When Christ who is our life appears, then you also will appear with him in glory. (Col. 3:1–4)

The first thing to notice is that such language does *not* equate resurrection with eventual, complete "glorification." There is an "unrealized" dimension to this eschatology as well (Fuller 1976:23). But in order to accept this language of current "resurrection" we need to appreciate "place"-language, imagery of spatial "levels," as valid. That which is "above" versus that which is "below" requires that we accept, at least at the level of imagery, the basic mythological "three-storied universe" of heaven, earth's surface, and hell. Whereas the Pauline language of sharing in Christ's death does not require "places" or "levels" so directly in order to appropriate it, this evocation of the self, hidden with Christ "above," surely does. This was one, although only one, of the multiple objections to "resurrection"-imagery, as posed by Bultmann (Bultmann 1961:4).

Place-Language

Curiously, here the psychological theories turn out to be far more open than much of the theological writing we surveyed in Chapter 6. Although "eras" became a dominant concern for those focused upon eschatology, "places" more or less vanished as theological categories. Yet Freud and Jung depended upon reintroducing multiple levels within the self, and Becker, Hillman, and Lifton relied in different ways upon this metaphor to make claims about the self's capacities for multiple perspectives. Some of what needs to be said about the self and its relation to death perhaps requires such language, with its references to multiple "places" and "levels." Precisely because human beings are embodied, and require space as well as time as a category of existence, this imagery reappears even when no one would mistake it for a geologist's or astronomer's account of reality.

And following this lead, we may try to apprehend the self that is hid with Christ, the "real" and resurrected new Christian self, as also a perspective more than a separate entity. This image of hidden, heavenly self could suggest for us not a disembodied thing, but a new viewpoint from which to see reality. It is hidden, never fully "owned" and "claimed"; it is as yet unknown even to us. The author of Colossians does not introduce this image in order to have us flee this world's daily responsibilities. But the language of "resurrected with Christ" does require a sense of split between the ordinary and the hidden-resurrected perspectives, a split that terms such as "above" and "below" try to capture.

Resurrection language like this, that seems to counter the death-imagery in some New Testament spirituality, forces us to recognize how a dimension of "otherness" and "elsewhereness" is built into the Christian landscape and its language about persons. The language of hidden and resurrected self is so elusive, so noncontrolling and nonactivist, that it cannot be attributed to the ordinary self as agent. The resurrected self is the self who has died, and its life is now Christ. It is not "made by hands," the product of our own wills. No references to "resurrection" find this dependent upon the individual's own power to rise above ordinary nature. It is the farthest reach of our participation in Christ, and its "otherness" is his.

There appears to be no nonmythic way to capture this dimension of resurrection-imagery or to translate it adequately into other, ordinary categories. As with Grof and Halifax's "posthumous journey of the soul," a cosmic vision has swallowed up all attempts to keep the theory "psychological." If this is the case for twentieth-century psychology, then it helps us to apprehend how Christ's death and resurrection, as spiritual realities expressed in the biblical "strange new world," provide a vision of a landscape, a reality for Christians. The totality of death-imagery, the corresponding totality of resurrection as image and perspective, together open up a cosmos, one available to those who participate in Christ's identity. They chart for Christians the boundaries of death's presence within the cosmos, and give form to the landscape of faith.

8

Encountering Death: Christian Resources

Everyone—theologians, pastoral counselors, and psychologists—agrees that Christianity has always taken death seriously, and made it a central spiritual concern. Some rely upon traditional resources, and incorporate liturgies and spiritual guides from previous eras into their counseling methods. They acknowledge a gap between ourselves today and the tradition, one that prevents a wooden and repetitive incorporation of past resources. Nevertheless, they believe a look at past spiritual resources will help give us distance from our own cultural and ideological frameworks. Instead of preoccupation with the psychological management of emotions, for instance, such traditional resources will restore the sense of "awe and ultimacy" surrounding death. True, it is hard to make use of the Christian materials without assuming some level of commitment to the vision of reality they hold. If psychologists were willing to treat myth "psychologically" and find in the imagery of Hades or the posthumous journey of the soul something of value for contemporary persons, can the same be said of the vision of dying and death contained in the late medieval *Ars moriendi* writings? It is hard to know just how deliteralized a

reading such a text should be given. Nevertheless, in search of
an alternative to today's restricted vision, we should be prepared to take seriously materials that were once widely accepted by Christians, and be taught how to encounter death.

The relation of such materials to the biblical landscape of
faith is often shadowy. Some were considered authoritative
interpretations of that landscape, others self-consciously
attempted to build a bridge between the witness of the Bible
and their own day. Although these perspectives from Christian
tradition stand in deep contrast to contemporary popular
Christianity, as well as popular psychological approaches, they
are also in places at odds with what appears to be the main
thrust of the biblical texts. Even when this is the case, there is
something to be said for examining a viewpoint radically different from that of the twentieth century. None of the resources discussed in this chapter, however, have the foundational and authoritative role of the biblical texts; our discussion
of them will be focused on their capacity to incorporate some of
the images examined in the previous chapter.

"My Death"

The rise of concern over "my death" seems to coincide with
the beginnings of Western individualism, in around the twelfth
century A.D. According to Philippe Ariès, in *The Hour of Our
Death*, for the first millennium of Christian history, individuals died what he calls a "tame death." To die was to undergo
an untraumatic transition, like moving from one house to
another. There was a standard program for a "good death," and
this took the form of a ritual performed by dying persons. They
first sensed that death was immanent; "knowing that their
time was near" they called relatives and friends to their bed-
side, bade them farewell, and forgave them any harms done.
Then, with a modest degree of sorrow, they took leave of both
persons and possessions, and committed the self into God's
hands. Then, nothing remained but to wait passively for death
to come, face to the wall or with the body positioned in the form
of a cross. Ariès' point is that in preindividualized society,
death could take this form because each person could exemplify
the universally shared pattern (Ariès 1981 [1977]:18). The
(very ancient) model of "corporate personality" still held firm

for the average person. Given such a standardized pattern, no need would arise for special guidance. "Tame death" is the baseline, Ariès believes, against which all later developments and styles should be measured. Note that this pattern resembles Kübler-Ross' dying Swiss farmer; it has persisted down through the centuries as both a reality and a nostalgic ideal (Ariès 1981 [1977]:28).

What disrupted it? Ariès describes the second phase of Westerners' attitudes toward death as "the death of the self." In short, it is the emergence of the self, of my unique being and destiny as individual, which makes death much more threatening. If death destroys that which is irreplaceable, it also offers me an opportunity to become more truly myself. The state of dying becomes especially significant, for it constitutes my final and ultimate moments. For the individual, older versions of "corporate personality" will no longer suffice. The individual must personally relate to other persons, including Christ as person. A new devotional intimacy with Christ is born, just as Western spirituality discovers a new sense of Jesus' humanity.

One of the classic expressions of this intensified awareness of the self's death is also an expression of what we have called "collective death." The poem by Thomas of Celona, *"Dies irae"* ("Day of Wrath") became a normative liturgical way to link these two concerns. The scene is the day of judgment, the death of everyone:

> The day of wrath, that day,
> The world will dissolve into ash . . .
> Death and nature will be stupefied
> When creation will awake
> Going to make answer to the judge.

The tone is of abject terror, for Christ will judge all and "Nothing shall remain unavenged." Here the self's response is contrition, remorse, and fear in the face of divine wrath. Yet Jesus is appealed to as savior, as the one who suffered for the self as individual being, and who will now take pity on the sinner.

> Remember, sweet Jesus,
> That I am the cause of your journey;
> So that I may not perish on that day.

"Awe and ultimacy" clearly dominate, and in the vision of *"Dies irae"* no doubt remains of that link between "wrath" and death. Moreover, wrath, and not hope, determines collective eschatology, so that the world's death stands over against the precarious rescue of the self. This un-Liftonian mode of relating individual and collective death is also, by twentieth-century theological criteria, woefully "unbiblical" in its stress on destruction and judgment without reference to the "new heaven and new earth," and in its overall deemphasis on Christian hope. And yet, *"Dies irae"* clearly does what Becker believes all religion should: it sets the human drama on the largest possible stage. To encounter death is to encounter the finitude and guilt of the entire cosmos faced by divine judgment. Next to this, any goal of psychological "acceptance," or of death as "natural," seems trivial.

Yet there was a need for more attention to the dying individual's plight. Historically the rise of the "art of dying" literature coincided with mass death from bubonic plagues. The plagues were traumatic, ghastly intrusions of mass death, when death's nearness, horror, and suddenness oppressed everyone. Although certain measures, such as the isolation of towns, were used to stop the spread of plague, not until a much later period did an ideology of effective control over epidemics emerge (McManners 1981:44ff.). Moreover, due to mass death, sacramental absolution, the presence of a priest at the time of dying, was not possible for everyone. Hence the rise of "do it yourself" manuals for the dying and their friends.

The Book of the Craft of Dying, or *Ars moriendi*, is an anonymously authored late medieval treatise that promises practical knowledge. "For doubtless it is and may be profitable generally, to all true Christian men, to learn and have craft and knowledge to die well" (Comper 1977 [1917]:3). The spiritual friend or guide is to read the treatise to the dying person, and ask the appropriate questions. In short, this work provides a direct antecedent to today's pastoral care literature.

Although *The Craft's* first chapter exhorts that the wise man never fears death, the bulk of the treatise takes another approach: "Know all men doubtless, that men that die, in their last sickness and end, have greatest and most grievous temptations, and such as they never had before in all their life" (Comper 1977 [1917]:10). Far from being an anticipated release from life's miseries, dying is in fact itself a miserable experience. The temptations referred to above are: of faith (the threat of unbelief); of despair over unconfessed sin; of impatience, which can lead to anger at God; of spiritual pride; and of preoccupation with outward things, when it is clear that death is immanent. This remarkable list is strikingly similar to Kübler-Ross' five stages and the "data" noticed by Cabot and Dicks and others who work with twentieth-century dying patients. Occupation with outward things appears to be "denial," while impatience is linked to anger. Despair covers the same ground as "reactive depression," a morbid preoccupation with unfinished emotional business.

Yet the overall framework of faith, and some of the specific remedies to meet these temptations, are not necessarily those of modern pastoral counselors. To bolster faith, a friend is to recite the Creed to the dying person. Against despair, the latter is to remember divine mercy.

> But therefore should no man despair in no wise. For though any one man or woman had done as many thefts, or manslaughters, or as many other sins as be drops of water in the sea . . . yet should he never despair; for in such a case very contrition of heart within . . . is sufficient and accepted by God for to save him everlastingly. (Comper 1977 [1917]:13)

The remedy against impatience is to curb all expressions of anger. Those who complain against God show insufficient love for him (Comper 1977 [1917]:16); moreover, physical suffering in this life, when endured meekly by the sufferer, will possibly release that person from some time spent in purgatory. The remedy against pride is to think upon one's sins, although not to the point of despair. Finally, the entire book is a remedy against denial; the spiritual guide or friend should remind the dying person that continued concern with worldly life is a terrible mistake. This method of direct confrontation with otherwise-unconscious flight from death helps make conscious the hold of denial over one who ought to concentrate only upon dying.

Behind this advice is a vision of death as that solemn and ultimate time of encounter with God and divine judgment, just as in *"Dies irae."* When people have endured the pain of physical illness and moral self-knowledge, they have no choice but to cling to God's mercy. Death ought not to be easy, really; if it were, this would probably be a sign of complacency. In the hour of dying, the Christian has not only a merciful judge but a model to follow: Christ upon the cross. Christ did the following in his last hour: he prayed; he cried; he wept; he commended his soul to God; he willfully gave up his spirit (Comper 1977 [1917]: 27–28). Note that Christ did not experience despair or alienation from God, however "human" the text's portrait of him is here. Christ is not only a "role model" for dying; he is a passionately loved presence: "Take heed and see: His head is inclined to salve thee; His mouth to kiss thee; His arms spread to embrace thee; His hands pierced to give thee; His side opened to love thee; His body along strait to give all Himself to thee" (Comper 1977 [1917]:14). Thus, at the moment of death, Christ is less the judge on the throne than the fellow-human in suffering, and the beloved, almost maternal comforting presence. The spirituality of *Ars moriendi* is Christ-centered at these points, and brings an immediacy to the relationship between Christ and the self.

In *The Craft of Dying*, remarkably little is said about any afterlife. Yet the entire framework depends upon seeing dying as preparation, as final testing ground. The explicit reference to purgatory reminds the reader that pain and suffering do not instantly end after physical death. The hope for a "good death" puts an enormous burden upon the final hours or moments of a life; one's dying becomes, so to speak, one's signature, a summation of who one has been throughout one's life. This vision of preparation for individual death continues after the Reformation. The sense of one's dying as individual task, of near-death as a special spiritual situation, and of Christ's merciful presence at the time of death, all persist as motifs.

Reformation Perspectives

One of the themes of Reformation piety was what Max Weber refers to as its "rationalization." The pursuit of an ordered rather than sporadic godly lifestyle, a planned and intentional application of faith to daily life, was now the ideal for all Christians (not just those in monastic settings). Hence, the approach of Calvin to the encounter with death does not isolate "dying" as in *The Craft of Dying*. In Book 3, Chapters

6–9 of *The Institutes* Calvin provides a portrait of the Christian
life which, unsurprisingly, emphasizes self-denial and cross
bearing as its key motifs. "Soberness, righteousness and godli-
ness" are the three headings under which all behavioral and
dispositional qualities desirable for Christians are classified.
Calvin goes out of his way to argue against Stoicism. The
Stoics found that dispassionate acceptance of suffering was the
highest ideal. For Calvin, "Patiently to bear the cross is not to
be utterly stupefied and to be deprived of all feeling of pain"
(*Inst.* 3.8.9). Jesus himself "groaned and wept both over his
own and others' misfortunes." Patience in the face of sorrow is
better than repression of natural feelings. Like Gerkin, Calvin
wishes to sever the authentically Christian response to suffering from "heroic humanism."

Nevertheless, the bulk of Calvin's treatment is weighted
against what he or we would call "natural emotions." No matter what sufferings come our way, "The conclusion will always
be: the Lord so willed, therefore let us follow his will" (*Inst.*
3.8.10). No more room is left for anger here than in *The Craft of
Dying*; the contemporary theme that God is more our fellow-
sufferer than the one who ordains our suffering is also absent.
Calvin notes with dismay:

> But monstrous it is that many who boast themselves
> Christians are gripped by such a great fear of death, rather
> than a desire for it. . . . Surely, it is no wonder if the natural
> awareness in us bristles with dread at the mention of our dis-
> solution. . . . But . . . will not faith compel us ardently to seek
> what nature dreads? (*Inst.* 3.9.5)

In other words, the proper Christian response to death is to
desire it as liberation from this life's miseries—a position not
taken by *The Craft of Dying*. Compared to later models that
took up the theme that faith will "ardently seek what nature
dreads," however, Calvin is restrained and balanced in his
somber assessment of death's meaning for Christians.

This balance is also intrinsic to the portrayal of death in the
famous Puritan classic, *Pilgrim's Progress* by John Bunyan. In
Parts 1 and 2 physical death is symbolized by the crossing of a
river, which serves as a boundary between this world of pilgrimage and the Heavenly City. In *Pilgrim's Progress* the

entire journey is a series of mostly unpleasant and dangerous adventures, with little respite along the way. Thus, death is no unique event, and in fact is described less dramatically than some of the earlier struggles. Nevertheless, the river threatens to drown Christian, the hero of Part 1, and he falls into despair and hallucinates during the crossing. His friend Hopeful tells him: "These troubles and distresses that you go through in these waters are no sign that God hath forsaken you, but are sent to try you, whether you will call to mind that which heretofore you have received of His goodness, and live upon Him in your distresses" (Bunyan 1981 [1678]:144). Bunyan wants to insist that there is no relation between the difficulty of one's death and the quality of one's Christian life. Ignorance, one of Bunyan's many negative characters, receives a ferry ride from Vain-Hope, and so avoids the lesson of the river altogether. Bunyan wishes to separate being dead from being saved, too: Ignorance tumbles into hell after his easy death. Realism may have compelled Bunyan to deemphasize the hour of dying as the signature of one's character.

One of the main characters of Part 2, however, does die rather more "ardently," and without fear. Mr. Stand-fast prepares to enter the river, and tells his companions: "This river has been a terror to many; yea the thoughts of it have also often frightened me. But now, methinks, I stand easy. . . . The thoughts of what I am going to, and of the conduct that waits for me on the other side, does lie as a glowing coal at my heart" (Bunyan 1981 [1678]:282). It was this, more "triumphant" death that many later Protestants wished to use as a model, perhaps losing Bunyan's own restraint in the process.

We should note that nowhere in *Pilgrim's Progress* is Cullman's "death as enemy" motif apparent. Bunyan's own long imprisonment and other sufferings may have sensitized him to guilt and despair as worse enemies than death. The two most villainous figures in *Pilgrim's Progress* are Apollyon and Giant Despair; the hero and his friend are nearly done in by both of these. In contrast, death is not personified, does not in itself convey any sense of horror via its imagery. Given the prevalence of other negative imagery throughout the book— from the start at the City of Destruction, through beatings and starvation, to Ignorance's fall into hell at the very threshhold of the Heavenly City—the mildness of the river as image is even more telling.

An intrinsic part of traditional Christian treatments of the encounter with death was the warning against a "bad death." The negative characters in Bunyan's book play this role. Another, later example of "bad death" can be found in William Law's *Serious Call to a Devout and Holy Life*. Writing in early eighteenth-century England, Law's main goal was to show that the true Christian life actually promotes happiness, even within this lifetime. Nevertheless, the use of near-death as a human situation is to provide a negative example. Law wants to show that the devout life is not only morally superior, but also a more intelligent choice. What better means to this aim than to present to the readers an allegorical case study of a dying sinner, a man whose life had been so insignificant spiritually that "sinner" seems too grandiose a category for him.

"Penitens" is a thirty-five-year-old businessman, struck down suddenly by illness and now near death. He exhorts his friends to revise their lives while there is still time, and bitterly pities himself. Everything now appears in a different light than it had before: "When you are as near death as I am, you will know that all the different states of life . . . signify no more to you than whether you die in a poor or stately apartment. The greatness of those things which follow death makes all that goes before it sink into nothing" (Law 1979 [1728]:71).

Penitens does not have countless murders of which to repent; only a life wasted in emptiness, in business activities and shallow respectability. Here, death's awe and ultimacy serve to reduce the self not to proper contrition, or "holy fear," but to meaningless triviality. Consequently, he is not a candidate for divine mercy or forgiveness and, without time to reform his lifestyle, he lacks hope for an eternal existence with God. Unlike the author of *Ars moriendi* writings, Law refuses to believe that "a good death" can overcome the totality of a ruined life. A truly good death is one that draws upon a lifetime of faith and righteous efforts, that summarizes character rather than denying its relevance. Yet both writers share a belief that dying gives clarity of moral vision, revealing the inescapable limits of one's capacities, choices, and values. "The greatness of what follows death" is fundamentally God, who is the measure against which human pursuits are judged.

Although in his suspicion of "death-bed conversion" Law seems more contemporary, the use of a "bad death" as warning strikes the modern reader as problematic. Is this because its prudential underpinnings appear dubious to us? Do some of us recoil from a mentality that believes "Get smart, get saved" to be the way to present Christian faith? Or do we need no reminder of "bad deaths," since our culture has convinced us that death is always a catastrophe, and all deaths will be "bad" and ought to go unmentioned? If we rely upon the autobiographers' testimonies, some deaths do indeed appear "bad" although not quite in Law's sense. Long-drawn-out illnesses, treated by means that leave the person diminished and terrified, result in "bad deaths" in our world. Or, closer to Law, there are persons whose major effort is denial and manipulation of their families, or who prefer isolation and despair to any emotional consolation. Perhaps these are today's variant of "Penitens." They have lost an opportunity to turn death as fate into death as "free act," or for an encounter with the true shape of their lives. But neither their relatives nor pastoral counselors would see these failures so harshly as Law sees Penitens' end. Today, like Bunyan and the author of *The Craft of Dying*, we would admit that some faithful Christians die "bad deaths" in the sense of deaths filled with temptations, pain, and distress—not, however, of extended denial or manipulation of others.

"Ardently to Seek . . ."

In the Wesleyan revival, and the form of evangelical spirituality derived from it, this admission was overshadowed by the other side of Calvin's picture. "Ardently to seek what nature dreads" became, as it had not generally been earlier, an idealized norm for all to follow. Although such an idea does not sound foreign to ancient accounts of martyrs' deaths, neither the "tame death" pattern described by Ariès, nor the sources already examined, stress this. Wesley argued for a state of "Christian perfection," full sanctification, within this life as a possibility toward which Christians were to strive. Complete freedom from sin did not mean infallibility or Godlikeness, but it did involve a conscious sense of full liberation into divine life. And Wesley himself admitted that "the generality of believers whom we have hitherto known were not so sanctified 'till near death" (Wesley 1981 [1777]:320). Perhaps something about "near-death" as a state may have served to release persons into this condition that Wesley called "perfection."

To support his claim, Wesley offers the case history of a Ms. Jane Cooper, whose "perfection experience" took place several months before her death. Ms. Cooper's assurance of Jesus' love became completely overwhelming before impending death. Although very sick, she said to a friend, "I have been worshiping before the throne in a glorious manner, my soul was so let into God." The account continues: "Some hours after it seemed as if the agonies of death were just coming upon her. But her face were full of smiles of triumph, and she clapped her hands for joy. . . . Afterward, she strove to speak, but could not. However, she testified her love, by shaking hands with all in the room" (Wesley 1981 [1777]:345–46). Ms. Cooper dies in an ecstatic condition, passing well beyond the solid trust of Mr. Stand-fast, into a "heavenly" mode of consciousness. She has been released not so much from sin as moral error, but from the restricted vision of earth itself. All that she is, is now identified with Christ, and she dies fully conscious of this as her true identity. In her we have reached the Christian equivalent to the case histories and perspective of Stephen Levine; the sanctified Ms. Cooper knows "who dies."

This pattern, although not directly intended by Wesley to represent an ideal for *dying*, did in fact become such among early Methodists (Schneider 1987:361). Joyous, ecstatic near-death scenes became a witness or testimony of one's love for heaven, one's ardent desire for that which nature dreads. Although in reality many persons continued the restrained, somber approach of a Bunyan to the deaths they saw and grieved (Rosenblatt 1983:68), it is this "joyous" pattern, and not Bunyan's or Calvin's, that determined the selection of *Death-Bed Scenes*, an anthology composed by David Clark, an American clergyman, in the 1850s. Clark saw Christian dying as joyous, eager, triumphant dying. It is neither stoic nor fearful nor filled with the kind of conflict earlier authors allowed for.

For instance, in one of the "case histories" a young woman missionary, very recently married, is dying. She is joyous and exuberant at the prospect. No word is so pleasant to her as "death." "Glorious!" is her first association to it. She knows she

will meet her dead mother very soon, but insists that to be with
God is far more important to her. As for her husband, she
assures him "Jesus will be your best friend" and adds: "We
shall soon, very soon, meet in a better world. If I thought we
should not, it would be painful indeed to part with you" (Clark
1855:330). But it is clearly not painful for her to die, and even
the temporary separation is minimized.

Note, however, that ties with relatives now occupy some of
the space reserved by earlier writers for the encounter with
God. This motif of "family reunion" came to dominate popular
nineteenth-century piety. The era of *Death-Bed Scenes* was also
the time of "the death of the other" or sentimental death, to use
Ariès' terms. Ariès studied French Roman Catholics rather
than English or American evangelicals, yet notes precisely the
same focus on ecstasy and family. Death and dying become glorious, sought-after experiences, unions with God and/or dead
relatives. His own case study is based on the diaries of one particular family, whose "baroque" piety and fascination with
romantic ecstatic dying mystified their old-fashioned
Calvinistic grandmother (Ariès 1981 [1977]:412ff.). It baffles
the modern reader of thanatology and pastoral care literature
as well. Dying seems to have brought young married couples
or parents and children together; it was not a separation but a
bond between them. In contrast, the few "ecstatic" deaths from
the transpersonal psychologists—we noted none in the autobiographies—do not serve to reinforce the family, but heighten a
sense of individual eternal selfhood.

Awe and Ultimacy

In confronting these varied resources from the past, we may
ask "Are these truly *resources* for us today?" Their approaches
to dying and to individual death as human situation are sufficiently varied, as well as different enough from our own, that
we cannot just embrace all of them with equal enthusiasm.
Most of us will find the Wesleyan "ecstatic death" ideal an ille-
gitimately generalized pattern, whose unfortunate result was
to make "joyous dying" a badge of authentic Christianity. When
Rahner claimed that the martyr is the model for true
"Christian death," this was *not* the feature of martyrs' deaths
he had in mind. Not ecstasy but "free act" should be the signifi-

cant feature of this ideal. Yet at the other extreme is the far more penitential and fearful tone of the *"Dies irae"* truly compatible with Christian hope? Not according to all of the twentieth-century theological writers on eschatology. Although Calvin may leave far more room than Wesley (or rather, than Wesley's possibility-become-norm) for natural affections and emotions, one intrinsic element of his outlook remains a firm insistence that all affliction is "God's will." Does this lead to worship of the executioner, in Soelle's words? How does it help us face the fact or possibility of humanly caused mass death?

Nevertheless, all of these Christian perspectives do manage to convey "the awe and ultimacy" of death. It is not ultimate because it marks "the end of everything," but because it forces an encounter of the self with God, and in turn of one's life as totality before God. "The Christian must surely be so disposed and minded that he feels within himself it is with God he has to deal throughout his life" (Calvin, *Inst.* 3.7.2). But near death, that fact looms more overwhelming and inescapable. God uses our weakness and affliction to make us recognize how we were always weak and afflicted, always in need of divine mercy. We may or may not directly benefit from this self-knowledge. But this emphasis upon total accountability makes death a situation where we can become totally disposed toward God. This theme all the writings discussed in this chapter share.

They also share a number of other features. Suspicion of "cheap consolation" is there, and certainly no one reviewing these traditional materials could equate belief in God and an afterlife with simple "wish-fulfillment." Even "easy dying" could be a sign of spiritual pride, of Ignorance and Vain-Hope. To die is not the same as to be saved. Although no one wants to rule out definitively all possibility of "last minute" or deathbed repentance, it is clear that a godly life is more of a witness than a "good" death.

There runs through most of these writings the sense that, for Christians, death ought to be faceable, for across the river awaits a Heavenly City. Therefore, to rely solely upon the theme of "the last enemy" is to misrepresent what the tradition held to be the proper mixture of awe, fear, and hope. Moreover, to what extent is death truly interpreted as a loss in this literature? For Law's Penitens, and others who die "badly," death turns all of worldly existence into "nothing," showing that it was "nothing" all along. Those who die "well," especially the ecstatic Ms. Cooper, lose nothing and gain heaven even before the point of death. For her, and for the others, dying is more a "gain" than a loss. Is this what Cullman would call "Platonism"? Or an exaggerated awareness of a legitimate spiritual possibility, that of glorified, resurrected identity with Christ?

On the whole, "awe and ultimacy" win out over consolation in the portrayals of what death as transition involves. It is a transition into Reality with a capital R. Moreover, God as judge, as that Reality whom we cannot avoid, figures just as centrally if not more so, than Christ as the beloved presence who will meet us at the time of death. When these are both participants in the drama, as for the *Ars moriendi*, it reinforces the sense that judgment and salvation go together. We can allow these writings to unlock the doors of our prejudices, our theological biases and beliefs, even when we do not wish to make complete, literal acceptance of everything in them a Christian norm. But all of these materials convey an expanded perspective on what death and near-death involve, and how to make these into Christian experiences of special significance.

A Christian Critique
of Contemporary Depth
Psychologies of Death

$\mathbb{W}$e now come to the final stages in our examination of perspectives on death. How can the visions of contemporary psychologies of death be placed in dialogue and mutual critique side by side with the roles of death in the Christian landscape of faith? To "critique" means to evaluate in accordance with certain norms or criteria. In any model of dialogue between two perspectives or bodies of knowledge, each has the opportunity to critique the adequacy and coherence of the partner-perspective. Christians who reflect on the contribution and challenge of psychology to their faith have produced critiques of psychological theory and practice in great number. In this chapter, we will attempt still one more critique of the psychological materials, based upon the insights we discovered in the Christian resources.

Situating Our Critique

Within the selection of materials we have examined, "critiques" abound. Their distance from contemporary American avoidance of death was indeed what led us to take these particular few theories so seriously. The depth psychological writers scrutinized here work with some awareness of the Freudian-Jungian tradition, and are in dialogue with each other about the adequacy of that legacy. Moreover, because virtually all the depth psychological and transpersonal theorists discussed unanimously oppose what they perceive to be the dominant values of North American society in regard to death, we may say that they join with Kübler-Ross in vigorously trying to awake us from our cultural sleep of silence and ignorance.

Yet in turn the autobiographers of Chapter 1, although often falling victims to the dominant pattern of denial, would not write on the topic of dying and death were they not hostile to silence and ignorance. They are as much the critics of our culture as are the psychological theorists and the theologians. Bitterness and anger run through many of the narratives as they chart the inability of Americans to face illness and death honestly. This is powerful testimony to their critical stance, however much it also at times exemplifies the distorted attitudes these authors themselves often share. In short, no one who writes on this topic is content with the manner in which our society encounters death, and *all* find something false and distressing to criticize in our cultural inability to face it.

What this means is that no "Christian" critique will likely be unique, if it begins with a call to overcome denial and repression of death. Almost everything along that line which Christians might want to say has already been voiced by the perspective of ethical naturalism. Then, too, as we have already seen, the weaknesses of naturalism as an approach have been well reviewed by exponents of the alternative depth psychologies of death. We saw how Hillman, for example, complained about our culture's "literalism" in equating all death with the physical process of dying, under the sway of the naturalist outlook. In fact, we may note how in some regard the theologians and pastoral care writers have been more naive than the depth psychologists in their enthusiasm for the ethical naturalist perspective.

Another reminder for those who support the need for a Christian critique of psychology is that the traditional "resources" of Christian faith do not all hang together tightly, or speak with one single voice. Not only do the traditional ones surveyed in the previous chapter differ greatly from the twentieth-century perspectives, but they do not all concur with each other. As for the biblical materials, these—as I hope we have shown—share a complexity that makes a wide variety of interpretations and extrapolations possible. For this reason, a project like that of Oden, who hopes to rely upon "tradition" in order to reveal the shallowness of the contemporary pastoral approaches, including those to death, will require a great amount of generalization and selectivity in regard to that tradition. Although all of the resources discussed in Chapter 8 do indeed stress the "awe and ultimacy" of death over any task of emotional adjustment to it, their outlooks do include quite a range of suggestions for handling the emotions that arise in response to death's nearness. Should dread or joy be the norm? How much room should be given to "natural" feelings? Here the materials critique each other, even if in other ways they stand united against certain twentieth-century assumptions.

Given all these potentials for mutual critiques, it nevertheless seems to us necessary to offer some evaluation of the depth psychological perspectives, based upon the images, norms, and visions generated by the Christian landscape of faith. We will assume that of all the depth psychological theories summarized in Chapters 2 to 5, that of Robert Lifton is probably the most powerful and comes closest to addressing the need for a comprehensive psychology of death. On the other hand, all three contemporary theorists—Becker, Hillman, and Lifton—demonstrate certain key advantages that make their ideas serious candidates for such a role. Certainly, all three self-consciously avoid the oversimplifications of the more popular and prevalent ethical naturalisms, and also avoid some of the reductionism and literalism of the classic Freudian heritage.

To state this more clearly, the trio of contemporary writers manages to accomplish the following three tasks. First, in their own ways, they leave space for the divine. They do not directly move "God" as an ontological reality into the middle of the psyche, but they leave room for the divine presence or image or encounter within their picture of who human beings are. That the shape of this space differs greatly among them is clear; yet all three find that some such opening up toward transcendence is necessary for an adequate apprehension of human experience. This is all, I believe, that Christians can ask of any psychological theory; Christ himself need not be named directly, nor need the shape left for the divine correspond precisely to his contours.

Even more directly, all move "death" from the edge or the ending of human life, into its center. Death as presence, as element to be taken into account, lies in the midst of life—and this they all agree is the central insight our culture represses and from which it frantically hides. Regardless of their very different imageries for death's presence, they all find it the missing dimension or ingredient in ordinary experience, however covertly. Because of this, all are engaged in an attempt to wrest encounter with death from its medicalized setting. All find deficient the current entanglement of mortality as human fact, with the political struggle over issues of institutional power and the health-care establishment. Whereas in the autobiographies and in Kübler-Ross the assumption or the claim often lurks, that were hospitals to become more humane, and were the power of the medical establishment curtailed, "death" would no longer be a human problem. It would be "natural" and "acceptable," and that would be that.

This confusion of levels of conflict, or oversimplified vision of the human psyche, is one of the targets Becker, Hillman, and Lifton all share. Not one of them finds death itself so reducible to external conditions, and even though Hillman and Lifton do not share Becker's position that denial is inevitable and death always catastrophic, they do not want to restrict its role to the chronological ending of biological life. In this, they join with the Christian and other religious traditions, none of which view the medical aspects of dying as ultimately significant. All religious traditions devise ways to stress the dying individual's need to move beyond preoccupation with bodily health and decay.

Finally, and as we will see, somewhat paradoxically, all three depth psychologists share with the Freudian tradition a deep ambivalence in regard to the body. In Becker, this ambivalence fades into hatred; in Hillman, it borders upon the Jungian forgetfulness of embodiment. In Lifton's work, there is a perhaps too "healthy-minded" an acceptance of vulnerability and limitation as necessary facets of embodiment. But in each case, they avoid a vision of human being that denies the problematic quality of embodiment, in favor of one that leaves room for this.

We may say that in one way or another, all three hold fast to Freud's dictum that "All organisms die for internal reasons," and try to weave such a claim into their views of persons and death. Their own vocabularies take them far from Freud's biological speculations about instincts and amoebas. Yet here again, all three appear aligned against a view, prevalent in our culture, that bodies are always young, healthy, beautiful, sexually attractive; and that when they fail, the sources of the catastrophe must be external to the person, accidental and too horrible to endure. The autobiographies, once again, provide indirect testimony to such a view, as all the while their narrators attempt to see through its destructive and illusory qualities.

Our critique, then, begins after this acknowledgment of the strengths of the best of the contemporary depth psychological perspectives. Nevertheless, there are still some weaknesses, gaps, and misformulations within these perspectives, in the eyes of Christian reflection. In spite of their strengths, these do not sufficiently move beyond naturalism, beyond twentieth-century individualism, and beyond the one-story nonmythic cosmos of our era. These criticisms depend of course upon our own portrayal of what the Christian landscape of faith requires, upon its vision of persons, God, the cosmos, and death. At least, it is this vision that will provide our foundation for the criticisms that follow.

Beyond Naturalism

This is the criticism that will no doubt sound most familiar to theologically oriented readers. The association of psychology, particularly Freudianism, with biological reductionism, is an established one, even if it does not do justice to the nuances of Freud's own thought (or to his ambiguous and confusing use of terms such as "instinct"). "The present development of human beings requires . . . no different explanation from that of animals," Freud insists during his arguments in *Beyond the Pleasure Principle*. This is the form of ethical naturalism that does easily equate to "reductionism," and is a sure target for theological and other critics. It is also not the variety we most frequently encounter in contemporary perspectives.

Instead, there are all sorts of ways to make "nature" into an ontological, trustworthy foundation upon which to build a positive, "human," and humane vision of life, with death as the "natural" ending of that life. All of the ethical "naturalists" would deny that humans and animals require "no different explanation," and all would use imagery of "nature" in ways vastly different in emotional tone from Freud's. Typical of this would be autobiographer Joan Gould's contrast between personal-human relationships that disappoint and bonds established by nature, of interlocking generations of mothers and daughters that endure and provide meaning and stability. Such a use of "nature" has been far more appealing than Freud's, and is frequently shared by Christians, including some of the pastoral writers on death.

From our perspective, however, this imagery represents a misguided, off-center starting point for authentically Christian reflections on the role of death in the midst of life. Up to a point, all three of the depth psychological thinkers we prefer agree with this criticism. For Becker, simplistically, "human" and "natural" are set in direct opposition. "Nature's values are bodily values, human values are mental values" (Becker 1974:31). Thus, nature is a negative force, an opponent, a feared presence of which the young child's mother is the psychic representative. Hillman, far more subtly, also relativizes the role of "nature" as foundation. No longer a "given," it is an image, and so returns to psyche as "earth," which is other than the "underworld" of psyche that interests Hillman most. It became one of the many Gods, or fantasies of soul, and so lost its nonpsychic, objective foundational quality.

Lifton's critique combines the insights of both Becker and Hillman, along with a touch of Jung. Humans are primarily symbolizing beings. This is our way of being "natural" and it implies that any opposition between "nature" and "culture," so dear to popular ethical naturalists, is not well grounded. If humans are as a natural species inveterate symbolizers, then our essence unites what Becker and Kübler-Ross manage to split apart, in different ways and for different purposes. Lifton carefully rejects the language of "instincts" as developed by Freud, for exactly this reason. It requires that we think, as Freud did, of explanations drawn directly from the behavior of nonhuman organisms. Neither death nor life can be, for us, "instincts." Nor does either lie beyond our human capacity for meaning. They are both, Lifton claims, symbolizable possibilities. His discussion of the five modes of symbolic immortality and the three experiential clusters of death-imagery depend upon this revision of ethical naturalism. Lifton's accommodation of nature and culture, organism and symbolism, is of a piece with his theme of reforging the broken connection between life and death.

Yes, but can there be a Christian critique of even this chastened view of naturalism? If we accept Hillman–Lifton's criticisms of Becker's (and Freud's) use of "nature" as a given, then can we still say that imagery drawn from the organic, "natural" realm is given too central a role in Lifton's theory? Does Lifton not join together too neatly, too "healthy-mindedly," dimensions of human existence that should be held in disjunction? If the answer is yes, then must Christians endorse a view that splits—at the level of imagery—human from "nature" in a way congruent with Becker's existentialist legacy? We will save this latter question for Chapter 10, in which we will deal directly with the construction of a Christian spiritual perspective on death. Still, in building a critique of contemporary depth psychology that directs attention to its most sophisticated rather than its crassest expressions, we may find that even these share certain biases and defects. Does Lifton rely too heavily, and at the wrong places, upon imagery of "nature" in his portrait of human beings and death?

The answer to this appears to be both yes and no. In stressing the validity of "symbolic immortality" Lifton builds upon the fact of human generational and historical continuity. For him, it is obvious that the human species is linked together over time, as each generation lives in mutual relatedness to its parent generation, and its progeny. This vision, which he derives from Erikson's work on "the lifecycle" and the cycle of generations, guides his understanding of the function of symbolic immortality modes. These express not our "horror" and denial of death, but the actuality of our link to other members of our species. The human race is made up of parents and children, not isolated atomistic individuals such as Becker postulates. Thus, biological continuity is a foundation for symbolic life.

When Lifton writes about the current situation, where the complete annihilation of all life is an imaginal possibility, he is particularly anxious to stress the foundational quality of "biological" imagery of survival. Not the hero or martyr, but the one who survives, is his ideal. The one who survives to build a world, establish a family, found a new generation, gives hope that out of death life may come. In contrast, the vision of nuclear annihilation—or other, less sudden catastrophes—is of a world without a future generation, without "nature" as humans hope for it to continue. All this is to emphasize that Lifton is rooted in a "biologically" grounded vision, even if he is sophisticated enough to treat this "biology" as imagery, as itself a partial product of human symbolization.

Is this wrong? Why should a Christian perspective find it inadequate? Isn't Lifton's outlook here congruent with Christian reverence for creation, and honor of the family as the "natural" unit through which individuals emerge, and within which they find their being? Although Lifton's insights may not be "wrong," the real heart of our critique is that they make biological generational continuity just too central a foundation for what we, and Lifton, ultimately want to affirm. It is not the tie to one's immediate family, or one's community or nation, but to the divine that provides the kind of ground for human existence, for death and immortality symbolizations, that Lifton seeks. It is in God, and not in the cycle of generations, that Christian faith sees the foundation for the human. Or, rather than pit these two possibilities against each other, Beckerian-fashion, we may insist that the levels at which each belongs are different. The cycle of generations will, like the human individual, have an end. As Brunner reminds us, "progress" within history is not the same as God's "eternal hope."

And this is where Lifton himself provides just the insight to express or leave room for such a possible revision of his theory. For, as we learned, the one mode of symbolic immortality that actually seemed to him to be the most "foundational" was the experience he called "transcendence." It was this, and not biological continuity, which grounded all four other modes. Transcendence is not itself "divine" but is a possibility for direct experience of the larger, more universal life that comes through death-immersion. "Transcendence" as Lifton describes it indeed leaves space for God, leaves space for a person to "see God and die," born anew into a wider, more profound, transfigured existence. At this point, then, however important the cycle of generations may be elsewhere in Lifton's psychological theory, it cannot serve to support what Lifton finally wishes to claim about death and immortality. Just as "transcendence" alone needs fleshing-out, so to speak, through one of the other four modes of symbolized immortality, so none of these modes can bring the person into a final and ultimate experience of this imagery.

Now this Liftonian priority cuts several ways. Not only does it require that "nature" and "biological continuity" become secondary expressions of some more basic core-experience. It also requires that "theological immortality" play this same role. Doctrines of immortality or resurrection cannot, in Lifton's view, be the "foundation" for an experience of transcendence. The relationship works in the reverse. Even identification with the sacred hero-founder, whose encounter with death helps followers integrate death and life, is itself made possible only because of the human capability for symbolization and "transcendence."

However, it is this form of theological immortality—and Lifton obviously thinks primarily of Christianity here—which comes closest for Christians to being the "foundation." From the Christian perspective as we have presented it, were it not for our tie with Christ, we would not have the possibility of moving from death to life, nor of symbolizing this adequately. In Christ, we share both his death and his resurrection, although the manner of the latter remains a matter of some ambiguity and debate among contemporary interpreters. "Transcendence" may represent whatever it is in human beings that makes such a tie possible from our end. But the "theological" mode of symbolic immortality is that which gives it form, which conveys for us the meanings that Lifton assigns partly to "transcendence." In neither case does "nature" or "biological continuity" play a central role. This is not to pit "nature" directly against Christ, who died to redeem it and us. Nor should it require us to pit our "natural" life so violently in opposition to our life in Christ that we must forcibly accept Calvin's vision of Christians who "ardently seek what nature dreads" in all things. But we should leave room for this as a possibility, for the Pauline disjunction between the "natural" person and the person made "new" in Christ, in a manner that "naturalism" at all levels fails to do.

Beyond Individualism

As we saw, the tie with Christ as presented in the biblical sources depends upon a mode of personal identity that is unfamiliar to those of us in twentieth-century Western culture. "Corporate personality" requires that what is unique to me, as myself, is less central to my "self" than my tie with some larger unit or collectivity. In the most ancient forms, it was clearly the social-collective unit such as the family, tribe, or nation whose life gave identity, and whose death would have been "the end of everything" for participants in these units. Such a model of selfhood is already replaced by an alternative form of "corporate personality" in the New Testament, where Christ is the one who binds together Jew and Greek, free and slave, male and female. In Christ we are all "one"; we share "in him." It is Christ who now "lives" in Paul, and who as the "new man" is the collective identity—the deepest self—of all members of his body. Although political and economic factors such as nationality and class undoubtedly influence who we are, it may be that older forms of "corporate personality" are simply inaccessible for postindividualized cultures. Nevertheless it seems as though some mode of identity other than our own culture's form of individualism must remain a norm for Christian faith.[1]

The difficulty with this claim is that, at another level, Christianity does indeed stress individual existence, life, and death in many ways. Not only is Christ himself a unique human individual, but the act of joining his body—whether as a single person, family, or household member, or as one of a tribe or nation "converted" en masse—requires a certain wrenching into individual choice or awareness of alternative options. Even if Baillie sentimentalized it, Christian faith has traditionally affirmed that "individuals matter to God." No vision of collective-communal identity should obscure this, or should dismiss the role of the individual (as a few of the theological writers on eschatology tried to do). The style of "individuality" endorsed by Christians, however, should be compatible with the theological affirmation that we are who we are "in Christ."

1. An interesting recognition of this point of view may be found in David Augsburger's *Pastoral Counseling across Cultures* (1986). Aware that in many third world cultures patterns of selfhood resembling those we have labeled "corporate personality" are still the norm, Augsburger attempts to describe counseling strategies appropriate to those settings, severing pastoral counseling from dependence upon individualistic models of personhood familiar to us (Augsburger 1986:79–110). Persons in cultures that value embeddedness and interdependence are just as fully "human" as those from cultures that extol independence; they are just as capable of leading mature Christian lives. This outlook both relativizes the "universality" of our psychological models, and draws attention to features of Christianity that implicitly critique these.

A critique of psychological theories on this point requires that we ask them to leave space for such alternative forms of identity. We can only ask that psychologists refrain from identifying the Western, contemporary isolated self with "universal human nature," in such a way as to make all alternatives appear pathological or immature. Of all the thinkers we examined, Kübler-Ross and those, like Becker, influenced by the existentialist legacy appear most vulnerable to this criticism. Becker in particular paints a portrait of a self so isolated, defensive, and terrified of bonds to others, that each dependency spells "death." And death, to this self, can never be less than the end of everything.

Kübler-Ross as well, in spite of her very different attitude toward "nature" and death, accepts in principle a self whose individual uniqueness is all. This self's emotions, desires and psychological processes know no bounds, and exist in a universe where they will spontaneously harmonize with all other selves' emotions, desires, and processes. This is where her view departs greatly from Bowlby's equally naturalistic but far more somber vision. In the eyes of Kübler-Ross, no constraints should be placed on each self, no possible criteria for behavior exist externally or should be imposed upon the self. This was Miller-McLemore's criticism of Kübler-Ross' popular mixture of ethical naturalism and humanistic hedonism, and it is a criticism that extends to all who reduce ethical obligation to the self's need to follow its "natural" spontaneous inner promptings.

These selves inhabited the autobiographies, indeed dominated many of them. Each self conveyed its fragile set of meanings independently, each set of meanings gained at least some validity because a unique self had discovered them, held them. Everywhere in those testimonies we found not only the obvious evidence of Becker–Kübler-Ross selves, such as emotional isolation and denial of dependencies. We found ethically dubious paths of action justified entirely on the ground that a particular individual chose freely to pursue them. We also found, in the very autobiographical process, endorsement of individual selfhood as the foundation, the center and creator of meanings. Whether naturalist meanings, Christian or existentialist, whether sacred or secular, each framework was secured upon this precarious rock.

Given this massive commitment to a contemporary form of individual identity, Lifton's theory becomes a significant alternative. As we have already seen, Lifton does not find that death at the individual level is "unimaginable," for it is far from being an "end of everything." This phrase might best be reserved for the total destruction of all life and potential for life on earth, the "petulant blasphemy" that is indeed unimaginably horrifying. Lifton insists that human continuities precede human isolation; that mutual dependence is not a threat, but a constituent ingredient of normal selfhood. Here, Bowlby's vision of nature, the human situation of childhood helplessness, and the universal need for "attachment" would fit as well. Distortions of human connnectedness, such as totalitarian ideologies support, are indeed among Lifton's targets. But, unlike so many who received the existentialist legacy, Lifton does not eschew all forms of community and connection as "inauthentic."

As we have seen, Lifton's own way to establish connectedness is through the imagery of generations, of the past as the realm of parents and the future as the realm of progeny. This, I believe, is more effective in regard to this issue, than it was as a foundation for the ultimate source of death and immortality imagery. It is surely more effective than the "Jungian" solution of interiorizing all communal realities into the archetypal imagery of "the collective unconscious." Although Jung sometimes uses the term "collective" to function as a synonym for "social" or "national" or "ethnic" (Jung 1953 [1943]:#240 and note 8) the most fundamentally "religious" or mythic levels of the collective unconscious are depicted stripped of such connotations. These can be retrieved by an individual in magnificent isolation from other empirical selves, as indeed Jung portrays himself throughout his autobiography. Jungian writers such as Hillman perpetuate this use of "collective" to substitute for what we might normally call "interpersonal," and indeed Hillman's vision of the role of death in soul is particularly weak here. Plurality within soul, but not of souls, seems to be his ideal.

And yet, once again, Christian faith does not require a renunciation of all forms of individuality, nor should it entirely renounce its legacy of "Platonism" (Cullman) and the "authenticity paradigm" (Wyschogrod) in favor of a "social self" too flat or one-dimensional to be "soul," to live as an interior self in relation to God. It is these depressing alternatives, appearing so often in theological and philosophical writings, which may have led psychology to take over the role of counselor to the dying. At this point, however, we merely need to insist that, contra Hillman at his angriest, Christianity does not confirm "the heroic ego," the isolated, autonomous self for whom death is terror and total annihilation. The "self" that lives hidden with Christ in God, or the "self" whose life has been replaced by the life of Christ: these are the eschatological "subjects" of Christian hope. Such a self is a long way from the self of twentieth-century individualism, the frantically fearful and finally pathetic self of Becker and so many of the autobiographical narratives.

Beyond the Demythologized Cosmos

The categories of "myth" and "demythologizing" have had a controversial and confused history both in and out of theology. It has been one of the pervasive themes of this work that "myth" is the necessary and appropriate framework within which the encounter with death can come to expression. "Myth" builds a landscape of faith for Christians, and the central narrative cannot be adequately transferred into other frameworks without catastrophic reduction and impoverishment. Even existentialist experiments in "demythologizing" seem steeped in mythic categories, and the best of such thinkers (Brunner, for one) clearly recognize the futility of abandoning these altogether. We cannot necessarily ask that psychologies of depth directly endorse our own "myth," but we need psychologies that recognize myth, and when pushed to their own limits deploy its categories. We also need psychologies that are aware of doing this, aware that their own language more properly belongs to "myth" than to natural science.

Depth psychology uses the language that we have called "myth." It has done so from its own beginnings, in Freud's "mythology" of dual instincts at war against each other. In its contemporary representatives whose work we examined, this adherence to myth is retained and strengthened, as all three recognize the need to liberate psychological discourse from its biological-mechanistic framework. Our argument has been that to encounter death at the level of thought and theory, at the level of imagery and personal experience, requires a language of

206 Death in the Midst of Life

206   Death in the Midst of Life

myth. Even when myth is "seen through" and treated as myth, it preserves that which no alternative language can convey.

We can now see how, in these selected depth psychological thinkers, "death" functions powerfully as an image of a transition from one mode of being into another. For Freud, the movement from organic to inorganic is a retracing and a return to the primordial beginning. For Jung, death/rebirth are paired together, as symbols of inner psychic transformation. And for the three more contemporary theorists, the self who can die "out of life" and into "soul"—to use Hillman's style—is the human self renouncing ordinary, restricted, denial-based existence.

It is here that Kübler-Ross' perspectives, both earlier and later, provide both confirmation and contrast. In the more obviously "naturalist" period, death as biological ending stands unchallenged, although as a "final stage of growth" it offers a promise of fulfillment for the organically imaged self. In this sense, death is not truly "transition" although the dying process provides exactly that movement from inauthentic to authentic that the other theories want to express. The "later" Kübler-Ross, of the caterpillar-into-butterfly vision of automatic, universal transition, has literalized psychologically powerful symbolism into religious doctrine, so to speak. At this point, as with some of the transpersonalists, one may speak of an obvious conflict of myths between the Christian landscape of faith and the alternatives such as Kübler-Ross' "harmonialist" spiritualism. There really is a conflict here, as almost all parties have recognized, but it is no longer that of psychology versus theology.

Moreover, the caterpillar-into-butterfly image is so certain, so grounded in "nature," and thus so inevitable, that "death" ceases to serve as the drastic rupture, the transition during which the ego, or the finite self, must "die" in order to see God. "Caterpillar into butterfly" is inadequate to the way Becker, Hillman, and even Lifton wish to employ "death" as symbol of drastic transition. From the perspective of Christian faith, the totality of death as negation and destruction—something stressed by theological writers—makes imagery drawn from "natural" continuities secondary if not suspect. According to Paul, seeds "die" in the earth before they can sprout; had he used Kübler-Ross' image, his emphasis would have been upon the drastic dissolution of form required for the emergence of the butterfly from its cocoon. Yet Kübler-Ross' own transition is surely additional testimony to the human need for myth, for imagery that claims ultimacy for the encounter with death. Emotional acceptance, and even "the final stage of growth," is not enough to do justice to what death as human situation means—even if we do not find her own mythic solution adequate.

The language of myth appropriate to either a psychology of death, or a theological system, requires both "times" and "places." It requires perspectives, points of view beyond that of "earth." Hillman, self-consciously advocating such "place"-language when he employs and extends the metaphor of "underworld," recognizes how restricted and confined ordinary psychological discourse has become. "Earth's surface" and the ego are its only territory, its only personage, childhood its major way to speak of existential beginnings (as in Becker's fantasies of *causa sui* ascribed to children). Not the material world, but materialism and literalism are the enemies of myth. In the world of the autobiographies, we found this as individuals struggle to express "awe and ultimacy" amid detailed descriptions of medical treatments and hospital policies. A mythic framework leaves room for earth's surface, but restores it to proper proportions, to one perspective out of several.

On this point pastoral writers such as Oden, anxious to liberate Christian counseling from captivity to psychological perspectives, may have confused two issues. The use of traditional Christian resources as alternatives to Kübler-Ross and other psychological exponents of naturalism is one strategy for critique of earlier trends, as we saw. Yet is the point of such moves to return to the past as Christian past, or return to a faith-perspective that leaves room for awe and ultimacy in the face of death? If the latter, then that need not lead to an irrevocable dismissal of all psychological theory, a rejection of all psychologies in the name of tradition. It is, however, a call for a different quality of psychological theory, as well as a more cautious endorsement of psychologists' imageries, than much of the pastoral literature reveals.

We have criticized these depth psychological theories for overreliance on "nature" and organic imagery, for adherence to contemporary individualistic models of selfhood, and for insufficient or oversimplified "myths." In the process, we seem to have reverted to a vision of Christianity that might easily be misperceived as Platonic, antimaterial, conservatively hostile to individual uniqueness and freedom, and finally overcommitted to an "otherworldly" and prescientific cosmology and eschatology. We have, in short, come close to advocating exactly what so many of the theological writers despise and regret, and what the majority of autobiographers would find opaque. Have we indeed merged Christianity to such unpalatable and unfashionable causes? I do not believe so. Yet, in the next chapter, I hope to show how a Christian vision of death within the landscape of faith can also liberate us from captivity to some of our era's most popular prejudices and dichotomies. This will be the cost, I believe, of an adequate integration of death into the midst of Christian life.

10

A Christian
Perspective
on Death

In the previous chapter, we presented a critique of the psychological theories of death, based upon a synthesis of the Christian "resources" surveyed in Chapters 6 to 8. In this, the concluding chapter, we turn to the task of presenting a Christian vision of the role of death in the landscape of faith, informed by the depth psychologies. We are interested in an understanding of what "death" means, how humans encounter it, and who we are in Christ as we encounter death. It is, I believe, within such a vision of the landscape of faith that our lives may be structured, and practical guidance sought. Lacking such a vision, Christians as well as their counselors will inadvertently depend upon the values and visions of the culture at large, or of the psychological theories that inform most of the pastoral psychology writers on death.

Were we conducting a totally symmetrical "dialogue," what ought to follow Chapter 9 is a "psychological critique" of the Christian resources. After all, not one of the texts discussed in Chapters 6 to 8 is immune from psychological analysis, and some of these seem to cry out for it. Why is this step omitted? Or is it?

Our answer is that twentieth-century Christian thought has been continuously embroiled in a "critique" of its own heritage. Indeed, this heritage is itself made up of successive "critiques," going back, I believe, to the materials of the New Testament itself. Far from merely reflecting first-generation Christian piety, Paul was, in many of the materials we have cited, "critiquing" the spiritual vision of his congregations. Mark's Gospel may be looked on this way as well, as a counter to the version of "the good news" proclaimed by a dominant party within the early Christian movement. Perhaps this is why the results, at least in regard to death, are a less than fully consistent set of statements, stories, and claims, embedded in contexts that are anything but straightforward—hence the subsequent variety of Christian theologies of death, as potentially valid elaborations of the biblical materials.

On the other hand, the theological and pastoral materials discussed in Chapter 6 also contain many critiques and reformulations based upon nontraditional sources. Freud, Marx, and the existentialists all were incorporated as voices in the rereadings of Christian eschatology we surveyed, or in the agenda to purge Christianity of supposed "Platonism." The heavy pastoral reliance upon Kübler-Ross could also be seen as a "critique" of traditional perspectives, and some of the authors who relied upon her ideas did indeed embark upon a severe criticism of the religious tradition's unwillingness or inability to deal with death "realistically," that is, according to the standards set by ethical naturalism.

On the other hand, we did not see evidence of sustained, careful use of depth psychological materials to reinterpret the tradition in ways that, to us, seem most necessary and most exciting. Most frequently, Freud was invoked to show how Christian hopes for an afterlife were vulnerable to dismissal as "wish fulfillment," following the Freud of *The Future of an Illusion*. Yet in one way or another, authors both traditional (Calvin) and modern (Gerkin) recognized how the Stoic alternative, the attitude upheld by Freud himself, was *not* adequate to the deepest insights of Christian faith. Even if it may be dismissed as "wish fulfillment," Christianity has something to say about dying and death that does not correspond to the "heroic humanism" that others find noble and appealing.

We will base our re-visioning upon points where the tradition can either be most sharply differentiated from the psychological theories, or where these contribute greatly to a clarification of what is at stake. The latter can, I believe, help in gaining distance from some of the polemical agendas of the theological writings, so that we can return to the traditional sources and encounter them with more attention to the nuances of their claims. The result will not be a systematic theology of death, but a psychologically informed spiritual vision that encompasses the role of death in Christian faith.

Death-Immersion

Our central, most basic motif emerges out of Christianity's own central narrative, that of Jesus' death and resurrection. And if "what happened to Christ, happens to the Christian," then the role of death in the landscape of faith is also central. We do not have to begin by a return to the fall narrative, as Augustine and so many subsequent Christian thinkers have done. We do not have to answer an impossible question such as "Is death natural to humankind?" based upon an ironic mix of ethical naturalism and the narrative of Genesis 2–3. Or, at least, if we wish to do this, I do not believe it is the only or the most appropriate starting place for a Christian perspective on death. Following the insight of theologians who emphasize divine involvement, pain, and suffering as intrinsic to God's character as well as Christ's redemptive death, we may see this as a far more appropriate narrative upon which to ground our reflections. Even if it is the case that "God did not intend death. . . . In God there is no death," it is Christ's death that brings death and God most closely together. And it is this that brings us, as baptized Christians, into relation to both Christ and death in a new way. It is this that makes possible the characterization of our past, our old self, as given over to death. And it is this that gives us power to claim, "For we have died, and our lives are hid with Christ in God."

"Death" in this landscape of faith ceases to be a moment at the chronological ending of biological life. It becomes a moment, a movement, a transition, available at every point where the infinite life of God touches our finite human selfhood. It is a continuous possibility, as Paul's many exhortations to "put to

death" behaviors and attitudes from the old, "dead" self indi-
cate. The body's dying may indeed be a sign of this process, but
the two are not equivalent. Were we to diagram this relationship, we would depict "death" as a border impinging upon every
moment, not a final closure at the end of a straight line.[1]

Here, I believe, the value of depth psychology has been to
rediscover the human need for some form of "death-encounter"
or "death-experience" within the midst of our existence.
However awkward Freud's version of a biologically based
"death instinct" may be, he along with Jung and contemporary
figures help sensitize us to the biblical insistence that at no
time is human life "death-free." There is no such thing as a
deathless person, in or out of Christ. We cannot image ourselves as if we could shed this relation to death, or invoke it
only as a final and entirely external happening. The "death-
immersion," the moment when the self "sees God and dies," is a
way to bring this continuous relation to awareness, and to seek
consciously (if not ardently) what "nature" in the sense of ordinary selfhood, dreads. Such death-immersion is built into
Christianity, is in fact so central to its landscape of faith that
no promise of "life abundant" should or could exclude it.
Relation to Christ links our life, and our death, to his; it never
exempts us from needing such a relation. To read our tie with
Christ as "freeing" us from death, as if it did, would be to fall
into Christianism, Hillman's caricature of Christian faith.

Alas, at least some of the twentieth-century theological and
pastoral materials come close to this descent. In their reaction
against the sentimental religious colonization of the afterlife,
as exemplified by the Victorian evangelicals' death-bed scenes
we examined, contemporary religious thinkers have gone over-
board in stressing how "life-oriented" and "this-worldly" the
authentic "Hebraic" vision of Christianity really is. The polemic
of Cullman et al. against "Platonism" and "otherworldliness"
may have been in a good cause (even if as biblical scholarship it
misrepresents ancient sources) if it tried to break the link

1. What is by all means to be avoided in any such possible diagram is the
clear division of human existence into "margins" and "center," with God ban-
ished beyond the "edges" while the center is self-sufficient, the locale of death-
free, confident life. Dietrich Bonhoeffer both vividly draws this picture and
then rebels against it in his own near-death reflections (Bonhoeffer 1967:175).

forged among faith, joyful dying, and a too-cozy heaven. Christians should be engaged with "history," with embodied fullness of life—not a sickly, escapist yearning for death.

But an alternative reading of this campaign against "Platonism" is that it expresses at the level of theology the same intensified fear and denial that one finds in American culture at large, prior to Kübler-Ross and the death-awareness movement. If Christianity is a religion of life, not death, if any "befriending" of death is dismissed as "Platonism," then our common everyday denial can be justified. And so, a tremendous break with the tradition of Calvin and Bunyan was created within theological reflection, and a gap left in care for the dying that Kübler-Ross and psychological thanatology was able to fill. If even a traditionally oriented spiritual writer such as Nouwen had to seek out and cite Hillman in order to justify establishing a continuous relation to death ("befriending"), then we may see the depletion worked by the twentieth-century theological campaign. To promote a "Hebraic" vision dedicated only to "fullness of life" would be a fine thing in a culture that had established some viable, nonrepressive relation to death. Within contemporary America, it likely serves the same function as "Americanized Freudianism," which assures us that the unconscious cannot ever conceive or imagine death. It legitimates our own denial.

This harsh verdict may be unfair. The purge of "Platonism" was in origin a move to reinvolve Christians with history, with the political and military catastrophes of the World Wars, and with the search for justice among the world's peoples. The rediscovery of biblical eschatologies was clearly an expression of this agenda. Nevertheless, its indirect and perhaps more typically Americanized effect has been rather different. It seems to support a vision of human fulfillment stressing health, youth, material prosperity, and individual subjective satisfaction, a vision of Christ as the one who promises "wholeness" and "growth." It is hard to come out against wholeness, growth, or health as goals, but are these adequate reexpressions of the Christian's hope? That the words for "salvation" and "health" originally derive from the same root, does not settle the question as asked today, for us. Ironically, such goals as the twentieth century's rediscovered "Hebraic" vision holds forth, make it even harder for us to hear how central the "death-immersion" motif is within the New Testament and the

Christian tradition. They seem to promise exactly the exemp-
tion from death that Cullman et al. never intended, but for
which the war against supposed "Platonism" paves the way.

Death-immersion, death-encounter, reaches into the deepest
levels of the self. The "totality" of death, in its various imageries
of separation and mutilation, stresses this. This, as we have
seen in Chapter 7, is where the theories of Hillman and Lifton
are particularly helpful in illuminating the biblical imagery.
Whether the person is a union of body and soul, or a whole indi-
visible entity, the imagery of "death" works totalistically, as
does the imagery of "participation" in Christ's death. There is
no corner of the self that "survives," that emerges unscathed in
the Christian's following of what happened to Christ.

Here perhaps Jungian terminology is misleading in its original,
pre-Hillmanian form. For Jung, only the ego or the persona "dies."
The Self-archetype does not, cannot. Which is the "real I"? Some
Jungian Christian writers such as David Cox have found this
ego/self division quite adequate to the Pauline claims about "new
life" and Christ's "I" living within. I am not so sure that it retains
the necessary quality of "totality" for the original imagery's intent.
Hillman, who breaks with Jung's legacy and eliminates "the Self"
as a monotheistic replication of the heroic ego, may be closer to the
original Pauline intention, ironically! Do not reserve a cornerstone
of the "real person" that will make the soul's death less sweeping,
his view would remind us. To befriend death is to open oneself up
to a sweeping, total encounter with its reality as hidden presence
in one's ongoing life. And it is this "totality" of death as negation
and destruction, as separation from the past, from which all the
Pauline death-language derives its power.

If death-immersion reaches down into the uttermost depths
of soul, does it also tear us as far away from earth's surface in
the other direction? Or, to put this in theological language, how
ultimately do we want to link "death" with God? Is there, as
Moltmann believes the crucifixion proclaims, "death in God"?
Or is this to overdo a valid and critical insight, perhaps for reasons similar to those that fueled the original campaign against
"Platonism"? Recall that Nouwen, on the farther side of
"befriending death" and after a period of intense personal identification with the Christ of the Passion narrative, nevertheless
maintains more firmly than ever that "In God there is no
death." God did not intend death, does not want it. In the final

eschaton, death will be ended forever, and the role it once played and now plays in the totality of existence will be no more. Note that this concern is not identical to that of *human* "nature," mortal or immortal. But it is a question about the limit of death-imagery, its final and ultimate scope.

Although my own reading of the New Testament and interpretation of the tradition tend toward Nouwen's perspective on this issue, at this point I should repeat the caution about theological agendas that legitimate American society's denial and ignorance. Were there no death in God, there would still be death in us, in ways our cultural context finds very difficult to acknowledge. To claim that "God did not intend death" is not to say that finally "There is no death," or that the transition mislabeled death is no real rupture, loss, or negation at all. To die for Paul may indeed be "gain," but that is on the farther side of a life given over to sharing Christ's death. It would, I believe, be a distortion of the Christian tradition, and of Nouwen's insight into the heights of its landscape of faith, to endorse a view that looked and felt so much like Kübler-Ross' caterpillar-into-butterfly vision. That is not the invariable, inevitable result of reaffirming a level of meaning, transcendence, and reality "beyond death," but it is a possible liability of such a claim. Nevertheless, I believe that some such claim is indeed intrinsic to Christian faith.

The Body as Ambivalent Sign

Christianity has, from its beginnings, been filled with bodies— Christ's body on the cross, his broken body and shed blood in the Lord's Supper, and the church as his "body." Not only does body-imagery pervade the New Testament, but the Pauline treatment of "body" as category has been the topic of much research and debate. Although this continues today, for our purpose it is important to acknowledge that the campaign against "Platonism" on behalf of "Hebraic" holistic views of body/self, is on one point entirely well grounded. "Body" could serve as a complex sign in early Christian thought only if it counted for something. Persons in Pauline writings are embodied enough so that the self, however divided and at war, is so precisely through its body. Measured over against a world whose common slogan was "The body is a tomb," early Christians appeared to hold a relatively positive and appreciative stance toward embodiment.

Their world, however, is no longer our world. The North American context of today apprehends embodiment in an entirely different manner, and pins hopes upon bodies as vehicles of self-fulfillment. Whether our attitudes would have amazed or disgusted those of Hellenistic persons is beside the point. As Hillman states it, literalism and materialism in regard to bodies is our problem, not overspiritualization. We have tried for too close an identification of psyche with body, or at least the wrong kind of identification. The testimony of the autobiographies on this point is disturbing. Bodily decay, mutilation, and deterioration bring social and existential humiliation to many of the sufferers. To some, the choice of isolation is preferable, for to be gazed upon as dying body is more than they can bear. This was not a universal problem, but it would have been incomprehensible to the author and readers of *Ars moriendi*, and goes unmentioned in the list of "temptations" peculiar to dying. As a concern, it appeared in enough of the contemporary narratives to make the alternative of a "Platonic" dichotomy between body and true self seem surprisingly appealing. The Platonist would be far less likely to interpret the body's decay as personal failure and humiliation.

Is this indeed an argument for a return to Christian Platonism? Should the theological purge of "Greek" elements be discarded in favor of a stance that once again encourages a dualistic view of the self? I believe the Cullmanian diatribe against "Platonism"—whatever its original reasons or motivations—has hardly helped in guiding Christians today, in our society, come to terms with the mortality and vulnerability of their bodies. Nor has the Christian enthusiasm for "holism" and the unified person led to a more complex and compassionate approach to dying as human experience. Ironically, it seems to legitimate the message of our culture about bodies as unproblematic equivalents of selves. To say this, and to argue against reliance upon the dichotomy of "Hebraic" (good) versus "Greek" (bad) is to take a fairly unfashionable position. It appears that "wholeness," "wellness," and "holistic" models of the person have popular appeal, and have been linked enthusiastically to the authentic "Hebraic" biblical view by many.

The confusion on this question is very great in our culture. For illustration, recall the several positions of Kübler-Ross. As pure ethical naturalist, organic imagery controls her vision in *On Death and Dying*. The body's ending is the closing of life's circle, and the ending of personal identity. These images could be upheld, even when the case history that supposedly illustrated them was of a pious Christian for whom personal postbodily continuation ("being with the Lord") is an intrinsic expectation. For the consistent ethical naturalist, body or organism equals self, and "death" is the closing of both (or their return to the "inorganic state," in the case of Freud). To "accept" death here means to face this prospect of annihilation or personal extinction, and assent to it.

Yet when Kübler-Ross titles an anthology *Death: The Final Stage of Growth*, there is implied in this a separation of psychic from somatic. Death is most surely not well described as the final stage of bodily "growth," and the upbeat title must only refer to the self's own completed quest for actualization and fulfillment at the time approaching death. This implicitly dualistic picture is indeed what the book supports, and is also quite compatible with a writer such as Bunyan insofar as he too depicts the struggle of the self to fulfill its vocation, as it heads into the final passage. Both body and psyche undergo something drastic, but their respective adventures must be described using two different narratives.

Finally, there is the Kübler-Ross of caterpillar-into-butterfly, the dominant and entirely dualistic "Platonic" image of *On Death and Children*. Here, no longer does the body's death count at all, and everyone may expect a transition from one form of selfhood to an improved form of selfhood, without fail. This is the view that dominates writing on near-death experiences, and appears to be near-normative for New Age spirituality. It is anything but "holistic," and confident that "the person" can experience quite severed from the "cocoon" of a body, left behind at death.

It is against this background that we must ask how embodiment is construed in the Christian landscape of faith and how depth psychology can help us in portrayal of the body's meanings. The Pauline writings have a special status as a resource for the first question, because they deal so explicitly with "body" as category. The answer they provide is that the body is an ambivalent sign of the self. In some ways, it is the person, pure and simple. At other points, especially in situations of stress or conflict, it is itself divided into "inner person" and "members," and these divisions both take on what we would call "psychological" qualities. At still other points, the body is discardable. It is a garment, a tent—or can be left behind in ecstatic states. Overall, this body, the one we are or

have or wear now, is mortal and weak and fallible. It may be the
temple of the Holy Spirit, but it is also given over to death. As we
have seen the death-language of the New Testament, explicitly
"symbolic" as it is, is also intended to cover embodiment. Hence the
confusion when Paul describes the destruction of the old body/self
in baptism, and the new life given to what is nevertheless still the
"mortal" body of the old age. At minimum, our categories of symbolic versus physical, or our dichotomy between "holistic" and
"dualist" do not do justice to this array of usages.

And it is here that the depth psychological theories can
really assist us, I believe, in sorting through these. For depth
psychology as well ranges from pure materialism (the Freud of
Beyond the Pleasure Principle) through a partial separation of
psychic from biological forces into a relationship that appears
clearly "dualistic." But in all cases, what interests its theorists
is not just the question of whether the person is one entity or
two joined together. It is concerned above all with motivations,
drives, forces, instincts, desires; to name and trace these is to
tell the story as both Freud and Jung read it. Both claimed
that the person as motivated is the person divided. The language of "levels" and Jung's "balance" model are only two of the
many metaphors generated by these theorists to unravel the
tangled pathways of the self-as-desiring. All of these involve
the creation of "agencies" within the self—forces and powers
and archetypes and Hillman's Gods—at work against each
other and engaging the physical organism in their warfare.

Those who inherit from the Freudian legacy vary as greatly as
Becker and Lifton do in regard to their appropriation of his materialism. For Becker, the warfare of two instincts becomes the
warfare of real self against body, a solution at odds with the complexity of the Pauline-"Augustinian-Lutheran" tradition itself.
For Lifton, the language of instincts has to be purged from depth
psychology, because it is insufficiently "psychological." Yet the
body contributes to the person's and culture's symbolizations for
death and life, and its vulnerability to pain, its sleep and waking
cycle, and its boundedness are intrinsic to its potential for symbolism. For Lifton, unlike for Becker, we *are* rather than *have*
bodies—but we are not bodies in the way Freud's amoebas are.

The Jungian tradition is far more "dualistic" on this issue, rele-
gating the body to oblivion insofar as the individuation process is
construed as purely intrapsychic. Hence, Hillman's appropriation

and transformation of this legacy could split soul from body as perspectives, assigning one to the underworld (the unconscious) and the other to earth's surface. Hillman's adaptation of "Greek" language and Greek gods emphasizes this psychological version of "Platonism." It is the ego who lives on earth's surface, however, and the ego for whom body equals material organism. Hillman is still a depth psychologist, more interested in charting psychic conflict and its pathos than in doing metaphysics. The body, the heroic ego, and psychology's own materialism and biologism all go together. This, Hillman believes, is our era's blindness. He would clearly find the theological campaign on behalf of "Hebraic" holism direct evidence of this, a sign of "Christianism's" own brand of cultural materialism.

Virtually all of these psychological theorists caution against naive endorsement of a "holistic" embodiment that allows no room for conflict and civil war within the self. All would find the campaign against "Platonism" fought by theological writers to be based on a false idealization of embodiment as potentially unproblematic. Depth psychology teaches somber caution about the ambiguities of embodied, vulnerable selfhood. It is, in this respect, un-healthy-minded in regard to the possibilities of embodiment. This does not lead it to direct contempt for the body (Becker is really the exception here), but its overall message is far closer to the ambiguous and conflict-laden imagery of Paul than is that of many of the theological writers. Pain, weakness, and decay are the stuff of embodiment. These become symbolized and psychologized into forces and desires that range from rage to humiliation and self-hatred. Yet the self must somehow learn to affirm and integrate its embodiment, even if that goal lies beyond our psychic means.

This convergence of biblical and psychological thought should not be oversimplified. We do not need to claim that Jung and Paul are saying the same thing. Certainly, Freud is not saying the same thing as Paul. But all unite in finding the body a pathway through which death becomes a psychological factor to be taken into account. All find "mortal body" a meaningful term, without necessarily postulating a contrasting "immortal" entity, whether resurrection body or Platonic soul. In their enthusiasm for holism, it is this somber ambiguity, the link of living organism with potential for death, which disappears from the Christian writers rediscovering the positive value of embodiment. Death can then become for them, as Cullman supremely illustrates, an external "enemy" with no interior representation within the self.

Here, I believe, Christians might do well to recover their tradition and its resources. Not just the "awe and ultimacy" of death, but the role of the "mortal body" as carrier and reminder of death, is a valid expression of the Pauline strand of New Testament spirituality. Since our era's worldview is not that of the Hellenistic age, but on this point its dubious opposite, we do not need more versions of "Christianism's" healthy-minded endorsements of embodiment as "good" and death as external evil. We do not need any encouragement for views that exclude weakness, pain, and mortality from our sense of ourselves as embodied beings. Civil war within the self is not the final Christian or depth psychological *telos*, but it remains an expression of our life within a yet-unredeemed existence. The body plays a part in this civil war, its energies and "members" recruited by psyche and spirit on both sides of the conflict. The body as mortal is a sign of Christ's real and present work of redemption, but also of the "futility" and death to which all creation is nevertheless still subject. This, and no vision less complex and ambiguous, is the appropriate vision of the body as bearer of meanings, and of the embodiment of the self in the landscape of faith.

Death and Justice Imagery

One theme that runs through this work is the inadequacy of imagery drawn from "nature" and organic life to encompass what Christians have traditionally wished to say about death, and what we still should continue to say. The theological ground for this, explored in Chapters 6 and 7, was the insight that the death of Christ is the central, formative death in Christianity; it gives shape to the landscape of faith as no other death can do. Hence it becomes a beginning place for further reflection on the roles of death. Christ's death was organic (there were medical causes of death by crucifixion) but the overall manner of death can best be described, in Moltmann's words, as "judicial murder." Categories of justice, judgment, punishment, and what we call "politics" enter into the accounts of this death, and into the subsequent theological elaborations of its meaning. These elaborations include the motif of Christ as victorious conqueror of evil spiritual powers and principalities, even as he became victim of their earthly representatives. Because of this, questions as to whether death in general is "natural" or "unnatural" should, I believe, not be allowed to determine the scope and direction of a Christian perspective on death.

Yet is there any role for this language of judgment and justice and military conflict today, in Christian thinking about death? Should we relegate to the past the view of death as "punishment for sin," and with it the entire theme of "judgment"? Are these ideas the relics of a prescientific age, or a wrong-headed theology? Or do they continue to offer an alternative language and imagery to that of ethical naturalism?

We have seen how completely such images have been discarded by Kübler-Ross and the ethical naturalist death-awareness movement. Alas, the enormous rise in litigation surrounding medical services and malpractice may be a testimony to the continuing relevance of "justice" as a concern, at least as this touches on death in a medical context. Malpractice as a legal category depends upon a notion of the doctor's personal responsibility, but also upon the hope that some deaths are preventable, and those that should not have happened are "unjust." Two strands of imagery, now severed entirely, both appear in the contemporary culture's very contradictory responses to death. The autobiographies testify as well to both, often asserting that death was "natural" while affirming a language of rights and blame that depends upon categories of justice. Our society is deeply conflicted and confused about how these two imageries should relate to each other, and the roles given to each. It should not be surprising that no clear directives come from the pastoral psychology literature, as this was deeply embedded in the pervasive cultural assumptions. The theological sources, however, tell a slightly different but still confused, unhappy story.

A Theological Paradox

It is important to note a paradox among the theological sources. Even Cullman, for whom death is "horror" and "terror," does not invoke the traditional link between death and guilt in order to make his point. As separation from God, death is construed as God's enemy, a quasi-personified enemy. But this is done without reliance upon the "justice" imagery referred to above. Moltmann, for whom Christ's death as "judicial murder" is a divine verdict against human institutional power, especially legal and religious institutions, wishes to press for a "political" reading of the narrative and for a "political" theology altogether.

Yet he shares with Cullman an aversion to a traditional use of "judgment" categories in regard to death. Moltmann's theology may indeed be a re-visioning of those categories, so as to avoid the simple theological equation of death with punishment for sin at the level of individual persons.

Moreover, both these thinkers and many others are engaged in a battle on behalf of "Hebraic" and historical thought, and against the "Greek" ideas they believe had infected Christianity. The categories we are now discussing—divine justice and the entire legal imagery elaborating it—are clearly a legacy of the "Hebraic" side of this dichotomy as it has been developed by the twentieth-century religious thinkers. There is indeed a paradox. While opting for history, for God's involvement with social justice and with the struggle against injustice and oppression in all its human forms, there has been a major reluctance to suggest that guilt, judgment, and punishment are necessary images for the Christian encounter with death. Certainly at the individual level, and among the pastoral psychology writers, such ideas play no role whatsoever. Since my view is that the Hebraic/Greek dichotomy represents an agenda of our era, not necessarily an empirical description of ancient patterns, this is indeed a paradox.

Although the imagery of justice and judgment has been expressed in systematic theological statements, starting with those in Paul's letters, it has also dramatically influenced the direction of personal spirituality. This imagery connects the individual's final encounter with the "awe and ultimacy" of death, to issues of personal accountability before God. This cluster of ideas, as we saw in Chapter 8, dominates the meaning of dying for *Ars moriendi*, Bunyan, and Law. For all of these sources, not to mention *"Dies irae,"* depend upon a view of the individual as free, active, and engaged upon creating a personal history. Such a unique history makes "my death" unique, a stress that in itself is far from ahistorical. Certainly, it is accountability before God and not acceptance of "nature" that counts at death, for the Christian thinkers discussed in Chapter 8. To know "who dies" is the central task of the dying person, and this can only be stated in terms of personal relation to God.

These motifs, brought to life again in existentialism (although with some basic and obvious differences), also influence pastoral psychology literature. They certainly hold sway in many of the autobiographies, where emphasis on death as "free act" of the self often becomes literalized and concentrated upon the question of "active euthanasia" and personal control over the timing and circumstances of one's death. Those with an existentialist framework seem paradoxically closest to the vision of a self as finally and ultimately accountable for its own acts and history, unsupported and unconsoled by any imagery of harmony with nature.

Yet the link between the existentialist autobiographers and any overarching imagery of justice and judgment is weak or nonexistent. And curiously, as if to complicate matters, in Wyschogrod's dichotomy between the "authenticity" model and the "social self," her version of Cullman's immortality/resurrection dichotomy, the existentialist appears on the first, negative end of the dichotomy. (The opposite is true for Gatch; Camus' focus on human solidarity is enough to place him on the "Hebraic" end of the scale.) Similarly, Brunner, the theological existentialist, is relegated to the role of twentieth-century "Platonist" in Moltmann's similar dichotomy of *Theology of Hope*. In short, the effect of the "Hebraic" versus "Platonic" dualism has not been to restore imagery of justice and accountability at the individual level, or to rediscover the key role this imagery has played in the Christian tradition of facing death.

Is this an issue that our selected psychological theories can address? Arc the sole alternatives a repetition of the traditional death equals punishment link, upon which the tradition of personal accountability before God seems to rest, or an abandonment of "justice" imagery altogether? Can the depth psychological theories offer anything to help reintegrate what contemporary religious thought has split apart or discarded?

Depth Psychological Responses: The Death of Everyone

To answer this difficult question, we may recall that direct references to justice and death play a peculiar role in these psychological theories. First, in the most popular and naturalistic theories, including Kübler-Ross', any references to "guilt" reduce it to an emotion ("guilt-feelings") whose resolution will lead the dying patient out of "reactive depression" and toward acceptance. Contrast this superficial placing with the complex role of guilt in Freud's legacy, especially the very explicit "castration" motif. Death, guilt, and punishment for desire are linked

together in the Oedipal conflict, as childhood fantasy and
Freud's mythic "primordial history" in *Totem and Taboo*. Freud
reads this Oedipal conflict into Christian theology of the atonement, with its Father-Son imagery and drama of sacrifice. One
might even say that Freud represents the early twentieth century's rendition of Anselmian substitution theology, where sexual themes are made explicit and the underlying rage against
the father is interpreted from the child's point of view. The
"band of brothers" who triumph over their despotic father in
Totem and Taboo are the ones who have Freud's sympathy;
their marred and guilt-ridden solution, based upon repetition
and renunciation, is a somber commentary upon our own possibilities, but not a defense of the primordial father's reign.

Yet this entire Oedipal narrative, the connection among
guilt, death, and castration as Freud expounds it, is laden with
enormous problems. Even when one allows room for "myth"
and dismisses Freud's claims to be reconstructing empirical
prehistory, his equation of death-fear with castration-fear leads
(as Lifton points out) to the classic statement of sexual reductionism. Every fear of death is *really* fear of castration, for
death itself is unsymbolizable. Thus American Freudianism
manages to literalize and repress death at the same time, legit-
imating a cultural pattern already at its height.

Moreover, Freud's formulation is so "gendered" as to turn
the entire connection among death, guilt, and punishment into
a male-only issue. Women, already "castrated," do not then
experience this as threat, and for this reason, do not develop
superegos and the capacity for justice as men do. Nor do they
play any role in the creation and maintenance of religion. They
exist as objects and spectators in a male drama. Although
there is room in Christian faith for potential variations due to
gender (as to other factors) there is no room at all for this
assumption that women are psychological nonparticipants.

Becker, of course, simply denies both these correlates, and
tries to maintain Freud's formulation as if it were not based
upon the primacy of sexual meanings or gender asymmetry.
His attempt at least shows his awareness that the link
between guilt and death is an intrinsic depth psychological
category, and also intrinsic to the "Augustinian-Lutheran" tradition. Becker's psycho-mythology is far more guilty of
"Platonism" than almost any of the other materials we have

discussed, and the unhelpfulness of his reading of Freud and his theological sources has already been established. It is curious how among the very few direct advocates for this aspect of the tradition, one finds a depth psychologist and Japanese theologian. Kitamori too retains the "Lutheran" motif of wrath and punishment in his view of "the pain of God."

I do not believe the route to reconnecting death and justice imagery can be helped by recourse to the Freudian legacy. But there may be another pathway. An alternative link among political categories, justice-imagery, and death is embedded in Lifton's theory. For Lifton, like Moltmann, is certain that collective, institutional, and historical forms play a role in human experience, that "death" is not solely a matter of individual, interior experience. The possibility of connection between death and life rests upon the assurance of historical connectedness among generations. Under the current threat of mass death, of total annihilation, this connection breaks. When death-imagery takes the form of the death of everyone, of all life, no individual "integration" of death with life can flourish. Although for the "normal" situation, the freedom to connect death and life via symbolic immortality is one of the deepest routes of individual action, this capacity is now endangered. Universal death overshadows it as imaginal possibility. This runs parallel to Wyschogrod's argument about mass death as historical reality; the collective quality of the Holocaust in particular, she believes, undermines the "authenticity paradigm" that has dominated Western thought since the days of both Jesus and Socrates.[2]

2. Hiroshima and the Holocaust dominate the twentieth century's vision in regard to this topic, prompting claims such as Lifton's and Wyschogrod's for these events' "uniqueness" and unprecedented horror. But one is left with the possibility that victims of past "collective deaths," especially those met at human hands, could have shared in this same annihilation of traditional cultural ideals, this same sense of unbearable rupture of the lived world. Perhaps the voices of nonsurvivors, silenced and unavailable to us—for those who write the historical record are normally both victors and survivors—would speak of connections broken beyond repair and life too poisoned by death to be livable. At the extreme are those groups who sought self-extinction in response to such a prospect, whether at Masada, Tasmania, or Jonestown. But in all these cases, and in others which to us might seem localized or small-scale relative to the examples selected by Lifton and Wyschogrod, the victim-participants themselves might see in such judgments their final humiliation and dehumanization.

If to encounter individual death evokes the awe and ultimacy of God and reveals the totality of my own life as a unique,
accountable self before God, then what will this prospect of
mass or universal annihilation evoke? Is there room for "collective death" as a possibility within the landscape of Christian
faith? During the age of the ancient Hebrews, "collective
death," the destruction of the nation, source of "corporate personality" for its members, was indeed a central fear. And as the
vivid imagery of *"Dies irae"* testifies, the vision of universal
death, when "the world will dissolve in ash," has in the past
been included within the scope of Christian vision. But should
it have been? And should such a "collective death" be construed
as a meaningless, final blasphemy, as Lifton clearly believes,
or an act of a God who is judge of humankind as well as creator, redeemer, and the one who will resurrect the dead?

The majority of twentieth-century writers on biblical eschatology wish to stress its often-forgotten universal, collective-
communal dimensions. They disagree over the space left for
divine wrath, for destruction, for judgment as a prelude or
dimension of this eschatology. They do not disagree that God's
ultimate intentions are for justice, and include the whole cosmos. God's "eternal hope" reaches beyond the salvation of individual persons, and is a reflection of the divine character. If
"hope" and "glory" and "resurrection" have this collective-communal scope, then does "death" as well? All of the positive
aspects of this eschatological consummation depend upon a
specific imagery of God as concerned for justice and the
redemption of the entire creation. But if that is the case, is
such a character at all compatible with a negative yet equally
collective polarity, a "death of everything" at the end of this
age, such as that which *"Dies irae"* foretells?

On this point, let us explicitly avoid the literalizations of this
imagery that became notorious post-Hiroshima, and which control even Lifton's presentation of his theory. Mass death as historical reality can be charted for the twentieth century, in the
World Wars, genocides, and other human-made or assisted
catastrophes that are part of "earth's surface." But along with
this, and far more relevant to Lifton's theory, is the accompa-
nying image of massive or total annihilation, as a possibility of
our spiritual landscape. To literalize this so as to imply that
pre-1945 death was not a problem because no technology

existed to bring about the complete destruction of life, is mistaken. It is just as mistaken as to apply the biblical scenarios of world destruction and final judgments to historicized predictions of "World War III." There is indeed a connection between historical experience of mass death and these images, but the two are not identical.

Historical events have, however, evoked and led us to rediscover the ancient biblical imagery of "the death of everyone." Brunner, for example, is at least willing to consider that the human-caused destruction of all life—Lifton's "final petulent blasphemy"—might also be an eschatological act of God. Certainly, the "ending" of humanity, the final death of everyone, plays a role in Brunner's theological vision. The power of this image serves to reinforce his critique of human historical "progress" as a valid translation of Christian "eternal" hope. One way or another, there will be collective death in the picture for us, whether by means of natural catastrophe far off, or human destructiveness nearer in our future. In this sense, "Armageddon" is something we might postpone, but not something we can truly prevent. Thus Brunner tries to encompass the possibility raised by Lifton, within the theological framework. His aim is to relativize all forms of Liftonian symbolic immortality save those of "transcendence" and the "theological" mode. It is precisely by evoking the most collective level of "death" that he severs the Christian hope in God from all lesser and less ultimate hopes.

Does this return us to the fearful picture of *"Dies irae"?* Or to scenarios of world destruction whose chief psychological function may be, as Lifton believes, to assure believers of a total immunity from death, while their own ambivalences and fears can be projected onto the longed-for destruction of enemies? In the Christian tradition, some room is reserved for the imagery of collective death. Just as there is no move at the individual level from life into "resurrection" without death as a point of transition, so too the hope for God's justice, his consummation of redemption, also seems to require a "purgative" negation, a verdict of "Guilty" against that which blocks this goal. Yet "the end of the world" or the "day of wrath" should not overshadow the final consummation of God's will for the total creation. The day of Christ and not the "day of wrath" is the day for which Christians hope, even if the two remain inseparable.

It is a far cry from the confusion of the contemporary world's approaches to death, the mixture of "naturalism" and legal categories of justice, rights, and blame, to this ultimate final vision of the death of the entire "old heaven and earth" in preparation for the new. The imagery of justice unites both ends of the contrast. Perhaps we should retain the theological centrality of Jesus' own death at the hands of human justice, a "judicial murder." This ought to make us even more aware of misuses of this imagery. The judge on the last day was once the victim of courts and political rulers. We may nevertheless try to develop categories to link justice, death, and accountability before God. If we can do so in ways that will be liberated from denial and projection, we can simultaneously affirm the fallibility and sinfulness of human individuals and the institutions within which our individual experience is shaped.

Were this task possible for Christians, perhaps our own society's quests for justice in the midst of death might take on a more compassionate and less self-serving quality. The current situation generates and perpetuates furious anger against hospitals and doctors. Psychologically this becomes a literalized and medicalized strategy by which we express outrage at the presence of death in a world from which we had exiled it. This has become our way to maintain the alleged "injustice" of all death, or of those deaths that matter to me. In contrast, the task of reconnecting political categories of justice and judgment to death, requires that issues of responsibility, accountability, and guilt be taken as intrinsic to death-imagery, at both the individual and collective levels. It does not demand a repetition of the motif of death as punishment for sin, but certainly does require that Christians be willing to engage once again with this strand of our own tradition. Imagery of justice and judgment remains an important dimension of the landscape of faith.

Death, Resurrection, and the Self

"Resurrection" must be present in any Christian perspective on death. The central Gospel narrative and the Pauline theology based upon it both pair death with resurrection, so that two movements, two moments, and two realities are intended. Even if one collapses both, as in Liftonian "transcendence," there is still a duality, and so a paradox of transfigured life in the midst of death. As with Freud, for whom death and life instincts form two mythic eternal forces, and unlike Becker for whom death is sole reality, Christian faith must rest upon this pairing. At this fundamental level, a transition model of death to resurrection takes priority over an extinction model, which makes of death an absolute negation with no corresponding affirmation. We have seen in many ways how difficult it is to affirm this without seeming to opt for a "transition" so smooth and nondisruptive as to trivialize "death" altogether. Without assenting to caterpillar-into-butterfly imagery, a transition from finite and mortal to an alternative, nonmortal mode of being appears to be the necessary model for a Christian spirituality of death.

The theological writers on eschatology and the biblical scholars all affirm the priority of resurrection, hope, and divine consummation over imagery of destruction and negation. At the very last day, the consummation of the eschaton, there will no longer be a need to proclaim "death in God," and death will indeed be defeated and annihilated as a presence in any corner of the restored and recreated cosmos. The "then" of the end time is established as a perspective separate from the "now," and a necessary perspective of distance and "otherness" from ordinary death-infested existence as we, even as Christians, continue to experience it.

The same theological writers disagree over how much the category of "resurrection" exists as *current* reality for Christians. Does Paul's spiritual imagery of death to resurrected life depend upon "realized" or "unrealized" eschatology? Is the "self hid with Christ in God" a prematurely resurrected self, or is it the true and secret source of identity and action? To what extent is the world as we live in it, this world, "unredeemed" in spite of the coming of Christ? Death certainly seems to remain as a residue, a reminder of its and our incomplete redemption. All who contribute to the debates on these questions admit that two situations, two "times," are needed in order to ask the questions. "Then" and "now"—however construed—are the eschatological categories. Times, as well as Hillman's "places," are essential to the Christian landscape of faith.

But then, are these two "times" to be equated with "this life" in contrast to our personal existence immediately after death?

Does "resurrection" become linked to our continued existence
in intimacy with Christ, which will be actualized postdeath?
And to what, given the very complex meanings of "death," does
"postdeath" refer? What counts as pre- and postdeath in a landscape where an author can announce to his readers, "For you
have died"? Does physical, bodily death play no role any longer,
if we the believers in Christ have already died with him?

We should reject this possibility right away. However much
emphasis "death" is given as a factor in the midst of life, however much death-imagery is employed to identify ruptures and
transitions within this life, the physical death of the body/per-
son is still something. It is not cancelled out by all the earlier
"deaths" that have occurred within the landscape of faith; these
may be its prefigurations. To use the imagery of the later tradition, even if the river in Bunyan's allegory is not the only or
the greatest danger, a danger it still remains.

What of the theologians' insistence that "resurrection" is
actually a communal-universal category, for which my own
individual death is no adequate substitute? Christ is the first
fruits of all the dead who will be raised, and it is to this collective hope that the imagery of resurrection ultimately points.
We have suggested in many places how twentieth-century individualism ill-prepares us for encounter with biblical models of
selfhood, which lack any absolute opposition between individual and collectivity. If there is indeed "collective death" in the
Christian landscape of faith, there is even more surely collective-communal resurrection.

The more acute and balanced of theological thinkers saw the
choice between individual and collective as another false
dichotomy. The individual who is "in Christ" is embedded in
and correlated to a collective, communal reality. The New
Testament's dependence upon "corporate personality" as an
alternative form of identity serves as a critique of our forms of
individualism. Whatever the ultimate scope of divine redemption, of final and complete resurrection—the eschatological
vision as yet "unrealized" in our world—it will include space
for the depths of individuality and be worked by a God to
whom individuals matter.

To the individual who has been brought from death to life in
Christ, the transition of personal death from this life can
become a sign of that greater, and not-yet-realized transition

of the cosmos from "old" and decayed into "new" and resurrected. The death of the self is total, in that it affects the entire person. Yet this death becomes an opening for the self's new and radically universalized ("pan-cosmic") relation to God and to reality as a totality. This new relation is an expression of hope for a new embodiment yet to come, a new mode of existence that awaits the final and universal triumph of God and redemption of creation. "Resurrection" as image points forward toward both these hopes.

In this work, we have alternatively stressed the roles of death in the midst of life, as power and hidden presence all through our journey into the landscape of faith, and have continued to link death to "ending," to the conclusion of the biological organism's existence. The death known in Kübler-Ross and discovered in the autobiographies is primarily this "final stage" of biological dying, while that of the depth psychologists and the New Testament clears the way for the first view, death as ongoing continuous presence within life. Christians do not need to choose between these two perspectives on death, but should be careful to affirm the first as spiritual priority. This will help us avoid that pitfall of the past, to literalize and overstress the final hours of dying. Such an isolation of dying is not always appropriate or meaningful. Yet behind such elements of the tradition lies the insight voiced by Calvin, that it is with God all along with whom the Christian has to do. Death's nearness erases a boundary that was never so firmly in place as our ordinary lives assume. The boundary between God and the self hides us from ourselves as well. Like the boundary between life and death, it may serve as a defense against the "awe and ultimacy" that surround human mortal existence all the time.

Death as transition is the completed crossing into a landscape shaped by this reality. And yet, for the self of the Christian hid with Christ in God, the true completion will occur only when "Christ who is our life" will appear, and we too with him in glory. The hidden, resurrected self is itself an eschatological perspective, although present in the landscape of faith's highest reaches. Heaven and earth's surface, "now" and "then": these terms may indeed be those of myth. Yet it is here that we may locate and pass beyond death and its presence in the landscape of faith. Both depth psychology in its different voices and Christian tradition in its own variations testify to the need for such a framework, for a vision of the widest, deepest, highest, and most complex divinely centered cosmos within which our pilgrimage toward death and from death to life is set. To participate in Christ's death and resurrection is to enter and abide within the fullness, pain, and glory of this landscape.

References

Albanese, Catherine. *America: Religions and Religion*. Belmont, Calif.: Wadsworth, 1979.

Albertson, Sandra. *Endings and Beginnings*. New York: Random House, 1980.

Anderson, Hugh. *The Gospel of Mark*. London: Oliphants, 1976.

Ariès, Philippe. *The Hour of Our Death*. Trans. Helen Weaver. New York: Alfred A. Knopf, 1981 [1977].

Augsburger, David. *Pastoral Counseling across Cultures*. Philadelphia: Westminster, 1986.

Autton, Norman. *The Pastoral Care of the Dying*. London: SPCK, 1966.

Bailey, Lloyd, Sr. *Biblical Perspectives on Death*. Philadelphia: Fortress, 1979.

Baillie, John. *And the Life Everlasting*. New York: Charles Scribner's Sons, 1933.

Bakan, David. *The Duality of Human Existence*. Chicago: Rand McNally, 1966.

Bane, Donald, ed. *Death and Ministry: Pastoral Care for the Dying and the Bereaved*. New York: Seabury, 1975.

Barth, Karl. *Word of God, Word of Man*. Trans. Douglas Horton. New York: Harper and Row, 1957 [1928].

Becker, Ernest. *The Denial of Death*. New York: Free, 1974.

Beker, J. Christian. *Paul the Apostle: The Triumph of God in Life and Thought*. Philadelphia: Fortress, 1980.

Best, Ernest. *The Temptation and the Passion: The Markan Soteriology*. Cambridge: Cambridge University Press, 1965.

Binswanger, Ludwig. "The Case of Ellen West." In *Existence*, ed. Rollo May, Ernest Angel, and Henri Ellenberger. New York: Simon and Schuster, 1967 [1944].

———. *Being-in-the-World*. Trans. Jacob Needleman. New York: Harper and Row, 1968 [1955].

Bonhoeffer, Dietrich. *Letters and Papers from Prison*. New York: Macmillan, 1967.

Boros, Ladislas. *The Moment of Truth: Mysterium Mortis*. London: Burns and Oates, 1969 [1962].

Boss, Medard. *Psychoanalysis and Daseinanalysis*. Trans. Ludwig Lefebre. New York: Basic, 1963.

Bowers, Margaretta, et al. *Counseling the Dying*. San Francisco: Harper and Row, 1981 [1964].

Bowlby, John. *Attachment and Loss*. 3 vols. New York: Basic, 1969, 1973, 1980.

Branson, Roy. "Is Acceptance a Denial of Death? Another Look at Kübler-Ross." *Christian Century* 92 (1975): 464–68.

Bregman, Lucy. *Through the Landscape of Faith*. Philadelphia: Westminster, 1986.

———. "Dying: A Universal Human Experience?" *Journal of Religion and Health* 28 (1989): 58–69.

Brown, Norman O. *Life Against Death*. New York: Random House, 1959.

Brown, Raymond. *The Gospel According to John*. Vol. 2. Garden City: Doubleday, 1970.

Browning, Don. *The Moral Context of Pastoral Care*. Philadelphia: Westminster, 1976.

Brunner, Emil. *Eternal Hope*. Trans. Harold Knight. Philadelphia: Westminster, 1954 [1953].

Bultmann, Rudolph. *Theology of the New Testament*. Trans. Kendrick Gobel. New York: Charles Scribner's Sons, 1951.

———. *Kerygma and Myth: A Theological Debate*. Ed. H. W. Bartsch, trans. Reginald Fuller. New York: Harper and Row, 1961.

Bunyan, John. *The Pilgrim's Progress*. New York: New American Library, 1981 [1678].

Cabot, Richard, and Russell Dicks. *The Art of Ministering to the Sick*. New York: Macmillan, 1951 [1936].

Calvin, John. *Institutes of the Christian Religion*. Trans. Ford Lewis Battles. Philadelphia: Westminster, 1960 [1559].

Camus, Albert. *The Myth of Sisyphus and Other Essays*. Trans. Justin O'Brien. New York: Alfred A. Knopf, 1955 [1942].

———. *The Plague*. Trans. Stuart Gilbert. New York: Alfred A. Knopf, 1977 [1946].

Cassirer, Ernst. *The Philosophy of Symbolic Forms*. New Haven: Yale University Press, 1953–57 [1923–29].

Clark, David. *Death-Bed Scenes*. Philadelphia: Carlton and Phillips, 1855.

Comper, Frances, ed. *The Book of the Craft of Dying*. New York: Arno, 1977 [1917].

Cooper, John. *Body, Soul and Life Everlasting*. Grand Rapids: Eerdmans, 1989.

Cox, David. *Jung and St. Paul*. London: Longmans, Green. 1959.

Cousins, Norman. *Anatomy of an Illness*. New York: Bantam, 1979.

Cullman, Oscar. "Immortality of the Soul or Resurrection of the Dead." In *Resurrection and Immortality*, ed. K. Stendahl. New York: Macmillan, 1965.

Episcopal Church. *The Book of Common Prayer*. New York: Church Hymnal Corporation, 1979.

Farmer, William. *The Last Twelve Verses of Mark*. London: Cambridge University Press, 1974.

Foos-Graber, Anya. *Deathing: An Intelligent Alternative for the Final Moments of Life*. Reading, Mass.: Addison-Wesley, 1984.

Frankl, Victor. *Man's Search for Meaning*. Trans. Ilse Lasch. New York: Pocket, 1959.

Freud, Sigmund. *Totem and Taboo*. Standard Edition 13. Trans. James Strachey. London: Hogarth, 1957 [1913].

———. *Beyond the Pleasure Principle*. Standard Edition 18. Trans. James Strachey. London: Hogarth, 1955 [1920].

———. *The Future of an Illusion*. Standard Edition 21. Trans. James Strachey and W. D. Robson-Scott. London: Hogarth, 1961 [1927].

———. *Moses and Monotheism*. Standard Edition 23. Trans. James Strachey. London: Hogarth, 1964 [1939].

Fromm, Erich. *Psychoanalysis and Religion*. New Haven: Yale University Press, 1950.

Fuller, Reginald. "Christian Initiation in the New Testament." In *Made, Not Born: New Perspectives on Christian Initiation and the*

Catechumenate. Notre Dame: University of Notre Dame Press, 1976.

Galvin, John. "The Death of Jesus in Contemporary Theology: Systematic Perspectives and Historical Issues." *Horizons* 13 (1986): 239–52.

Gatch, Milton. *Death: Meaning and Mortality in Christian Thought and Contemporary Culture*. New York: Seabury, 1969.

Gerkin, Charles. *Crisis Experience in Modern Life: Theory and Theology for Pastoral Care*. Nashville: Abingdon, 1979.

Gould, Joan. *Spirals: A Woman's Journey Through Family Life*. New York: Penguin, 1988.

Grof, Stanislav. *Realms of the Human Unconscious*. New York: E. P. Dutton, 1976.

Grof, Stanislav, and Joan Halifax. *The Human Encounter with Death*. New York: E. P. Dutton, 1977.

Gundry, Robert. *Soma in Biblical Theology with Emphasis on Pauline Anthropology*. Cambridge: Cambridge University Press, 1976.

Gunther, John. *Death Be Not Proud*. New York: Harper, 1947.

Hawkins, Anne H. "A Change of Heart: The Paradigm of Regeneration in Medical and Religious Narrative." *Perspectives in Biology and Medicine* 33 (1990): 547–59.

Hendriksen, William. *New Testament Commentary: Exposition of the Gospel According to Mark*.Grand Rapids: Baker, 1975.

Hick, John. *Death and Eternal Life*. New York: Harper and Row, 1975.

Hillman, James. *Suicide and the Soul*. New York: Harper and Row, 1964.

———. *The Myth of Analysis*. New York: Harper and Row, 1972.

———. *Revisioning Psychology*. New York: Harper and Row, 1975.

———. *The Dream and the Underworld*. New York: Harper and Row, 1979.

Homans, Peter. *Jung in Context*. Chicago: University of Chicago Press, 1979.

Hostetler, Helen. *A Time to Love*. Scottdale, Pa.: Herald, 1989.

Hulme, William. *Pastoral Care and Counseling Using the Unique Resources of the Christian Tradition*. Minneapolis: Augsburg, 1981.

Jewett, Robert. *Paul's Anthropological Terms*. Leiden: E. J. Brill, 1971.

Juel, Donald. *Augsburg Commentary on the New Testament: Mark*. Minneapolis: Augsburg, 1990.

Jung, Carl G. *Modern Man in Search of a Soul*. Trans. W. S. Dell and Cary Barnes. New York: Harcourt, Brace and World, 1933.

———. *Psychology and Religion*. Collected Works 11. Trans. R. F. C. Hull. Princeton: Princeton University Press, 1958 [1938].

———. *Two Essays in Analytical Psychology*. Collected Works 7. Trans. R. F. C. Hull. Princeton: Princeton University Press, 1953 [1943].

———. *Psychology and Alchemy*. Collected Works 12. Trans. R. F. C. Hull. Princeton: Princeton University Press, 1968 [1952].

———. *Memories, Dreams, Reflections*. Ed. Aniela Jaffe, trans. Richard and Clara Winston. New York: Random House, 1963.

Kamerman, Jack. *Death in the Midst of Life: Social and Cultural Influences on Death, Grief and Mourning*. Englewood Cliffs, N.J.: Prentice-Hall, 1988.

Kaufman, Walter, ed. *Existentialism from Dostoevsky to Sartre*. New York: Meridian, 1956.

Keck, Leander. *Paul and His Letters*. Philadelphia: Fortress, 1979.

Kierkegaard, Søren. *The Concept of Dread*. Trans. Walter Lowrie. Princeton: Princeton University Press, 1957 [1844].

Kitamori, Kazoh. *Theology of the Pain of God*. Richmond: John Knox, 1965 [1958].

Kübler-Ross, Elisabeth. *On Death and Dying*. New York: Macmillan, 1969.

———, ed. *Death: The Final Stage of Growth*. Englewood Cliffs, N.J.: Prentice-Hall, 1975.

———. *On Children and Death*. New York: Macmillan, 1983.

Küng, Hans. *Eternal Life?* Trans. Edward Quinn. London: Collins, 1984.

Lane, William. *The Gospel According to Mark*. Grand Rapids: Eerdmans, 1974.

Law, William. *A Serious Call to a Devout and Holy Life*. Classics of Western Spirituality. New York: Paulist, 1978.

L'Engle, Madeleine. *Two-Part Invention*. San Francisco: Harper and Row, 1988.

Levine, Stephen. *Who Dies? An Investigation of Conscious Living and Conscious Dying*. Garden City: Anchor, 1982.

Lewis, C. S. *A Grief Observed*. New York: Bantam, 1976 [1963].

Lifton, Robert. *The Broken Connection*. New York: Simon and Schuster, 1979.

Lindemann, Erich. "Symptomatology and Management of Acute Grief." *American Journal of Psychiatry* 101 (1944): 141–48.

London, Perry. *The Modes and Morals of Psychotherapy*. New York: Holt, Rinehart and Winston, 1964.

McManners, John. *Death and the Enlightenment*. Oxford: Clarendon, 1981.

McWilliams, Warren. "Divine Suffering in Contemporary Theology." *Scottish Journal of Theology* 3 (1980): 35–53.

Malraux, André. *Man's Fate*. Trans. Haakon Chevalier. New York: Random House, 1934.

Maslow, Abraham. *The Farther Reaches of Human Nature*. New York: Viking, 1971.

May, Rollo. *Man's Search for Himself*. New York: New American Library, 1967.

May, Rollo, Ernest Angel, and Henri Ellenberger, eds. *Existence*. New York: Simon and Schuster, 1967.

May, William F. *The Physician's Covenant: Images of the Healer in Medical Ethics*. Philadelphia: Westminster, 1983.

Miles, Margaret. *Fullness of Life: Historical Foundations for a New Asceticism*. Philadelphia: Westminster, 1981.

Miller-McLemore, Bonnie. *Death, Sin and the Moral Life*. Atlanta: Scholars, 1988.

Mills, Liston, ed. *Perspectives on Death*. Nashville: Abingdon, 1969.

Mitchell, Juliet. *Psychoanalysis and Feminism*. New York: Random House, 1974.

Moltmann, Jürgen. *Theology of Hope*. Trans. James W. Leitch. New York: Harper and Row, 1965.

———. *The Crucified God*. Trans. R. A. Wilson and John Bowden. New York: Harper and Row, 1974.

Monette, Paul. *Borrowed Time: An AIDS Memoir*. New York: Avon, 1988.

Moody, Dale. *The Hope of Glory*. Grand Rapids: Eerdmans, 1964.

Moody, Raymond. *Life after Life*. New York: Bantam, 1975.

Morison, Robert. "The Dignity of the Inevitable and Necessary." In *Death Inside Out*, ed. Peter Steinfels and Robert Veatch. New York: Harper and Row, 1975.

Murphy Center for Liturgical Research. *Made, Not Born: New Perspectives on Christian Initiation and the Catechumenate*. Notre Dame: University of Notre Dame Press, 1976.

Newcombe, Nora, and Jeffrey Lerner. "Britain Between the Wars: The Historical Context of Bowlby's Theory of Attachment." *Psychiatry* 45 (1982): 1–12.

Nickelsburg, George. *Resurrection, Immortality and Eternal Life in Intertestamental Judaism*. Cambridge: Harvard University Press, 1972.

Nouwen, Henri. *A Letter of Consolation*. San Francisco: Harper and Row, 1982.

Oates, Wayne. *Pastoral Care and Counseling in Grief and Separation*. Philadelphia: Fortress, 1976.

Ochs, Robert. *The Death in Every Now*. New York: Sheed and Ward, 1969.

Oden, Thomas. *Pastoral Theology: Essentials for Ministry*. San Francisco: Harper and Row, 1983.

Otto, Rudolph. *The Idea of the Holy*. Trans. John Harvey. London: Oxford University Press, 1976 [1917].

Parkes, Colin. *Bereavement: Studies of Grief in Adult Life*. New York: International Universities Press, 1972.

Parkes, Colin, and Robert Weiss. *Recovery from Bereavement*. New York: Basic, 1983.

Pelikan, Jaroslav. *The Shape of Death: Life, Death and Immortality in the Early Fathers*. New York: Abingdon, 1961.

Perry, Shireen. *In Sickness and in Health*. Downers Grove: Inter-Varsity, 1989.

Rahner, Karl. *Zur Theologie der Todes*. Freiburg: Herder, 1958.

Raines, John, and Donna Day-Lower. *Modern Work and Human Meaning*. Philadelphia: Westminster, 1986.

Ricoeur, Paul. *Freud and Philosophy*. Trans. Denis Savage. New Haven: Yale University Press, 1970.

Rieff, Philip. *Freud: The Mind of the Moralist*. Garden City: Anchor, 1961.

Ring, Kenneth. *Life at Death*. New York: Coward, McCann and Geoghegan, 1980.

Robinson, John. *In the End God*. New York: Harper and Row, 1968.

Rollin, Betty. *Last Wish*. New York: Warner, 1985.

Rosenblatt, Paul. *Bitter, Bitter Tears*. Minneapolis: University of Minnesota Press, 1983.

Sartre, Jean-Paul. "The Wall." Trans. Lloyd Alexander. In *Existentialism from Dostoevsky to Sartre*, ed. Walter Kaufman. New York: Meridian, 1956 [1948].

———. *No Exit and Three Other Plays*. Trans. Gilbert Stuart. New York: Alfred A. Knopf, 1949 [1944].

———. "Existentialism Is a Humanism." Trans. Philip Mairet. In *Existentialism from Dostoevsky to Sartre*, ed. Walter Kaufman. New York: Meridian, 1956 [1946].

Schnackenburg, Rudolph. *Baptism in the Thought of St. Paul*. Trans. G. R. Beasley-Murray. New York: Herder and Herder, 1964.

Schneider, Gregory. "The Ritual of Happy Dying among Early American Methodists." *Church History* 56 (1987): 348–63.

Schreiber, LeAnne. *Midstream*. New York: Viking, 1990.

Schwartz, Hans. *On the Way to the Future*. Minneapolis: Augsburg, 1979.

Schweitzer, Albert. *The Quest for the Historical Jesus*. Trans. W. Montgomery. London: Adam and Charles Black, 1945 [1906].

Shilts, Randy. *And the Band Played On*. New York: St. Martin's, 1987.

Silberman, Lou. "Death in the Hebrew Bible and Apocalyptic Literature." In *Perspectives on Death*, ed. Liston Mills. Nashville: Abingdon, 1969.

Soelle, Dorothy. *Suffering*. Trans. Everett R. Kalin. Philadelphia: Fortress, 1975.

Southard, Samuel. "The Current Need for 'Theological Counsel.'" *Pastoral Psychology* 32/2 (1984): 89–105.

———. *Dying and Death*. Westport, Conn.: Greenwood, 1991.

Stacey, W. David. *The Pauline View of Man*. London: Macmillan, 1956.

Steinfels, Peter, and Robert Veatch. *Death Inside Out*. New York: Harper and Row, 1975.

Stringfellow, William. *A Second Birthday*. Garden City: Doubleday, 1970.

Tart, Charles, ed. *Transpersonal Psychologies*. New York: Harper and Row, 1975.

Thomas of Celona. "*Dies irae*." Trans. Peter S. Hawkins, mod. R. Boisclair.

Truman, Jill. *Letter to My Husband*. New York: Penguin, 1987.

Van Der Leeuw, G. *Religion in Essence and Manifestation.* Trans. Victor Turner. New York: Harper and Row, 1963 [1933].

Van Herik, Judith. *Freud on Femininity and Faith.* Berkeley: University of California Press, 1982.

Watson, David. *Fear No Evil.* Wheaton: Harold Shaw, 1984.

Wehr, Demaris. *Jung and Feminism: Liberating Archetypes.* Boston: Beacon, 1987.

Weil, Simone. *Waiting for God.* Trans. Emma Craufurd. New York: Harper and Row, 1973 [1951].

Weisman, Avery. *On Dying and Denying.* New York: Behavioral Publications, 1972.

Wesley, John. "A Plain Account of Christian Perfection." In *Selected Writings and Hymns.* New York: Paulist, 1981.

West, Jessamyn. *The Woman Said Yes.* Greenwich, Conn.: Fawcett, 1976.

Whitmore, George. *Someone Was Here: Profiles in the AIDS Epidemic.* New York: New American Library, 1988.

Wiesel, Elie. *Night.* Trans. Stella Rodway. New York: Avon, 1969.

Wink, Walter. *Naming the Powers.* Philadelphia: Fortress, 1984.

———. *Unmasking the Powers.* Philadelphia: Fortress, 1986.

Wyschogrod, Edith. *Spirit in Ashes: Hegel, Heidegger and Man-Made Mass Death.* New Haven: Yale University Press, 1985.

Zaleski, Carol. *Otherworld Journeys: Accounts of Near-Death Experiences in Medieval and Modern Times.* New York: Oxford University Press, 1987.

Index

243